THE MONEY SANDBOX

Smart Wealth
How to build wealth, carry risk and still sleep at night

Hemant Goyal

Kappa Koffee LLC

Financial clarity, one cup at a time

Copyright & Legal

Disclaimer

This book is for **educational and informational purposes only**. It is not intended as, and does not constitute, personalized financial, investment, tax, legal, or other professional advice.

Nothing in this book creates an advisory, fiduciary, attorney-client, accountant-client, or other professional relationship between the reader and the author or publisher. Readers should consult with qualified professionals regarding their individual circumstances before making any financial, investment, or legal decisions.

Every effort has been made to ensure the accuracy of the information provided as of the time of writing. However, laws, regulations, financial products, and market conditions change over time. The author and publisher make no representations or warranties regarding the completeness, accuracy, reliability, or suitability of the information contained in this book and disclaim liability for errors, omissions, or outdated information.

All investing involves risk, including the risk of loss of principal. Past performance is not indicative of future results. Any examples, case studies, or scenarios described in this book are illustrative only and may be composites or modified to protect privacy. They are not guarantees or predictions of any particular outcome.

Third-party product names, services, platforms, trademarks, and brands are the property of their respective owners and are used in this book solely for commentary, or illustrative purposes. No affiliation, sponsorship, or endorsement is implied

By reading this book, you agree that you are solely responsible for your own financial decisions and outcomes, and that neither the author nor the publisher shall be held liable for any loss or damage arising from your reliance on the information contained herein.

For my parents & in-laws,

> who have showed me what hard work looks like

and especially my dad,

> who taught me what honesty, consistency and good money habits actually mean.

For my wife & daughter,

> who have always stood by me, are there for me and make it worth it.

For all my friends,

> who shared coffee, questions and money stories, this book started with you.

Money isn't an exam you pass.

It's a language you learn, one conversation at a time.

For the smart ones

> who ever thought, "I'm smart… so why doesn't money feel simple yet?"; This one's for you.

For the quiet worriers, late-night spreadsheet builders & "I'll figure it out later" crowd,

> may this be your reset button.

For everyone,

> who is willing to step into the sandbox, make a small mess & build something better with their money.

Contents

Preface

I didn't grow up around financial advisors, but growing up in India did instill a mindset of financial responsibility coupled with habits emphasizing saving over spending, safety over risk and securing tangible assets like gold or property. Those early years stayed with me as I moved to the United States and spent two decades climbing the corporate ladder. But the kid in me still watched the adult me, and other adults around me, juggle with money hoping nothing broke.

Curiosity took over, and I started reading everything I could about finance and wealth building. I tried things. Some worked. Some didn't. I played with budgets, credit cards, 401(k)s, Roth IRAs, HSAs, side projects, real estate, crypto, collectibles and pretty much anything left in the whole messy buffet. Along the way, I learned that money can be unforgiving when you wing it but surprisingly kind when you give it a clear job and a calm system.

And a thought lingered: we're trained to work for roughly half of our lives to earn a living but never taught how to manage what we work for or lose sleep over. Not in elementary school, not in middle or high school, and not in most college programs. Instead, many of us hand money to someone we don't really know and hope they'll make the right decisions for "our" wealth, even when their incentives may not fully align with ours. That quiet gap has always bothered me.

Over time, friends and colleagues started asking for help. "Can you take a look at our situation?" "Should we prioritize this or that?" "We're overwhelmed, where do we start?" Those conversations, over coffee and shared spreadsheets, turned into my coaching practice, Kappa Koffee, and then this book.

This is not a book about getting rich overnight. It's not a day-trading manual and it's certainly not a tax loophole encyclopedia. It's a book about **holistic wealth**: money, yes, but also time, stress levels, flexibility and the ability to say yes or no without your stomach knotting up. It's about having a Tuesday you enjoy today and a future you don't have to dread.

You'll notice three themes running through these chapters:

- First, **everything connects**. Your bank account, your credit habits, your investments, your insurance, your taxes, your "shiny" experiments are all part of one system. We'll treat them that way.

- Second, **behavior matters more than brilliance**. The difference between chaos and calm is usually a few simple defaults and tiny rituals, not a secret stock picker.

- Third, you **don't have to sacrifice all joy for future safety**. A small, intentional "sandbox" for experimentation can live right alongside a boring, effective plan.

I write as a product leader, a GAFM Chartered Wealth Manager™ (CWM), a Chartered Financial Manager™ (ChFM) and as someone who has made mistakes, course-corrected and learned by doing. This is not individualized financial advice; it's education - a set of mental models and systems you can adapt to your own life. Your situation, tax rules and risk tolerance are unique. When in doubt, pair what you read here with a professional who knows your full picture, not just the slice of it they manage.

My hope is simple: that you'll finish this book feeling less anxious, more informed and in control because you now have a way to think about money that's **calm, holistic and human**.

Let's build a foundation, give your money a job, fence off a small sandbox to play in and design a Tuesday worth funding.

- Hemant

Redmond, WA

How to Use This Book

You don't need to "study" personal finance to get good at it. Same way, read the book like a conversation, not a curriculum.

On your first pass, just follow the flow. The early chapters give you the "language" for everything else. They set the mental model (how money works, what it's for, and how to build guardrails that don't feel like punishment). When that clicks, the practical chapters feel lighter.

In the second pass, jump around without guilt. Read tid-bits over coffee, let it sink and form your opinion over what you just read. Think of Parts 2 and 3 as your "modules" which explain credit, investing, retirement, real estate, insurance and the fun stuff (crypto/collectibles) with a sandbox fence around it. In future, come back to the chapter that matches the decision you're making *right now*.

Each chapter has two sections. **Reflection Pause's** to help you think what's true for you, and **Worksheet** to help you turn insight into simple actions. You don't have to do them all. Treat them like menu items, not homework.

When you're ready to connect the dots, the later "stitch-it-together" **Toolkits** help you build a system using levers (spend/earn/invest) your timeline and your willingness to explore new frontiers without blowing up the plan. They also have checklists and one-pagers you can use in an hour, once a month or once a year.

If you're reading as a couple/family, use the prompts as conversation starters. If you're outside the U.S., translate the labels (401(k), Roth, etc.) into local equivalents and keep the underlying behaviors and guardrails. Personal finance is older than the borders and follows the basic rules of money, much older than the current money system.

The goal isn't to do everything. The goal is to have a calmer relationship with money - one cup at a time. If this book leaves you with fewer questions, a handful of clear actions and thinking of money as a tool, it will have done its job.

Part 1: Foundations of Money

"We are what we repeatedly do with our money. Stability, then,
is not an act but a habit."
— *Adapted from Will Durant*

1

What is Money, really?

When my daughter was about six years old, she loved shiny things. She would pick up buttons, bottle caps, or marbles and hold them as if they were treasure. One afternoon she found a few quarters and dimes on the dining table that had slipped out of my pocket. To her, they were nothing more than little silver discs. She stacked them like building blocks, slid them across the table like race cars and giggled when they dropped, making the clinging sound to irritate me.

At that age, she had no concept of what those coins really represented. They were just toys, no different from the colored beads she strung into necklaces or the pebbles she collected in the park.

That evening we went out for ice cream. She proudly carried the same coins in her small fist. When we reached the counter, I let her place them in the cashier's hand. A moment later, the cashier handed her an ice cream cone, dripping with sprinkles. My daughter froze for a second, staring at the cone and then back at the cashier. Her eyes widened in wonder. She had just transformed shiny discs into ice cream.

In that moment, money stopped being a toy. It became something powerful.

That ice cream story reminded me of my own childhood. Growing up, we didn't call it "economics" or "currency exchange." We just called it trading. On the playground, I'd swap marbles with a friend. One marble for a shiny sticker. Sometimes a comic book for a plastic figurine or collectible sports cards of my favorite sportsperson.

But every trade carried a problem: only if my friend wanted what I had could the deal work. If I had a bag full of marbles but my friend already had plenty, the trade died before it began.

I didn't know it then, but I was bumping into what economists call the **double coincidence of wants**, the condition that both sides must want exactly what the other is offering, at the same time. Without that match, no trade can happen.

That day with my daughter, I saw the exact opposite. The cashier didn't want coins for their own sake. She wasn't collecting quarters as shiny tokens. She accepted the coins because she trusted that later, she could use them to get ice-cream, buy chocolates or even her own toys.

That's the first big shift in understanding money: it isn't valuable because of what it is.

Money is valuable because of what people agree it can do.

For my daughter, coins turned into ice cream. For me, marbles turned into nothing when the other kid didn't want them. The two moments, decades apart, carry the same lesson: money is a tool that solves the problem of trade.

But here's where it gets interesting. That shift in my daughter's mind didn't happen slowly. It happened instantly. One second, coins were toys. The next, they were ice cream. And once she saw that power, she couldn't "unsee" it.

As adults, we forget that shift. We handle cash, swipe cards, tap phones, move numbers between accounts. We treat it as normal, mundane, routine. Yet the truth is, money is nothing short of magical when you first discover its purpose.

Reflection Pause

Do you remember the first thing you ever bought with money? How did it make you feel?

Maybe it was candy from the corner shop, maybe a toy car, maybe a slice of pizza. That moment stays with you because it transforms your understanding of value. That feeling of power, control and independence is what makes money so compelling.

I often tell my clients: until you reconnect with that sense of wonder, you'll always see money as a burden. Bills, taxes, credit cards, debt - all the "adult" baggage drowns out the basic truth.

At its core, money is just a bridge. It connects what you have to what you want. It connects your effort today to your dreams tomorrow. It connects strangers in a society, allowing trust to flow between people who may never meet again.

My daughter didn't realize she was stepping onto that bridge when she bought her first ice cream. But that tiny transaction captured the essence of money better than any economics textbook. So let me ask you: is money, to you, still just paper and metal or numbers on a screen that stress you out? Or is it a tool, a bridge, a language of trust?

If we can relearn to see money the way a child does in that first moment of wonder, then personal finance stops being about numbers and budgets and starts being about power, freedom and possibility.

THE IMPRACTICALITIES OF BARTER

Imagine living in a small farming village thousands of years ago. You raise cows. Your neighbor grows wheat. Another villager weaves cloth. Life seems simple, until you need something you don't produce yourself.

One day, you decide you're tired of milk and butter and want bread. So you walk to the farmer who grows wheat and say, "I'll give you a cow for ten sacks of grain." The farmer laughs. "I don't need a cow. I need shoes. Go talk to the shoemaker."

So now you carry your cow to the shoemaker, who tells you, "I don't need a cow either. I need apples for my children." Off you go again, tugging your cow through the village. By the time you finally get someone who wants the cow, you're exhausted and you still haven't eaten.

This is barter; trading one good for another. And while it seems natural, it's also incredibly messy. It runs into the same "double *coincidence* of wants" problem we just saw: for a trade to work, both sides must want exactly what the other has at the same time.

And that's only the first headache.

Even when you find a willing partner, you hit the fairness problem. How many sacks of grain equal one cow? What if you want just a little bread? Are you supposed to chop your cow in half? Barter struggles with *divisibility*. Some things can be split without losing value; many can't. A cow, a house, or a plow doesn't divide neatly like a bag of rice.

Then there's *storage* and *durability*. Chickens don't last forever. Grain can rot. Apples can spoil. Carrying around perishable or bulky items makes trade inconvenient and inefficient.

And finally, barter doesn't scale. In a small village, maybe you can afford the time to search for the perfect match. But in a growing town, let alone a city, where thousands of trades need to happen every day, you'd spend more time hunting for the "right" trading partner than actually producing anything of value.

But... Barter isn't entirely dead. Children still practice it instinctively.

I've watched children swap books, toys and cards at school. One day it's crayons for stickers, another day it's half a sandwich for an extra cookie. Think of Pokémon cards. A rare holographic card can be worth ten common ones. No money changes hands, but both kids walk away happy; when the match exists.

And notice what happens when it doesn't. If one child doesn't want the card you're offering, the trade collapses on the spot. Or the negotiation turns into a courtroom drama: "Is this Pikachu really worth three Charmanders?" I've seen kids argue with more passion about the fairness of a card swap than world leaders bring to a summit.

Barter can be simple, even fun, when the group is small, trust is high, and the stakes are low. But beyond that, it collapses under its own weight.

That's why societies eventually realized they needed something better: a **common medium of exchange.** Something everyone would accept, regardless of their immediate wants.

Instead of dragging cows through the village, you could carry small, portable tokens. Instead of debating how many apples equal a goat, you could agree on a shared measure of value. Instead of relying on luck to find the right trade partner, you could transact with anyone, anytime. This was the birth of money.

Money solved this double coincidence of wants. It created a shared language of value that allowed trade to flourish. It made economies more efficient, scalable and fair.

And yet, deep down, the spirit of barter never fully left us. From Pokémon cards to sports memorabilia, from neighborhood favors to corporate barter deals, we still practice it in pockets of our lives. But the fact that we do so voluntarily, in fun or limited contexts, proves the point: barter works only in small, specialized exchanges. For everything else, we need money.

Reflection Pause

- ☐ Think about the last time you bartered. Maybe it was swapping a shift at work, trading a skill, or exchanging collectibles as a kid. How did it feel?
- ☐ Now imagine if every transaction in your life worked this way — groceries, rent, electricity, medical bills. Could you function?

That thought experiment alone explains why money became humanity's greatest invention.

THE AGREEMENT OF TRUST

At its core, money is nothing more than trust.

Take a currency bill out of your wallet. Look at it closely. It's a piece of paper with some ink, numbers and a portrait of a long-dead personality. On its own, it has no real use. You can't eat it. You can't wear it. You can't build a house out of it. Yet you and I both know that if you walk into a coffee shop with that piece of paper, you'll walk out with a latte.

Why? Because the barista trusts that later, she can use that same bill to buy groceries, pay rent, or get gas for her car. And the grocer, the landlord, the gas station all trust it too.

That's what makes money extraordinary: it's not the paper, the coin, or the digital number on your screen. It's the belief behind it. I once had a client who put it perfectly. We were going through his finances and he said with a chuckle,

Money is just a wallet full of IOUs.

He was right. A dollar is basically a promise. It's a note saying, "This piece of paper will be accepted in exchange for something of value." A credit card swipe is just another kind of promise that the bank will pay the merchant. Even your paycheck is a promise, backed by your employer's ability to transfer money into your account.

Strip away that trust and the entire system collapses. And... history is full of moments when trust in money cracked, followed by chaos.

Take Zimbabwe in the late 2000's. Inflation there spiraled so out of control that the government printed a 100 trillion-dollar bill. You could carry a suitcase full of cash to the bakery and still not afford a loaf of bread. The bill was still ink and fibers. What changed was people's trust in it.

Or look at Venezuela more recently. Hyperinflation reached millions of percent in a single year. People abandoned their currency entirely. They started trading in U.S. dollars or even returned to bartering goods like rice and cooking oil. Trust in the Venezuelan Bolívar had vanished, so the Bolívar itself became useless.

These examples may seem distant, but they show just how fragile money really is. Without collective belief, money reverts to being just paper, metal, or digits.

Digital Trust

A book in 2026 would be incomplete without mention of Crypto, the new(er) trust experiment. Trust is the reason why Bitcoin fascinates so many people. It is designed to operate without centralized trust. Instead of relying on banks or governments, Bitcoin relies on math and networks. Bitcoin exists because enough people trust the code, the blockchain and the idea that someone else will accept it tomorrow.

For some, a currency outside government control feels liberating. For others, it feels something pulled out of thin air "How can code be money?". But at its core, Bitcoin doesn't break the rule. It still requires belief. Whether it's a Dollar or a Bitcoin, the principle is the same: money only works when enough people trust it.

Imagine waking up tomorrow and discovering that no one accepts money anymore. You hand over a $20 bill at Starbucks and the barista shakes her head. "Sorry, we don't take that." You go to the grocery store and the cashier refuses your card. Gas stations shut down because no one will exchange fuel for worthless bills.

How long before society collapses? Hours, not days. That's how fragile money really is. We go through life spending money without thinking twice. Strangers hand you goods in exchange for slips of paper because of an invisible agreement: "I'll accept this because I know others will too". It is one of humanity's greatest achievements, a silent contract billions of people uphold every single day.

Reflection Pause

☐ Take out a note or coin from your pocket. Really look at it. Without trust, it's just paper or metal. Why do you believe it has value?
☐ Now think about your digital balance. It's not even tangible. Why do you feel safe that those numbers will buy you real goods?

That quiet confidence you feel *is* trust. And the invisible glue holding the financial world together.

THE JOURNEY OF MONEY

Once societies realized barter was too clumsy and that trust needed a vehicle, money began to evolve. And that evolution is one of the most fascinating journeys in human history.

In many coastal regions, seashells were once used as money. They were beautiful, durable and relatively scarce. In parts of Africa, salt became a currency. It was so valuable that Roman soldiers were sometimes paid with it and where the origins of word *salary* lie.

Picture a market in ancient Rome. A soldier walks in with a pouch of salt. He hands it over to buy bread, wine and oil. Today, it would feel strange but to them, it made sense. Everyone needed salt to preserve food and everyone trusted its value.

Eventually, societies gravitated toward precious metals like gold and silver. They were shiny, rare and didn't spoil. Kings and emperors minted coins stamped with their seal. That seal wasn't just decoration but a guarantee. When you held a coin with Caesar's face, you trusted its weight and value.

Coins solved many problems of barter: they were portable, divisible and widely accepted. Trade expanded. Empires grew. But coins were heavy and as trade spread across continents, carrying sacks of gold and silver became impractical. Leading to the birth of paper money.

The Chinese pioneered paper money as early as the 7th century. Instead of lugging coins, merchants carried notes backed by the government. The notes said, in effect: "This slip of paper represents value you can redeem later."

Centuries later, Europe adopted the practice. Banks emerged as safe places to store gold and silver. Instead of moving the metals themselves, people traded the paper claims. Over time, the paper itself became money. People stopped asking for gold. The government's promise was enough.

The Gold Standard and Its End

For a long time, countries tied their money to gold. A dollar represented a fixed amount of gold in a vault. This was The Gold Standard. It reassured people: "Your paper is backed by something real."

But as economies grew more complex, the gold standard became limiting. Governments needed flexibility to respond to crises, wars and recessions. In 1971, the U.S. formally ended the gold standard. From then on, money was no longer tied to gold. It became fiat money, valuable only because the government declared it so and people trusted it.

To some, this felt risky. But in practice, fiat money gave economies more room to grow. It was a reminder that at the heart of it all, money was still trust.

Fast forward to the 20th century. Carrying cash was still common but new innovations made spending easier. Enter the credit card. A small piece of plastic suddenly replaced wads of cash. Swipe it, sign a slip and you could walk out with goods.

What made it work? Again, trust. The store trusted Visa or Mastercard. You trusted your bank to honor the payment. Everyone trusted the system. Debit cards followed, linking directly to bank accounts. Then came ATMs, letting you withdraw cash anywhere in the world. Money was becoming less physical and more digital. And then came cryptocurrency. Bitcoin was born in 2009, created to be money without banks or governments. Instead of trusting institutions, people are pivoting to trust code.

Whether you love it or doubt it, crypto highlights the same truth: money has always been an evolving agreement. Shells, salt, coins, paper, plastic, digital numbers - each stage only worked because enough people believed in it.

Reflection Pause

- ☐ Imagine you're holding a Roman coin, a paper note from 1700s Europe, a 1950s credit card and your smartphone today. They look nothing alike. But all four served the same role. Which one would you trust most if you had to buy lunch right now?
- ☐ Now ask yourself: what might money look like 50 years from today? Will we still carry wallets or just digital identities?

From shells in a village market to QR codes at shops, the principle hasn't changed. Money is whatever we agree it is. Its power lies not in the thing itself, but in the belief that tomorrow, someone else will accept it.

MONEY AS MORE THAN NUMBERS

If money were only about math, life would be simple. Earn more than you spend, save the difference, invest it wisely and watch it grow. Anyone who can count should be rich, right?

But we know that's not how it works. If it were just math, people with six-figure salaries wouldn't be living paycheck to paycheck. If it were just numbers, credit card companies wouldn't exist, because no one would pay 20% interest willingly. If it were just logic, lotteries would have no buyers, because the odds are absurd.

Money isn't math. Money is psychology.

Ask ten people what money means to them and you'll get ten different answers. For some, it means freedom with the ability to travel, take risks and retire early. For others, it means safety buffer against emergencies. For some, it symbolizes power or status like the car they drive, neighborhood they live in or the watch on their wrists. And for many, it's the stress of bills, debt and uncertainty.

I once worked with a client, Andy, who earned well over $200,000 a year. On paper, he was thriving. But every month, he felt anxious. He described money as "sand slipping through my fingers." Despite his income, he had no savings. For him, money was about the fear and not about freedom or power. He was afraid of losing it, afraid of not having enough tomorrow, afraid of confronting his own spending habits.

Contrast that with Jessi, another client who earning half of what Andy did. She lived modestly but intentionally. She had savings, no debt and a clear plan. When I asked her how she felt about money, she just said a single word... "Calm." Same dollars, different psychology.

Behavior Beats Math

This is why two people with identical incomes can live entirely different lives. The difference is in the mindset, it is not about the math

Think about dieting. Everyone knows the formula: eat less, move more. Yet billions are spent every year on diet programs, gyms, supplements and "hacks." Why? Because it's not about knowledge, it's about behavior.

Money works the same way. The formula is simple. The execution is hard, because humans are emotional, not calculators.

For many people, money becomes tied to identity. A luxury car is a statement. A big house is the proof of success. A designer bag is the stamp of social approval. There's nothing inherently wrong with enjoying nice things. The problem comes when your self-worth rises and falls with your net worth. When that happens, money stops being a tool and starts being a mirror. And mirrors can be cruel.

I've seen clients who felt ashamed of earning less than their peers, even though they lived comfortably. I've also seen people earning millions who felt empty, constantly chasing "more" because money had become their scoreboard.

So, when I ask people their financial goals, they often say, "I want to be rich." But when I push further with "What does rich mean to you?", the answers vary. Some describe specific numbers: "a million dollars." Others describe lifestyles: "travel whenever I want." Still others describe feelings: "peace of mind." The truth is, most people don't actually want to be rich. They want what they believe money will give them: freedom, security, joy or peace.

Money may be counted in numbers but it's lived in feelings. Until you understand your own psychology of money, no budget, no plan and no investment strategy will stick.

Reflection Pause

Imagine two people. One has $10 million in the bank but feels trapped, anxious and constantly working. The other has $100,000 but feels calm, free and grateful. Who is richer? The answer depends on how you define wealth. And that's the point: money is subjective. It's not just numbers on a spreadsheet; it's emotions, values and perspective.

☐ What does money mean to you right now? Freedom? Safety? Stress? Status?
☐ Does that meaning empower you or does it limit you?
☐ If your relationship with money were healthier, what would change in your daily life?

MONEY AS A TOOL, NOT THE GOAL

One of the most common mistakes I see people make is treating money itself as the destination. They set goals like, "I want to have a million dollars" or "I want to be rich." When I ask why, the answers become fuzzy: "Because then I'll be secure," or "Because then I'll be respected." But nothing is further from the truth. A million dollars is just a number. Money sitting in an account does nothing by itself. What matters is what money enables you to do.

Think of money like a car. If you buy the most expensive, luxurious car but never decide where you're driving, what good is it? You'll sit in the garage, polishing it, showing it off, maybe revving the engine to impress the neighbors. But the car isn't fulfilling its purpose.

That's how many people treat money. They collect it, chase it, even worship it, but never ask what journey it's supposed to take them on. The purpose of money is to serve you just as the purpose of a car is to move you.

The Chasers vs. The Builders

Over the years, I've noticed two broad mindsets when it comes to money:

1. **The Chasers** *These people are always running after money. A new job, a side hustle, the latest investment trend. They measure their worth by how much they make. No matter how much they have, it never feels enough, because there's always someone richer. Chasers live in comparison mode.*

2. **The Builders** *These people use money as a tool. They focus less on accumulation and more on creation. Money helps them build security, experiences, freedom and impact. Builders may not always have the flashiest lifestyles, but they tend to feel more satisfied.*

The irony is that Builders often end up wealthier in the long run financially and emotionally, all because their money has purpose.

There's a famous saying: "Money can't buy happiness." That's partly true. Money can't buy love, purpose or health. But it can buy freedom from constant worry. It can buy time - the ability to work less and spend more with family. It can buy access to healthcare, education and opportunities that improve life. Money can remove barriers, but it can't create meaning. Meaning comes from how you use it.

So instead of asking, "How much money do I want?" let's reframe the question to:

> *"What kind of life do I want, and how much money do I need to support it?"*

This flips money from master to servant. It shifts the goal from "a number in the bank" to "a life well-lived." Money is a wonderful servant but a terrible master. If you make it your goal, you'll always feel empty, because numbers have no finish line. But if you make it your tool, you'll always feel empowered, because tools build something bigger than themselves.

Reflection Pause

- ☐ Imagine you woke up tomorrow with unlimited money. No restrictions, no limits. What would you do with your time? Travel? Write a book? Spend more hours with your kids? Start a charity?
- ☐ Now ask yourself: which of those things could you start doing today, even with the money you already have? Often, the gap isn't as big as you think.
- ☐ Are you treating money as a car in the garage, a hammer in the drawer, a trophy on a shelf? Or are you using it to build the road, the house, the life you want?

SEEING MONEY CLEARLY

We've covered a lot in this first chapter. We started with a child's wonder of shiny coins turning into ice cream. We traveled through the chaos of barter, where you couldn't chop a cow in half to buy bread. We saw how trust transformed shells, salt and coins into a global language of value. We explored how money isn't math but psychology, carrying emotions like freedom, stress, or power. And we reframed money not as the destination, but as the tool that helps us build the life we want. So, really, what is money?

Money is an agreement. A belief. A tool. A bridge. A servant.

It's the means, never the end itself. And when we forget that, when we let money define us rather than serve us, that's when we lose balance.

This foundation matters! Before we dive into spending, saving, investing and planning in the chapters ahead, we have to get clear on this foundation. Because the truth is: if you think of money only as numbers, you'll make financial decisions without meaning. If you think of money only as status, you'll forever chase other people's approval. If you think of money as scarce, you'll hold it so tightly you'll never enjoy it. But if you think of money as a tool, you unlock its real power. Tools build houses, bridges and futures. Money, used wisely, builds freedom, choices and peace of mind.

A Story of Reframing

One of my clients, Neeraj, once told me, "Money feels like a chain around my neck. I work for it, I stress about it, I fight with my spouse about it. It controls me."

Together, we worked on reframing. We explored what money really meant to him. Over time, he realized he didn't actually want "more" money for its own sake. He wanted flexibility to work fewer hours, to spend weekends with his kids, to travel once a year without guilt.

When he started budgeting with those goals in mind, money stopped being a chain and started being a set of keys. Same dollars with a completely different feeling.

Remember my daughter's eyes lighting up when coins turned into ice cream? That sense of awe is worth holding onto. Because money, when stripped of noise, really is magical. It takes effort and transforms it into value. It turns invisible trust into tangible outcomes. It bridges strangers into collaborators. If you can reconnect with that sense of wonder, money becomes less of a burden and more of a blessing. It becomes less about fear and more about possibility.

Money is not paper, coins or digits. It is trust, energy and possibility. The earlier you understand this, the faster you stop chasing money and start guiding it. Because at the end of the day, money is not the story. You are. Money is simply the pen in your hand. What matters is the life you write with it.

In the chapters to come, we'll break money into its four destinations: spending, saving, investing and giving. We'll explore how to budget without boredom, how to grow money through compounding, how to protect it with insurance and how to align it with your dreams.

But all of that will only work if you remember this first lesson: money itself isn't the goal. It's what you do with it that matters.

Worksheet: My Relationship with Money

Take 10–15 minutes to jot down your thoughts. Don't overthink. Be honest.

1. **Your First Memory of Money**

    o What's the first thing you remember buying with your own money?

    o How did it make you feel?

____

____

2. **What Money Means to You**

    o In one word, finish this sentence: "To me, money feels like _______."

3. **The Goal vs. Tool Test**

    o Do you think about money more as an end goal, or as a tool? Why?

____

____

4. **Your Barter Skill**

    o If money disappeared tomorrow and society went back to barter, what could you trade? (Your skills, your services, your resources).

____

____

5. **Reframing Exercise**

    o Write one sentence that reframes your relationship with money.

____

____

2

Spend, Save, Invest, Give

When I was young, my father told me something I didn't fully understand at the time. He said, "Every rupee that comes into your hands has only four places it can go. You can spend it, you can save it, you can invest it or you can give it away." Back then, I thought he was just giving me another one of his grown-up lessons, like "finish your homework before you play." But years later, after working, earning, saving and even struggling with money at times, I realized how profound that simple statement really was.

Every dollar you and I will ever earn has only those four possible destinations. That's it. No magic fifth option, no secret loophole. You can spend, save, invest or give.

The simplicity is deceptive. Because while those four choices look straightforward on paper, in real life they are anything but. How much do you spend? How much do you save? How do you invest? When and where do you give? Those decisions shape not just your finances but your peace of mind, your opportunities, even your relationships.

The problem is that most people tilt too heavily toward one or two of the jars and ignore the rest. Some people spend everything, chasing lifestyle upgrades and instant gratification. Others hoard money, saving endlessly but never enjoying it. Some invest aggressively but forget the importance of having a safety net. And some give generously to others while quietly neglecting their own security.

When one jar dominates, your financial life gets out of balance.

I've seen this in coaching countless times. High-earning professionals who seem successful on the outside but are drowning in expenses.

Frugal savers who look secure but secretly feel they missed out on life. Impatient investors who chase every "hot tip" but never let compounding work its quiet magic. And well-meaning givers who feel burned out because they forgot to take care of themselves.

The truth is, financial peace doesn't come from any single jar. It comes from balance.

A Simple Framework, A Lifelong Practice

When you zoom out, this framework of spend, save, invest and give is the foundation of personal finance. It's like the four directions on a compass. Every financial decision points one way or another.

You buy groceries → that's spending.

You put aside money in a savings account → that's saving.

You contribute to your 401(k) → that's investing.

You donate to a cause, help family or volunteer time → that's giving.

Everything you do with money fits into one of these buckets. The question isn't which you'll use. The question is <u>how much of each</u> and whether your choices align with the life you actually want.

If Chapter 1 was about redefining what money really is - *trust, belief, a tool, not the goal* - then this chapter is about giving that tool direction. Because without direction, money slips away. It gets consumed by impulse purchases, eaten by inflation or left idle in accounts that don't grow.

But when you consciously choose how to distribute your money across these four jars, you take back control. You stop wondering, *"Where did my money go?"* and start deciding, *"Here's where I want my money to go."* Because money is like water: if you don't direct its flow, it seeps away unnoticed. But if you channel it wisely; some for today, some for tomorrow, some for growth, some for others; it can nourish every part of your life.

This chapter will walk through each jar in turn. We'll look at real stories - some inspiring, some cautionary - and simple analogies that make the concepts stick. And at the end, you'll have a framework you can use for the rest of your life.

We'll start with the most obvious jar: spending. Because spending is where most of us live day to day. It's the fruit we eat today and it's also the place where financial leaks quietly drain the harvest.

Reflection Pause

Take a moment right now. If you had to guess, out of every $100 you earn:

- How much do you spend?
- How much do you save?
- How much do you invest?
- How much do you give?

Write down your best estimate. Don't overthink. Don't calculate. Just be honest. That rough guess is your starting point

---

SPENDING: THE NOW

Let me introduce you to *Carter*, a client I once worked with. On paper, he was living the dream. Mid-thirties, working at a top tech company, pulling in close to $300,000 a year. His colleagues envied him, his family praised him and his lifestyle was the kind you'd expect from someone in the top few percent of earners.

But when we sat down to review his finances, his first words shocked me. "Every month," he said, "I feel broke." How could someone earning three times more than the national average possibly feel broke?

As we dug deeper, the answer unfolded. Here's where Carter's money was going:

- A leased luxury European SUV: $2,200 a month.

- Two international vacations every year with his wife, five-star hotels and business-class flights included: about $50,000 annually.
- Frequent gadget upgrades - a new iPhone after every launch plus smartwatches, earbuds and the latest Macbook.
- Designer handbags and watches, which he and his wife treated as "investments" but really were status symbols: around $20,000 a year.
- Dining out: fine restaurants every weekend, brunches with friends, mid-week takeout. That bill alone topped $1,500 a month.
- Plus the small leaks: subscription boxes, luxury gym memberships, streaming platforms, impulse Amazon purchases.

Out of his salary, almost every dollar was spoken for.

Carter wasn't starving. He wasn't struggling to pay the bills. But he was trapped in something more subtle: <u>lifestyle inflation</u>. Every time his income rose, his expenses climbed higher. He had more fruit than ever, but he was eating it all.

This is where I introduced Carter to a simple analogy of the Fruit and the Seeds.

"Think of your income," I told him, "as a basket of fruit. Every month, you harvest fresh fruit. And you've been eating almost all of it right away: the vacations, the cars, the gadgets. The fruit tastes sweet, no doubt. But once it's gone, it's gone.

Here's what you're forgetting: inside every piece of fruit is a seed. You can eat the fruit now, freeze some for next month and also you can take some seeds and plant them. Seeds don't give you instant satisfaction, they look small and unimpressive compared to the juicy mango in your hand. But if you plant them, they grow into trees that keep producing more fruit, year after year.

If you eat everything you harvest today, there's nothing left to plant. And when tomorrow comes, your basket is empty. But if you plant wisely, one day you'll have more fruit than you could ever eat." I watched the realization sink in. For the first time, Carter understood why he felt broke despite his big paycheck. It wasn't his income that was the problem. It was his consumption. He was eating all the fruit and planting none of the seeds.

The Paradox of Spending

That's the paradox of spending: it feels good in the moment, but it leaves you vulnerable for the future. And the higher your income, the easier it is to fall into the trap. Because with more money, the fruit looks bigger, juicier, harder to resist.

There's nothing wrong with spending. We all need food, shelter, clothing and the occasional indulgence that makes life enjoyable. But when spending becomes the only destination for your money, you're not building a life; you're just treading water.

Spending everything you earn is like running on a treadmill. You're working hard, but you're not moving forward.

Here's the dangerous part: people who spend everything don't always realize the risk until it's too late. What happens if Carter loses his job tomorrow? With almost no savings and little invested, he'd be scrambling within weeks. The vacations and watches would suddenly feel hollow compared to the stress of covering his mortgage and bills.

The sweetness of spending today often hides the bitterness of insecurity tomorrow.

The solution isn't to stop spending altogether. That would be unrealistic, even joyless. The solution is to spend with intention.

When you spend, ask yourself if you are eating this fruit because you truly enjoy it, or because you feel pressured by status, habit, or impulse? Spending intentionally doesn't mean deprivation. It means aligning your spending with your values. For some, that might mean fewer gadgets but more travel. For others, fewer luxury dinners but more experiences with family. The point is to decide, not drift.

Spending is the most visible part of money. It's where most of us live day to day. But if you let it dominate, you'll always feel like you're running hard but staying in place. The key is to enjoy the fruit, but never forget to plant the seeds.

Reflection Pause

Take a moment to reflect on your own basket of fruit.

☐ Do you know where your biggest bites go — housing, dining, gadgets, vacations?

☐ If your income stopped tomorrow, how long could you keep eating at the same pace?

Write down your answers. Awareness is the first step toward balance.

SAVING: THE CUSHION

If spending is about enjoying the fruit today, saving is about keeping some aside for tomorrow. It doesn't grow like investing and it doesn't sparkle like spending, but it creates something invaluable: security.

I once worked with a couple who lived modestly, earned steady salaries and raised two kids. They didn't drive flashy cars, they didn't take exotic vacations and they didn't post pictures of luxury dinners on Instagram. What they *did* have was an emergency fund worth about twelve months of living expenses, tucked safely in a savings account.

Then the unexpected happened. Husband and wife lost their jobs within weeks of each other as companies downsized, markets dipped and economy started to slow. Suddenly, their primary sources of income disappeared overnight.

Most families in that situation would panic. Bills pile up, credit cards get swiped, loans start creeping in. Stress skyrockets and relationships strain. But the couple didn't panic. They dipped into their savings, covered their bills and bought themselves time. Wife found another job within six months, husband in ten. Their kids never felt the pinch, their mortgage was paid and their dignity remained intact.

That's the power of saving. It's not glamorous, but it's steady. Nobody claps for you when you quietly transfer money into a savings account. Instagram won't congratulate you for topping up your emergency fund. But in the real world, saving is what prevents financial earthquakes from becoming life-ending disasters. It's the difference between crisis and inconvenience.

The Seatbelt Analogy

I like to think of saving as wearing a seatbelt. Most of the time, you don't notice it. You buckle up, you drive and nothing happens. But the day something unexpected does happen, that simple seatbelt can save your life.

An emergency fund is your financial seatbelt. It won't make you wealthy, but it will keep you safe. It will prevent an accident from turning into a disaster.

If saving is so important, why do so many people skip it?

One reason is that saving feels invisible. When you buy a new phone, you see it, feel it, show it off. When you save money, nothing seems to happen. It just sits in an account, silently waiting. Human brains love instant rewards and gratification, and saving doesn't give you that rush.

Another reason is that people tell themselves they'll save "later." After the next raise. After the next vacation. After the next bonus. But "later" rarely comes, because lifestyle inflation always fills the gap.

That's why I often tell clients:

Saving isn't what you do with leftovers. It's what you do first.

Most people think of saving only as protection, as money for emergencies, unexpected expenses, job loss. And that's true. But saving does more than protect. It also creates opportunity.

I once coached a woman named *Leah* who always wanted to start her own business. She had the skills, the idea and the drive. What she lacked was the cushion. Without savings, she felt trapped in her job. But once she built a one-year emergency fund, she quit confidently and launched her venture. Today, she's thriving.

That's what saving buys: freedom. It doesn't just cover the downside; it opens the upside. It gives you the courage to take risks because you know you have a cushion to fall back on.

The most common question I hear: *So, How Much Should I Save?*. My Answer: **It Depends**. It depends to your specific situation. The common guideline is to aim for three to six months of essential living expenses, enough to cover housing, food, utilities and other basics if your income suddenly stopped.

But that's only a starting point. Your situation can tilt the number higher or lower:

- If you're the sole earner in your household or your job has ups and downs, lean toward the higher end - six months or more.
- If you're in a dual-income household with stable, predictable work, three months may be enough of a cushion.
- If you're planning to buy a house, it's wise to save more, because those first months often bring extra expenses - furniture, repair and all the little things you didn't budget for.
- If you're an immigrant, the uncertainty of relocation, visas or potential moves means you'll want a thicker safety net.
- And if you're a parent with kids heading to college, saving on the higher side helps you handle tuition surprises, living expenses and emergencies without panic.

The rule of thumb gives you a baseline. Your personal circumstances decide whether you should build higher walls around your financial safety net. The number isn't as important as the principle:

Build a cushion that helps you sleep at night.

Here's something worth remembering: saving is not a competition. Don't measure your success by someone else's bank balance. For some, saving $500 is a milestone. For others, it's $50,000. What matters is whether your savings protect you and align with your needs.

Saving isn't about deprivation. It's about preparation. It doesn't mean you stop enjoying life today; it means you make sure today's joy doesn't turn into tomorrow's regret. Because when you have a cushion, you live with confidence, knowing you're protected, prepared and ready for what comes next.

Reflection Pause

Imagine two people. One has a sports car worth $120,000 and no savings. The other has an old sedan worth $18,000 and $45,000 in the bank. Who is wealthier? The car looks flashy but depreciates every day. The savings sit quietly but protect, enable and empower.

- ☐ If your paycheck stopped tomorrow, how long could you cover your current lifestyle without borrowing?
- ☐ Do you save only what's left after spending, or do you save first and spend what's left?
- ☐ What opportunity could you create if you had six months of expenses saved?

INVESTING: THE GROWTH

If spending is enjoying the fruit today and saving is storing some fruit for tomorrow, then investing is planting the seeds. At first, seeds don't look like much - small, fragile, almost unimpressive compared to the juicy fruit you gave up. But given time, sunlight and patience, seeds turn into trees that bear fruit season after season.

Take *Maya*, a young engineer who started her career at 25. She wasn't earning a huge salary, but she made one wise choice: she set aside $500 a month into a retirement account, invested in a simple stock market index fund.

At first, the results felt underwhelming. After a year, she had around $6,000 saved, plus a little growth. Not life-changing. After five years, she had $40,000. Respectable, but still not jaw-dropping. But then compounding, the eighth wonder of the world, kicked in. By 35, her account crossed $100,000. By 45, assuming she stays consistent, it could grow past $400,000. By 55, it could be close to $1 million - all from the steady planting of $500 seeds each month with total contributions of just about $185,000. And the best part, another 10 years of contributions will double the amount to $2M+.

Maya didn't chase trends or gamble on hot stocks. She **simply planted, watered and waited**.

Now compare that to *Rahul*, a consultant who earned more than Maya. He wanted fast results, so he jumped in and out of the stock market depending on the headlines. He sold when markets dipped, chased the latest tech stock when it was already expensive, and "paused investing" whenever life got hectic. Over ten years, he contributed more than Maya - but his results were worse. Why? Because he never let compounding do its quiet work. He kept digging up his seeds to see if they had grown.

Investing isn't about chasing the shiny fruit on someone else's tree.
It's about planting your own orchard and letting it mature.

The Snowball Effect

Investing is like rolling a snowball down a hill. At the top, the snowball is tiny. With each roll, it picks up a little more snow. At first, progress looks slow. But as it keeps rolling, it gets bigger, heavier, faster. Eventually, it's an unstoppable force.

That's how money works when you invest wisely. The earlier you start, the longer your snowball rolls and the more powerful compounding becomes.

Let's do a simple exercise.

- *Lena* starts investing at 25, putting in $300 a month for 10 years, then stops. She contributes a total of $36,000.

- *James* waits until 35 to start. He invests the same $300 a month, but for 30 years straight. He contributes $108,000.

At age 65, who do you think has more? You can use excel or any online calculator.

Surprisingly, it's Lena, the one who invested less money, for less time. Why? Because her money had more years to compound. Her snowball started rolling earlier. That's the magic of time. When it comes to investing, time in the market beats timing the market.

The hardest part of investing isn't knowledge - it's patience. Most people know they should invest. What trips them up is the waiting. We live in a world of instant gratification - two-day shipping, on-demand streaming, same-day groceries. Investing doesn't work that way. Trees don't grow overnight. Orchards don't appear in a season. Investing rewards those who can delay gratification and let time do its work.

Investing vs. Saving

This is also why saving and investing are different. Saving keeps money safe but stagnant, like storing fruit in a fridge. Investing puts money at risk, but also gives it a chance to grow, like planting seeds. Both matter, but they serve different purposes.

You save for the short-term and emergencies. You invest for the long-term and growth. Confuse the two and you either stay stagnant (too much saving) or risk disaster (too much investing without a cushion).

Investing doesn't look the same everywhere.

- In the U.S., people often use 401(k)s, IRAs and brokerage accounts.
- In the U.K., there are ISAs and workplace pensions.
- In India, it might be mutual funds, PPFs, or fixed deposits alongside stocks.

- In Kenya, many people invest through SACCOs or community funds.

The vehicles differ, but the principle is universal: plant seeds, give them time and let them grow.

Investing isn't about luck or brilliance. It's about patience, discipline and time. The seeds look unimpressive at first, but one day, they grow into orchards you can live on and pass on.

Reflection Pause

☐ If you started investing today, how many years would your snowball have to roll?

☐ Are you more like Maya (consistent planter) or Rahul (impatient digger)?

What's one small seed you could plant this month, even if it feels insignificant?

GIVING: THE FULFILLMENT

If spending is about today, saving is about safety and investing is about tomorrow, then giving is about meaning. It's the part of money most people overlook, but often the part that makes us feel richest.

When I talk about giving, some people immediately push back.

"I barely have enough for myself — how can I give?"

"I'll donate once I'm rich."

"Charity is for people with more money than me."

But here's the thing: giving isn't about the size of your wallet. It's about the size of your heart. And the strange irony is, the act of giving often makes you feel wealthier, not poorer.

Take *Neha*, a marketing professional. She wasn't a millionaire. She earned a comfortable salary but lived modestly. One day she decided to sponsor a girl's education in India. The cost? About the same as one fancy dinner a month.

Every few months, she'd receive letters and drawings from the student. "Thank you for helping me go to school." "I want to be a teacher when I grow up." Neha once told me, "That little girl's success means more to me than any bonus I've ever earned." For her, giving turned money from numbers into meaning.

Here's how I like to put it: giving is like lighting another candle. When you light someone else's candle, your flame doesn't shrink. The room just gets brighter. Money spent only on yourself satisfies you briefly. Money given to others has a way of echoing, rippling, multiplying.

Different Faces of Giving

Giving doesn't always mean charity donations. It comes in many forms:
* ***Money***: *Donating to causes, helping a struggling friend, supporting community projects.*
* ***Time***: *Volunteering at a local shelter, coaching kids, mentoring younger professionals.*
* ***Skills***: *Offering expertise to nonprofits, helping someone with a résumé, teaching financial literacy.*
* ***Kindness***: *Covering a stranger's coffee, tipping generously, small acts that make someone's day.*
Each one creates impact. Each one reminds you that money is a tool, not just for you, but for others.

Another example: *Marla*, a retired nurse in Chicago. She had a modest pension, not a huge fortune. But every week, she volunteered at a local soup kitchen. "I don't have millions to give," she said, "but I can give my hands and my heart." Her presence meant people felt cared for. Her giving wasn't money, but it was priceless.

Even research backs this up. Studies show that people who give, whether money, time or support, report higher levels of happiness than those who only spend on themselves. It activates parts of the brain linked to pleasure and reward. In other words, giving makes us feel good. That's why giving isn't just noble. It's practical. It enriches your life as much as it helps others.

The Global Perspective

Giving also looks different across cultures.

- *In the U.S.,* philanthropy *often takes the form of donations to nonprofits or foundations.*
- *In Japan, people practice* osettai, *small acts of kindness and gifts that reinforce community.*
- *In parts of Africa, the concept of* ubuntu *emphasizes shared humanity where helping neighbors is seen as helping yourself.*
- *In India, the idea of* daan *(charitable giving) has been part of spiritual practice for centuries.*

Different names, same principle: money finds its deepest meaning when it flows outward.

Of course, giving doesn't mean neglecting yourself. You can't pour from an empty cup. The key is balance. Give in ways that are sustainable, joyful and meaningful. Even a small slice of your income or time can make a big difference.

When you give, you remind yourself that money is a tool, not a trophy.

Spending brings pleasure. Saving brings safety. Investing brings growth. But giving brings fulfillment. It reminds us that money isn't just a private tool but a shared resource. It connects us to something bigger than ourselves. Because at the end of the day, wealth isn't just measured by what you keep. It's measured by what you give and lives you touch along the way.

Reflection Pause

☐ Think of a time you gave - money, time or help. How did it make you feel afterward?

☐ If you could dedicate 1% of your income to any cause, what would it be?

☐ Beyond money, what skills or time could you give that might change someone's life?

THE BALANCE OF THE FOUR JARS

Imagine four jars sitting on your kitchen counter. Every dollar you earn flows into those jars. One jar is for spending, one for saving, one for investing and the last one for giving. At the end of the month, the jars show you where your priorities really lie.

Most of us, whether we realize it or not, already live with these jars. The trouble is that for many people, one jar dominates while the others sit nearly empty.

I once met *Daniel*. His spending jar overflowed, like Carter in the Spending scenario, with designer clothes, gourmet dining, concerts every weekend. But his saving and investing jars were nearly empty. When he hit a health setback and had to stop working for six months, he quickly fell into debt. His full spending jar gave him pleasure but no protection.

Then there was *Harper*, a meticulous saver. She hated spending money, even on herself. Every raise went straight into her savings account. But she never invested and she never treated herself. Ten years later, her account balance was respectable, but inflation had quietly eaten away at its power. She lived cautiously, yet she never felt truly free.

I also think of *Kenji*, who loved investing. He poured every spare yen into the stock market. For a while, he felt brilliant watching his portfolio climb. But when markets dipped, he had no emergency fund, no cash on hand. He was forced to sell at the worst possible time. His seeds were planted, but he had no fruit to eat in the meantime.

And then there's *Amira*, who had a heart for giving. She supported her extended family, donated to her community and often helped friends in need. But she never saved or invested for herself. When she faced her own financial hardship, she had to depend on others. Her generosity was beautiful, but it left her vulnerable.

Each of them was leaning too heavily on one jar. The balance was missing.

The Four Jars Together

The truth is, none of the jars are bad. Spending keeps you alive and brings joy. Saving protects you. Investing grows your future. Giving connects you to others and creates meaning.

But just like a chair needs all four legs to stand steady, your financial life needs all four jars in balance. Too much in one and too little in the others and things wobble.

Remember the basket of fruit analogy? Here's how it connects to the jars:

- The **fruit you eat now** goes into the spending jar.

- The **fruit you store for later** is your saving jar.

- The **seeds you plant for the future** fill your investing jar.

- The **fruit you share with others** belongs in the giving jar.

A healthy financial life has some of each. Eat enough fruit to enjoy life, but don't eat it all. Store enough to feel secure, but don't hoard until it rots. Plant enough seeds to ensure a future orchard. Share enough to brighten others' lives without leaving yourself empty.

There's no single formula for the perfect mix. For some, it might be 60% spending, 20% saving, 15% investing, 5% giving. For others, it might shift. What matters isn't the exact percentages but whether your jars reflect your values and goals.

The danger comes when you never look at the jars at all. If you don't pay attention, the spending jar fills by default. The others get whatever crumbs are left.

I once worked with *Sofia*, a teacher in Spain. Her salary wasn't high, but she divided it intentionally:

- 60% spending,
- 19% saving,
- 20% investing,
- 1% giving.

She told me, "I don't feel rich, but I feel at peace." Each jar was modest, but together they created balance. When emergencies came, she had savings. When opportunities arose, she had investments. When friends needed help, she could give. And she still enjoyed life today.

That's the beauty of balance. It's not about how much you have but about how well you direct it.

Money becomes powerful when it flows through all four jars. When you spend with joy, save with confidence, invest with patience and give with meaning, you stop feeling like money controls you. You begin to feel like you control money.

Balance doesn't happen by accident. It happens by design. The jars are already on your counter. The question is: how will you fill them?

Reflection Pause

☐ Which of your four jars is overflowing right now? Which one is almost empty?

☐ If you had to rebalance, which jar would you start strengthening first?

☐ What's one small shift you could make this month - 1% less spending, 1% more saving, 1% more giving - to bring the jars closer to your balance?

DIRECTING THE FLOW

By now, you've seen the four destinations every dollar has: spend, save, invest and give. These jars aren't optional. Every person on earth uses them, whether they realize it or not. The difference between financial chaos and financial clarity comes from how consciously you fill them.

Spending gives you joy today. Saving protects you tomorrow. Investing builds your future. Giving connects you to meaning beyond yourself. Each jar has its purpose. Each one matters.

Think about a river. If the flow is blocked in one direction, it floods or dries up in another. Money works the same way. Too much toward spending and you're left vulnerable. Too much toward saving and you stagnate. Too much toward investing and you starve today for a tomorrow that may never come. Too much toward giving and you risk running on empty yourself.

Balance isn't just a nice idea; it's the difference between feeling constantly anxious about money and feeling in control. It's what turns money from stress into strength.

The Stories Revisited

Remember Carter, the high earner who spent almost everything? He had fruit but no seeds. Remember the couple with savings who weathered a job loss calmly? Their cushion gave them security. Remember Maya, who planted her $500 seeds consistently and built an orchard over time? Patience turned her into a millionaire. And remember Neha, whose modest giving transformed not just her sponsored student's life, but her own sense of fulfillment?

Each of them illustrates a jar. Together, they show the whole picture.

Here's the truth: no one fills their jars perfectly. There will always be seasons when one jar takes more than the others. That's okay. What matters is awareness and intention.

Your jars tell the story of your values. If you want more security, strengthen your saving jar. If you want more growth, focus on investing. If you want more joy, rebalance your spending. If you want more meaning, commit to giving. *The jars don't judge you. They just reflect you.*

The Power of Small Shifts

One of the most encouraging lessons I've learned as a coach is that balance doesn't require massive changes. Sometimes just shifting 1–2% of your income makes a huge difference.

If you spend 98% of your income and save 2%, try flipping it to 90/10. If you never invest, start with $50 a month. If you've never given, try giving enough to cover one meal for someone else. Small adjustments compound - not just in your bank account, but in your mindset.

As I mentioned earlier in the chapter, money is like water. Left unattended, it seeps away. Directed with care, it nourishes everything it touches. The four jars are your channels. Together, they ensure your money doesn't just vanish but it flows with purpose.

And the beauty of the four jars is their simplicity. Anyone, at any income level, can use them. They remind us that money isn't about mystery formulas or complex spreadsheets. It's about choice. Every dollar you earn will end up in one of these jars. The only question is: **are you choosing the balance, or is the balance choosing you?**

Because at the end of the day, financial peace doesn't come from having the most money. It comes from knowing where your money is going and why.

Worksheet: My Four Jars

Take 15 minutes. Be honest. This isn't about right or wrong but about clarity.

1. **Where My Money Goes Now**

    o   Out of every $100 I earn, I currently spend: ___ %

    o   Save: ___ %

    o   Invest: ___ %

    o   Give: ___ %

2. **Jar Strengths and Weaknesses**

    o   My strongest jar is: ___________

    o   My weakest jar is: ___________

3. **My Next Small Shift**

    o   One action I can take this month to strengthen my weakest jar is:

    ____

4. **Values Alignment**

    o   Do my jars reflect what I truly value? If not, what would I change?

    ____

    ____

5. **Future Balance**

    o   What does a balanced set of jars look like for me five years from now?

    ____

    ____

3

Budgeting Without the Boring

The very word *budget* makes many people groan. It carries the same emotional weight as the word *diet*. Restriction. Rules. Guilt. No fun allowed.

I've seen this play out dozens of times. A client will sit across from me and say, "I know I should budget, but I just can't stick to one." They'll tell me about how they downloaded a fancy app, tracked every single transaction for three weeks and then gave up. Why? Because it felt like homework. Every purchase came with a dose of guilt and soon they were avoiding the app altogether.

One client, *Sarah*, told me she tried the "perfect budget" once. She created categories for everything...groceries, gas, streaming subscriptions and even coffee. She proudly tracked every cent for a month. At the end, she was exhausted. She said, "I spent more time updating my spreadsheet than enjoying my life." By month two, the budget was abandoned, replaced by guilt and avoidance.

That's the diet problem. Strict diets often fail because they're unsustainable. You can cut carbs, sugar or calories for a few weeks, but eventually life happens - you go to a birthday party, or someone brings donuts to the office. You indulge, feel guilty and the diet collapses.

Budgets work the same way. If they're too rigid, too complicated or too joyless, they collapse. People quit and tell themselves, "I'm just not disciplined with money." But the problem isn't discipline - it's design.

Here's the shift I want you to see:

A budget is not a restriction. A budget is a permission slip.

Think about it. Without a budget, money slips through your fingers. You swipe your card, tap your phone, pay your bills and by the end of the month, you're left wondering, *where did it all go?* That uncertainty is stressful.

A budget removes that stress. It tells your money where to go, instead of leaving you wondering where it went. Far from being restrictive, that's liberating.

Imagine planning a vacation. You book flights, hotels and activities. You know what's covered and you can relax because everything's accounted for. That's what a budget does for your daily life. It gives you the confidence that the essentials are covered, your goals are funded and most importantly, your fun is guilt-free.

Budgets Are About Choice

The truth is, budgeting isn't about saying "no" to everything. It's about deciding what you want to say yes to.

- *If travel lights you up, your budget can include a travel fund.*
- *If you love trying new restaurants, you can carve out money for dining out.*
- *If security matters most, your budget can emphasize savings and insurance.*

The point isn't to copy someone else's budget. The point is to build one that reflects your values. Just like a diet should fit your lifestyle (not everyone wants to live on kale smoothies), a budget should fit your life.

I'll never forget working with *Marco*, a young professional in Dallas, TX. He loved soccer, concerts and weekend barbecues with friends. When we first talked about budgeting, he looked horrified. "You mean I can't do those things anymore?". "Not at all," I told him. "In fact, a budget means you can do them guilt-free."

We set aside a line item called "fun fund." Every month, Marco put aside money specifically for those activities. Suddenly, instead of overspending and feeling anxious later, he enjoyed his weekends fully.

His friends teased him for being "organized," but Marco laughed. He said, "For the first time, I know my bills are paid, my savings are growing and I can party without stress." That's the freedom of budgeting. It doesn't take joy away. *It protects joy.*

So why do most people still hate the word? Because they associate it with punishment. Somewhere along the line, we were told budgets are about cutting back, denying yourself or living on scraps. That's simply not true.

A good budget isn't about scarcity. It's about clarity. It's about making sure your money reflects your values, not someone else's. It's about ensuring you're steering the car, instead of letting money drive you wherever it wants.

Here's the promise of this chapter: budgeting doesn't have to be boring. It doesn't have to be spreadsheets and guilt. Done right, budgeting is empowering. It's the bridge between your income and your dreams.

Over the next sections, we'll look at why most budgets fail, simple frameworks like the 50/30/20 rule, the power of automation and how to design a budget that reflects *your* values. By the end, you won't see budgeting as a diet you dread. You'll see it as a lifestyle you choose that gives you freedom, confidence and control.

Reflection Pause

☐ When you hear the word "budget," what's your first reaction — excitement, stress, or guilt?

☐ If you've tried budgeting before, what frustrated you the most? Was it too detailed, too rigid, or just boring?

☐ If a budget could feel like a permission slip instead of a restriction, how would your relationship with money change?

WHY MOST BUDGETS FAIL

If budgets are supposed to give us freedom, why do so many people abandon them within weeks? I've seen it again and again - the excitement of starting, the frustration of tracking and the guilt of quitting.

Take *Jamie*, a consultant. At the start of a new year, he resolved to finally "get serious" about his money. He downloaded a budgeting app, linked his accounts and created a dozen categories: rent, groceries, utilities, transportation, clothing, dining out, streaming services, gym membership, coffee shops, gifts, medical expenses, travel and "miscellaneous."

For the first week, he was on fire. Every expense was logged. Every dollar had a label. Jamie felt like he was in control. By week three, things started slipping. His app glitched and disconnected one of the cards, so he forgot to log a taxi ride. When he bought groceries, he wondered whether to put them under "groceries" or "dining" because some of it was pre-made food. His app kept sending reminders. He grew frustrated. By week six, he'd stopped updating it altogether. When I met him months later, he sighed. "I guess I'm just not disciplined enough."

But here's the truth: Jamie didn't fail because of discipline. His budget failed because it built on *The Complexity Trap*. Products and Apps create too many categories, track every cent and turn budgeting into a second job. To hit their engagement numbers, apps keep sending you notifications.

But life is messy. Some weeks you buy groceries, some weeks you order takeout, some weeks you do both. Some months you travel, others you don't. A budget with twenty categories sounds precise, but it collapses under the weight of real life. Budgets need to be simple enough to follow when you're busy, tired or distracted. If a budget requires perfect attention, it won't last.

Another reason budgets fail is _rigidity_. Some apps tell you exactly how much you "should" spend in each category. Housing should be 30%. Food should be 15%. Transportation should be 10%.

But here's the issue: people don't live cookie-cutter lives. Someone living in San Francisco or Singapore may spend 50% of their income on housing. Someone living with family in a small town may spend only 10%. Forcing both into the same mold is a recipe for guilt and failure. Budgets have to flex with your reality. If they don't, you'll either abandon them or live constantly frustrated.

Many people believe budgeting is about _willpower_ - resisting the urge to spend, sticking to strict rules. But willpower is unreliable. It's strong on January 1st, weaker on February 10th and nearly gone by March. Sustainable budgeting isn't about willpower, it is about seamlessness. The best budgets reduce the number of decisions you have to make, instead of multiplying them.

And then, there is also the _"all-or-nothing" trap_. People start a budget, stick to it for two weeks, then overspend one weekend. Instead of adjusting, they declare the whole budget a failure and give up.

It's the same with diets. You eat a slice of cake on day 10 and instead of moving on, you think, "I ruined it, might as well give up."

Budgets aren't meant to be perfect. They're meant to guide. A missed target doesn't mean failure - it means recalibration.

The Guilt Factor

Budgets fail because they're built on guilt. People design budgets that allow for rent, bills and groceries and nothing else. No room for coffee with friends, hobbies, or fun. Of course, those budgets fail! They erase joy. And joyless systems don't last.

A sustainable budget has room for living. It acknowledges that you'll buy the latte, take the trip, or see the concert. By planning for it, the joy becomes guilt-free instead of guilt-ridden.

The Lesson from Marco

When *Marco* and I revisited his budget, I asked him to throw out his app. We rebuilt it with just four categories:
1. **Needs** (housing, groceries, bills)
2. **Wants** (dining, travel, entertainment)
3. **Savings/Investing**
4. **Giving**

That was it. Four jars, not fourteen categories. Suddenly, budgeting was simple. Marco no longer stressed about whether groceries should be split between "meals" and "snacks." He just knew how much went into "needs," "wants," and so on. Within months, he felt in control again - not because he tracked every penny, but because he tracked what mattered.

Most budgets fail not because people are weak, but because the systems are weak. Complexity, rigidity, willpower dependence, guilt - they doom the process from the start.

But when budgets are simple, flexible and value-driven, they don't feel like punishment. They feel like clarity. And clarity is something you'll want to keep.

Reflection Pause

☐ Have you ever started a budget and abandoned it? What made it fail? Too much detail, too much rigidity, or too much guilt?
☐ If you had to track only four categories - needs, wants, savings, giving - how would your spending look?

THE 50/30/20 RULE AND ITS FLEXIBILITY

Once people realize their budgets don't need to be complicated, the next question is: *"Okay, but how do I decide what goes where?"*

One of the simplest and most popular frameworks comes from U.S. Senator Elizabeth Warren's book *All Your Worth*. It's called the **50/30/20 rule** and it's as straightforward as it sounds:

- 50% of your income goes to needs
- 30% to wants
- 20% to savings and investments

It's a clean, simple rule of thumb. Not perfect, but a great starting point. To see it in practice, let's say your take-home pay is $4,000 a month.

- 50% for needs = $2,000 (rent, groceries, utilities, insurance, transportation).
- 30% for wants = $1,200 (dining out, vacations, hobbies, shopping, entertainment).
- 20% for saving and investing = $800 (emergency fund, retirement accounts, index funds).

That's it. With three numbers, you've covered the big picture.

Of course, life isn't the same everywhere. A rule that works in one city may not fit neatly in another.

Take *John* in New York City. His rent alone eats up 45% of his take-home pay. Strictly following 50/30/20 would make him feel like a failure. Instead, he adjusted his rule: 60/20/20. He spends more on needs, trims wants and still saves 20%.

Meanwhile, *Ananya* earns a lower salary but lives with her parents. Her "needs" are only 25% of her income. That gives her room to save nearly 40% while still enjoying her wants. Her jars look more like 25/35/40.

And *Joseph* works a government job with modest pay. For him, 20% saving feels impossible right now. We started with 5% investing and aimed to increase it gradually. His first step wasn't perfection but momentum.

The principle is simple, but the application is flexible.

Why the Rule Works

The genius of 50/30/20 isn't the exact percentages - it's the categories. It forces you to think in broad buckets instead of obsessing over every coffee purchase. It also reminds you that savings and investments aren't optional. They're part of the plan, baked in from the start.

Another benefit: it's easy to remember. Whether you earn in dollars, rupees, yen or pounds, the categories stay the same. You don't need an app or a spreadsheet to keep track.

I once worked with *Lena*, a nurse. She hated spreadsheets and told me, "Numbers stress me out." When we tried 50/30/20, her shoulders relaxed. She grabbed a notebook and wrote three numbers at the start of each month:

- $1,500 for needs
- $900 for wants
- $600 for savings/investing

As long as her spending stayed inside those boundaries, she didn't stress over the details. For the first time, budgeting felt doable instead of overwhelming.

The danger with any framework is turning it into law. If you treat 50/30/20 as a strict commandment, it can backfire. People in expensive cities may feel discouraged. People in unique situations may feel guilty. Think of the 50/30/20 rule is like training wheels. It's not the ultimate destination, but it gets you moving. Once you find your balance, you can adjust the percentages to fit your own road.

The point isn't to hit the exact percentages. The point is to use them as a compass. If you're saving 2% today, the framework reminds you that the target is closer to 20%. If your wants are swallowing 60% of your income, it signals imbalance.

Flexibility makes the framework powerful. Rigidity makes it fragile.

Most importantly, budgeting isn't about chasing perfection. It's about awareness and direction. The 50/30/20 rule gives you both, without drowning you in detail. Even if your numbers don't match exactly, asking yourself, *"Am I closer to 50/30/20 or 70/25/5?"* instantly shows where you stand. That awareness alone can change your money habits.

Reflection Pause

☐ If you applied 50/30/20 to your current income, what would the three numbers look like?

☐ Do your actual percentages look very different? If so, which category is too high and which is too low?

☐ If you had to shift just 5% this month, where would it come from and where would it go?

THE "PAY YOURSELF FIRST" METHOD

One of the biggest reasons people struggle with saving and investing is simple: they wait until the end of the month to see what's left over. And by then, the answer is usually "not much." Rent, groceries, bills, dinners out, Amazon packages and the occasional emergency seem to eat everything. That's why one of the oldest, simplest and most powerful budgeting principles is this: **pay yourself first.**

Take *Amelia*, a project manager in Seattle. When we first talked, she told me, "I've tried to save for years, but every month something comes up". She wasn't careless. She earned well and managed her bills on time. But she was following the "leftover" method. She'd pay all her expenses, live her life and then hope there was something left to save. Most months, there wasn't.

When I suggested the "pay yourself first" method, she was skeptical. "How can I pay myself when there are so many bills?". She set it up anyway. On the first of every month, her paycheck hit. The same day, an automatic transfer moved 15% into a high-yield savings account. That money was gone before she even saw it.

Three months later, Amelia told me, "This is the first time I feel like I'm actually building wealth. It doesn't even hurt because I never see the money in the first place."

The Rock-in-a-Jar Analogy

There's a classic story about time management that applies perfectly here. Imagine a jar. If you fill it with sand first, then try to add rocks, the rocks won't fit. But if you place the big rocks in first, then pour the sand, everything fits together.

Your money works the same way. If you let the "sand" of daily spending fill the jar first, you'll never have space for the "rocks" i.e. savings, investing, long-term goals. But if you put the rocks in first (or pay yourself first), the sand still finds its way around them. You can live, enjoy and spend, but your priorities are already protected.

So, why does this work?

1. It removes willpower.

Willpower is like a battery. It drains throughout the day. If your savings depend on willpower at the end of the month, you'll usually skip it. Automation makes saving the default, not the exception.

2. It reframes priorities.

When you pay yourself first, you stop treating saving as optional. It becomes as non-negotiable as rent or groceries.

3. It scales with income.

If you set a percentage (say 15%), then when your income grows, your savings automatically grow too. Lifestyle inflation doesn't swallow it all.

When I share this method, people often say:

- *"But my expenses are too high to save first."* Start small. Even 2% matters. The habit is more important than the amount.

- *"What if I need the money later in the month?"* That's the point. If you save first, you'll learn to live within what's left. It's surprising how quickly people adapt.

- *"I'll start when I earn more."* No you won't. If you don't learn the habit at $50,000, you won't magically find it at $150,000. Habits grow with you.

I once worked with *Raj*, an IT consultant originally from India but now living in Texas. His salary was healthy but he admitted, "I keep upgrading my life every time I get a raise. It feels like I'm on a treadmill."

We set up a system: 10% went into his 401(k), 5% into a brokerage account, all automated - on payday. Six months later, he laughed. "I thought I'd miss the money, but I don't. My lifestyle adjusted without me even noticing. And now I have $12,000 invested." The treadmill stopped because Raj planted his rocks first.

The Global Reference

This principle shows up worldwide. In Japan, there's a concept called kakeibo - a household budgeting system where savings are planned first, not last. In parts of Africa, rotating savings groups (ROSCAs) enforce the same idea socially - everyone contributes at the start of the month and each member gets a turn receiving the pooled funds. Different cultures, same principle: you secure your future first, then live on the rest.

Paying yourself first is one of the simplest shifts you can make, yet it changes everything. It turns saving from a leftover into a priority. It builds wealth in the background, while you keep living your life.

Because here's the truth: no one ever "finds" extra money to save at the end of the month. You have to *take* it at the start. Pay yourself first and watch how quickly the jar begins to fill.

Reflection Pause

- ☐ Do you currently save at the start of the month or at the end?
- ☐ If you automated a small percentage — even 5% — on payday, how would your budget feel different?
- ☐ What's one "rock" you could put in your jar first this month?

BUDGETS THAT REFLECT VALUES

When most people think of budgets, they picture limits. "You can't buy this. You shouldn't spend on that." But the truth is, a budget done right isn't about limits. It's about alignment. A budget should reflect what *you* value, not what anyone else thinks you should value. Otherwise, you'll feel deprived or guilty and eventually, you'll quit.

Take *Ethan*, a software engineer living in Austin. During a session, he came to me frustrated. "I've tried budgeting, but it feels like punishment. It's all about cutting back. I want to enjoy my life". So I asked him a simple question: "What do you value most?". He didn't hesitate. "Travel. Seeing the world. Meeting new people."

But when we looked at his spending, there was no room for it. His money was going to random Amazon orders, impulse dining and endless subscription services he barely used. Travel, his top value, was squeezed out by noise.

So we restructured his budget. Every month, he created a "travel fund." It wasn't huge - just 5% of his income. But it was *intentional*. The next time Ethan bought plane tickets, he didn't feel guilty. He said, "I can now enjoy my trips without stressing over whether I'm being irresponsible." His budget didn't restrict him. It freed him to prioritize what mattered most.

Budgets as Permission Slips

Here's the reframe: a budget isn't a list of "no's." It's a permission slip.

- *Love concerts? Budget for them.*
- *Obsessed with coffee? Budget for it.*
- *Want to take annual family vacations? Budget for them.*

The point isn't to eliminate joy but to protect it. When your budget aligns with your values, every purchase feels intentional.

On the flip side, misaligned budgets cause frustration. I once worked with *Sofia*, a nurse in New Jersey. She loved reading and dreamed of building a home library. But she felt guilty every time she bought a book, because her "budget" didn't allow it. Meanwhile, she was spending hundreds every month on takeout she didn't even enjoy.

When we shifted her budget to include a monthly "book fund," her guilt vanished. She told me, "Every time I buy a book now, it feels like a gift I planned for myself." That's the difference between restriction and alignment.

I once spoke with a client group that included people from different backgrounds. It was fascinating to see how values shaped budgets.

- One family originally from China budgeted heavily for their child's education in tutors, classes, enrichment. For them, education was non-negotiable.

- Another couple from Brazil allocated more to gatherings and barbecues with family and friends. Their budget was a reflection of connection and community.

- A single professional in San Francisco built his budget around flexibility where savings and investments came first, because freedom from financial stress was his top value.

Different values, different budgets. No right or wrong, just alignment.

Budgets are not about saying no. They're about saying yes to the right things. When you align your budget with your values, you stop feeling guilty about spending. You stop feeling deprived. Instead, every purchase feels like an investment in the life you actually want.

Because at the end of the day, money is only as powerful as the meaning you give it. And when your budget reflects your values, your money becomes a tool for joy, not just a list of limits.

Reflection Pause

☐ What are your top three values? (Write them down: family, freedom, travel, security, health, fun, or something else.)

☐ Look at your last three months of spending and circle the expenses that actually reflect the values. Do your last three months of spending reflect those values? Or do they reflect distractions?

☐ What's one category you'd increase if your budget truly matched your values? What's one you'd decrease?

TOOLS, TECH AND TRACKING

Once people understand the "why" behind budgeting, the next question is always, *"Okay, but how do I actually do it?"* This is where tools come in. And here's the good news: there's no shortage of options. From high-tech apps to old-school notebooks, you can find a system that fits your personality. The trick is not to chase the fanciest option, but to pick the one you'll actually use.

Some people thrive on apps. Take *Jamal*, a data analyst in Chicago. He loved numbers, graphs and dashboards. For him, using Mint (now discontinued) was like a game. He connected his accounts, watched his transactions auto-categorize and got a little dopamine hit every time the app sent him a progress report. Others prefer more proactive apps like YNAB (You Need a Budget). YNAB forces you to "give every dollar a job." It's hands-on and for some people, that accountability is powerful.

Then there are envelope-style apps like Goodbudget, which let you divide money into virtual envelopes for categories like groceries, dining and travel. Once the envelope is empty, you stop spending. Simple, visual, effective. If you're someone who likes digital tools and notifications, apps can be great. They keep your budget top of mind and give you instant feedback.

Then there are people who have tried apps but found them overwhelming. "Too many notifications, too many categories".

They prefer tools like Excel enabling them to build their own simple sheet: income at the top, four categories (needs, wants, savings, giving) down the side. At the end of each week, spend ten minutes updating it. That is enough. Spreadsheets may not look flashy, but they're customizable, flexible and don't rely on third-party platforms. If you like control, spreadsheets are your friend.

And then there are people who keep it as simple as possible. *Luis* carried a pocket notebook. On payday, he wrote his income at the top of the page. Then he jotted down his planned expenses for the week. As he spent, he crossed things off. No graphs, no charts, no notifications - just a pen and paper. It worked for him because it was low-tech and fit his lifestyle. Sometimes, the simplest tools are the stickiest.

Here's the important part: **the tool itself doesn't matter** nearly as much as people think. The *best* tool is the one you'll actually use consistently.
- If you love apps and data, go digital.
- If you like structure but hate apps, use a spreadsheet.
- If you're visual and tactile, use envelopes or notebooks.

Budgeting isn't about impressing anyone. It's about clarity for yourself.

The Danger of Over-Tracking

One mistake I see is people choosing tools that are too detailed. They create twenty categories, track every cent and end up overwhelmed. Remember Marco from earlier? His budget collapsed because his app forced him into too much detail. A simpler system with fewer categories would have worked better. Tracking should give you clarity, not headaches.

Here's how I recommend choosing your tool:

1. **Ask yourself how you naturally think.** Do you like detail, or do you prefer broad strokes?
2. **Decide how much time you're willing to spend.** Do you want daily tracking, weekly check-ins, or monthly reviews?
3. **Try one method for 60 days.** If it feels like a burden, switch. If it feels like clarity, stick.

The tool should bend to your personality, not the other way around. A word of caution: don't let the tool itself become the focus. I've seen people get so obsessed with their app or spreadsheet that they forget the real purpose - aligning money with life.

There's no universal "best" tool. There's only the tool that works best for *you*. For some, it's a high-tech app with graphs and charts. For others, it's a plain notebook with numbers scribbled down. What matters is that the system gives you clarity, confidence and consistency.

Because at the end of the day, budgeting isn't about the tool in your hand. It's about the control in your life

---

Reflection Pause

☐ Do you prefer digital tools, spreadsheets, or pen and paper?
☐ Which system feels most natural to you? Detailed tracking or simple broad categories?
☐ If you tried budgeting in the past and quit, was the tool the problem?

REAL-LIFE ADAPTABILITY

If there's one thing life guarantees, it's surprises. Promotions, job losses, weddings, illnesses, relocations - none of these arrive neatly penciled into your budget calendar. That's why one of the most important qualities of any good budget is flexibility.

Take *Chinyere*, a healthcare worker in Houston. She built a thoughtful budget, tracking her needs, wants, savings and giving. For the first time, she felt calm. She told me, "I finally know where my money's going. It's like a weight lifted."

Then, one spring, her mother back in Nigeria fell seriously ill. Medical bills and travel expenses landed on her shoulders. Overnight, her budget was upended. The savings she'd carefully earmarked for a future home had to be redirected to cover flights and hospital care. For a while, she felt like a failure. "I worked so hard to build this plan," she said. "Now it's ruined."

But here's the lesson Chinyere discovered: her budget wasn't ruined. It was adapting. She hadn't broken it. She was using it - exactly as intended.

A common mistake is treating budgets like stone tablets. Once written, they're seen as unchangeable rules. Break them and you feel guilty. But budgets aren't commandments. They're living documents. They're meant to bend, adjust and reshape as your life shifts.

Think of your budget like a GPS. You set a destination and the GPS suggests a route. But if there's traffic, construction or you take a wrong turn, the GPS doesn't scold you. It simply recalculates. Your budget should do the same.

Here's how to think about it:

1. **Expect the unexpected.** Leave some room in your budget - even 2-5% - for "life happens." That way, you're not blindsided when things pop up.

2. **Revisit regularly.** Check in monthly or quarterly. Are your categories still realistic? Has your income changed? Do your values look different today than last year?

3. **Adjust without guilt.** If you need to redirect money from travel to medical bills, or from dining to savings, that's not failure. That's life.

The Danger of Rigidity

Rigid budgets often lead to two outcomes: burnout or abandonment.

- **Burnout** *happens when you force yourself into a budget that no longer fits. Every purchase feels like a violation and you end up resenting the process.*
- **Abandonment** *happens when you "break" the budget once and decide it's hopeless. You toss the whole system aside, like breaking a diet with one slice of cake.*

Both are avoidable when you embrace flexibility.

I also worked with *Maria*, a single mom in Florida. She budgeted carefully, but when her car broke down, the repair costs blew through her "transportation" category. Instead of giving up, we adjusted. For the next two months, she cut back on dining out and redirected those funds. By month three, she was back on track. Her budget didn't fail but flexed. That's what kept her consistent.

One of the hardest parts of budgeting isn't the math but the mindset. People often tie emotions to money. When the numbers don't go as planned, they feel guilt, shame, or frustration. But emotions fade when you reframe flexibility as strength, not weakness. You're not "failing" when you adjust your budget. You're proving that you're resilient enough to handle reality.

Think about it this way: if your budget only works in perfect conditions, it's fragile. But if your budget can bend and still hold, it's strong.

Chinyere didn't abandon her plan when her mother got sick. She adapted it. That's why, months later, when life settled down, she was still budgeting. The habit survived because it wasn't built on perfection. It was built on adaptability.

Budgets aren't meant to be prisons. They're meant to be maps. Maps get redrawn. GPS recalculates. Life changes and your budget should too. The goal isn't to stick perfectly to a plan. The goal is to **stay**

financially intentional, even when the plan changes. Because in the end, flexibility isn't a weakness of budgeting. It's the very reason it works.

Reflection Pause

☐ Has your life ever thrown a curveball that wrecked your budget? Did you quit, or did you adjust?

☐ If an unexpected $1,000 expense hit next month, how would you handle it?

☐ Do you view budget changes as failure, or as recalculating the route?

CONFIDENCE OVER GUESSWORK

By now, you've seen that budgeting isn't about punishment. It's about purpose. It's not about tracking every penny; it's about knowing your direction.

We began this chapter by talking about the "diet problem." Most budgets fail because they're too rigid, too detailed, or too joyless. Then we explored simpler, more sustainable methods: the 50/30/20 rule, the power of paying yourself first, aligning budgets with your values, using the right tools and keeping things flexible.

Together, these lessons reveal a simple truth: **a budget is not a cage. It's a compass.** It doesn't lock you down; it points you toward the life you want.

When you don't have a budget, money feels slippery. You swipe, tap and pay, then wonder at the end of the month, *Where did it all go?* That uncertainty is stressful.

With a budget, you're no longer guessing. You know your bills are covered, your savings are growing, your fun is accounted for and your giving is intentional. That confidence reduces stress and increases joy.

Budgets don't take the fun out of life. They take the fear out of money.

The Stories Revisited

Remember Sarah, who quit her "perfect" spreadsheet because it felt like homework? Her mistake wasn't discipline but design. Simpler systems would have worked.

Remember Marco, who abandoned his app after three weeks? His problem wasn't willpower but complexity. Once he switched to broad categories, budgeting became sustainable.

Remember Ethan, who loved travel? Once his budget reflected his values, he spent guilt-free.

Remember Amelia, who automated savings? By paying herself first, she built wealth in the background.

Remember Chinyere and Maria, whose budgets were tested by emergencies? Their success wasn't in sticking perfectly to a plan, but in adapting when life changed.

Each story points to the same lesson: a budget that works is one that fits your life.

Here's the reframe I want you to carry: a budget is not about cutting out lattes, dinners or joy. It's about making sure your money aligns with your values.

A budget says:

- "Yes, you can travel because you planned for it."
- "Yes, you can buy books because they're in your plan."
- "Yes, you can retire comfortably because you invested consistently."

It's not about *no*. It's about *yes, with confidence.*

Once you start budgeting, something else happens: you gain momentum. At first, it's about numbers. But soon, it's about mindset. You stop drifting and start directing. You stop reacting to money and start guiding it. This shift compounds. The longer you live with a budget that reflects your values, the more freedom you feel, the less stress you carry and the faster your goals become reality.

Budgets don't have to be boring. They don't have to be spreadsheets you dread or rules you constantly break. Done right, a budget is a reflection of your priorities and a tool for your freedom.

Because at the end of the day, money without a plan drifts. But money with a budget flows with purpose. And when your money flows with purpose, so does your life.

Worksheet: My First Budget Snapshot

Take 15–20 minutes to complete this. It doesn't have to be perfect. It just has to be honest.

1. **Income**
   - My monthly take-home pay is: $__________

2. **Needs (housing, food, utilities, insurance, transport)**
   - Amount: $________
   - Percentage of income: _____ %

3. **Wants (dining, travel, shopping, hobbies, entertainment)**
   - Amount: $________
   - Percentage of income: _____ %

4. **Savings & Investments**
   - Amount: $________
   - Percentage of income: _____ %

5. **Giving (charity, family support, community)**
   - Amount: $________
   - Percentage of income: _____ %

6. **Values Alignment**
   - My top 3 values are: ____________, ____________, ____________
   - Does my spending reflect them? Yes / No

7. **One Small Shift**
   - One thing I want to decrease: ______________
   - One thing I want to increase: ______________

Part 2: Building Wealth Step by Step

"You're sitting in the shade today because you planted a seed a long time ago."

— Adapted from Mr. Warren Buffett

4

Banking – More Than Just a Place for Your Money

Payday doesn't feel like a story, but it is. Long before you sip your first coffee, your money has already traveled farther than you did. In wee hours of the morning, your employer (or their systems) uploads a payroll file. It flows into a clearing network, bounces through a maze of servers and lands in your account before dawn. While you sleep, tiny messages move billions of dollars with the quiet precision of air-traffic control. You wake up, glance at your phone and see a new number. Tap. Smile. Move on.

Most of us never think about what just happened. We see the balance, not the journey. We use the card, not the rails under it. We assume money "shows up" and "goes out," as if by magic. But banking isn't magic. It's plumbing. It's pipes and valves and pressure, directing flow. When the pipes are clean, the flow is smooth. When they're clogged, everything backs up and life gets messy fast.

I realized this in a checkout line on a Saturday morning when the card terminals went down. The grocery store was humming until, suddenly, it wasn't. A chorus of beeps turned into a chorus of declines. "Try again." "Do you have another card?" "Do you have cash?" People stared at their phones like travelers staring at departure boards after a storm cancels every flight. Nothing was "wrong" with anyone's money; the pipes were blocked. The invisible system we count on every second had hiccupped and the room felt it immediately.

That moment crystallized something for me: we don't carry money as much as we carry **access** to money. Your debit card isn't a stack of bills;

it's a key to the pipes. Your checking account isn't a shoebox; it's a switching station. Your bank is the utility that keeps the pressure steady so your financial life runs when you twist the faucet - pay rent, tap for coffee, send a transfer, schedule a bill.

And like any utility, you can use it well or badly.

Some people treat banking as an afterthought: one default account, random fees, near-zero interest on savings, a tangle of auto-pays they barely remember. They lose dollars to leaks they can't see - overdraft charges here, maintenance fees there, low-yield balances that quietly shrink against inflation. *The pipes are working, but they're not working for them.*

Others treat banking like a tool. They separate spending from savings so the currents don't mix. They park their emergency fund where it earns more and can be reached fast. They automate bill pay to avoid late fees and automate transfers so "I'll save what's left" becomes "I saved before I spent." They choose institutions the way you'd choose a contractor: What's the quality? What's the cost? What's the service? They don't worship banks and they don't ignore them. They partner with them.

If money is the story of your goals, banking is the grammar that makes the sentences readable. Without grammar, even brilliant ideas are hard to understand. Without clean banking, even strong income feels chaotic. Think about the last time a small banking friction derailed your day: a frozen card while traveling, an account you couldn't log into, a surprise fee. Notice how quickly financial peace turns into agitation when the plumbing sputters. And notice the opposite: how calm you feel when the bills pay themselves, your balances are exactly where they should be and your savings grows every month without you thinking about it. Same income. Different pipes.

Let's follow a dollar for a moment. Your paycheck lands in checking. Some of it flows to **needs** - rent, utilities, insurance - through scheduled payments. Some of it flows to **tomorrow** - an automatic sweep into a high-yield savings account you rarely touch. Some of it flows to **later** - your 401(k) or IRA, routed out before temptation can grab it. A trickle flows to **joy** - your fun fund, the one that lets you book a concert ticket without guilt. If your banking is set up well, this choreography happens without drama. You're not "trying to remember" or promising yourself you'll do it after lunch. The pipes do what pipes do. Quietly. Reliably. In the background.

Of course, not all pipes are equal. Some banks are pricey for the pressure they provide in ways of monthly fees, overdraft charges, ATM costs, foreign transaction penalties. Some are generous with no fees, stronger interest on savings, early direct deposit, broad ATM networks. Some add tools that make life easier like sub-accounts, round-ups, instant transfers, alerts that actually help. Others make simple things confusing. The point isn't to learn every acronym in banking. It's to recognize that the choice of where you keep and move your money affects your daily life as much as the choice of where you live or what phone you use.

There's a second truth here: safety matters. Put simply, banks keep your cash from living under your mattress. Deposit insurance exists for a reason. Fraud monitoring exists for a reason. If you've ever lost a card and watched a fraud team reverse the mess, you've tasted the relief the system can provide when it works well. Banking isn't a headline until you need it to be. Then it's everything.

So, this chapter won't try to turn you into a banker. *It will make you a better **user** of banks*. We'll strip banking down to the parts that matter in everyday life: what accounts do, how banks make money (and how to avoid being the money they make), which institutions fit different needs and a few simple habits that transform your experience from reactive to confident. We'll keep it practical. No jargon blizzard. No lectures. Just clear choices you can make once that keep paying you back, month after month.

Reflection Pause

Before we dive in, ask yourself a few questions:

☐ Do I know, right now, what interest my savings is earning—and could it be earning more somewhere else?

☐ Am I paying any monthly fees I don't need to be paying?

☐ If my paycheck posted tomorrow, would my essential bills, savings and investments move automatically - or would I need to remember?

☐ If I lost my wallet today, would I be one tap away from freezing cards and staying calm?

If those questions make you uneasy, good. Not because you're doing anything wrong, but because it means this chapter will pay off quickly. Banking isn't the most glamorous topic in personal finance. It's the pipes. But when the pipes are sound, everything you care about - budgeting, saving, investing, even giving - flows more easily.

Let's open the walls, take a look at the plumbing and rebuild it so it serves you better than it ever has.

WHAT BANKS ACTUALLY DO

When you think of a bank, you probably picture a building with a logo, a vault and maybe a teller behind the counter. But that's just the surface. Banks are really more like the invisible plumbing of your financial life - they keep the flow moving in the background so you don't have to carry coins in your pocket or cash under your mattress.

At its core, <u>a bank is a safe</u>. Instead of hiding money in your dresser or between couch cushions, you park it in a place that's guarded, insured and organized. If the bank itself goes under, your money doesn't vanish into thin air - at least not in countries like the U.S. where deposits are insured. In the U.S. deposits are insured up to $250,000 per account by the FDIC. That peace of mind alone is worth a lot.

Banks are also <u>a middleman for money</u>. Banks don't just sit on your cash - they keep it moving. Your paycheck? It flows through a bank before it lands in your account. That coffee you bought with a tap of your card? A bank processed that too. They're like the stage crew in a play: mostly invisible, but without them the show can't go on.

Banks also wear another hat: <u>lender</u>. The money you deposit doesn't gather dust in a vault. It's lent out to people buying homes, starting businesses or paying for cars. Your deposits help fund someone else's goals and in return, the bank earns interest. They give you a slice of that interest (often a very tiny slice) for keeping your money there.

The Profit Game

Here's where it gets interesting. Banks make money by charging borrowers more than they pay savers. For example, you might get 0.5% on your savings while someone else pays 7% on a loan. That difference is the bank's business model. The wider the gap, the more they profit. Understanding that game is important, because it explains why some banks quietly "drain" your money with low savings rates and high fees, while others are more generous.

On top of the basics, banks throw in tools that make life easier:
- Online bill pay so you don't miss deadlines.
- Automatic transfers to help you save without thinking.
- Fraud protection if your card gets skimmed.
- Mobile apps to check your balance while in line for groceries.

Some of these tools genuinely help. Others come with sneaky fees if you're not careful.

Think of banks as pipes in your house. They bring money in, send it out, store it in a tank and even share it with neighbors. When the pipes work, you barely notice them. When they clog like when your card gets declined or a fee shows up, you suddenly realize how much you depend on them.

Banks aren't just vaults or apps on your phone. They're the system that makes modern money usable. As you understand how they actually work, you can start choosing banks the way you'd choose any service provider: based on how well they handle your flow, not just based on which branch is closest.

Reflection Pause

- ☐ When was the last time you actually thought about how your paycheck, bills, or card payments move behind the scenes?
- ☐ Do you see your bank as just a place that "holds" your money, or as the system that makes your money usable?
- ☐ If banks are the plumbing of your financial life, are your pipes working smoothly or leaking through fees and low interest?

THE TYPES OF BANK ACCOUNTS

Banks may feel like one big bucket, but in reality, they offer different containers for different purposes. Knowing which container to use makes your money easier to manage, safer and in some cases, more rewarding.

Checking Accounts: The Everyday Wallet

A checking account is like your wallet. Money flows in (paychecks, transfers) and flows out (bills, debit card swipes, ATM withdrawals). It's designed for constant movement, not long-term storage. That's why checking accounts usually earn little to no interest. Think of them as running water - always moving, never stored.

Savings Accounts: The Safety Net

Savings accounts are meant for parking money you don't need daily access to. They're your safety net for emergencies or short-term goals like setting aside cash for a new laptop or building your three-to-six-month emergency fund. Some savings accounts barely pay interest (close to zero), while others like online high-yield savings accounts, offer much more. Same "container," very different results.

Certificates of Deposit (CDs): The Locked Box

A CD is like a locked box. You deposit a fixed amount for a set period, say 6 months or 1 year and the bank rewards you with a higher interest rate. The catch: if you break the lock early, you usually pay a penalty. CDs work well for money you know you won't touch for a while, but they're less flexible if surprises pop up.

Money Market Accounts: The Hybrid

Money market accounts blend features of savings and checking. They may offer higher interest rates and limited check-writing or debit access. Think of them as a halfway point - safe for savings, but still accessible in a pinch.

Specialized Accounts

Some banks offer accounts tailored for kids, students, or seniors. Others let you create "sub-accounts" or "buckets" within one account - great for separating money for travel, holidays, or sinking funds. The idea is the same: give each dollar a home with a purpose.

Choosing the Right Mix

Most people don't need every type of account. A simple mix - a checking account for flow and a savings account for safety - is enough. As your goals grow, you might add a CD or money market. The key is knowing what each container is for and matching it to your needs. The clearer you are about what each one does, the easier it is to build a system where your money has direction. Instead of one blurry bucket, you create a set of containers, each serving its role in your financial story.

Reflection Pause

☐ Do you currently use separate accounts for spending and saving, or does everything sit in one bucket?
☐ Is your savings account earning interest that actually matters or is it quietly lagging?

☐ If you had to assign your money to "flow" (checking), "safety" (savings) and "future" (CDs or money market), how would your current setup look?

INTEREST, FEES AND THE BANK'S GAME

Banks may smile at you from their ads, but make no mistake - they are businesses. Their business model is simple: pay you little, charge you more and profit from the difference. Once you see that clearly, you stop being just a "customer" and start being a strategist.

Let's take interest. Suppose your bank pays you 0.01% interest on your savings. That's literally ten cents a year on $1,000. Meanwhile, the same bank might charge 20% on a credit card balance. They're borrowing from you cheaply and lending to someone else expensively. That spread which is tiny for you but massive for them, is how they win.

The same goes for loans. A mortgage at 5% sounds reasonable. A car loan at 8% adds up quickly. A payday loan at 300%? That's a trap. Interest isn't good or bad in itself - it's a tool. It can either grow your savings or crush your debt, depending on which side you're on.

Then there are fees. Overdraft charges. Monthly "maintenance" fees. ATM fees for using the wrong machine. Foreign transaction fees when you travel. None of these are illegal but they're all ways banks quietly drain your money.

I once had a client realize she'd paid $200 in ATM fees in a single year while her balance earned $3 in interest. That's not banking. That's leakage.

The Leaky Bucket Analogy

Think of your bank account like a bucket. Interest is water flowing in. Fees are holes drilled at the bottom. The wrong bank leaves you with a leaky bucket where you pour money in but much of it seeps out unnoticed. The right bank helps seal those holes and maybe even adds a little extra water on top.

You don't need to obsess over every decimal of interest or every $2 fee. But you do need to pay attention to the pattern. Over a year, the difference between a low-interest savings account and a high-yield one could be hundreds of dollars. Over a decade, thousands. The difference between always paying overdraft fees and never paying them is even bigger.

Banks will always play their game. The question is whether you're playing it blindly or whether you've learned the rules well enough to flip the advantage. Remember that interest and fees are two sides of the same coin: one builds you up, the other chips away. You can't avoid the game, but you can choose how you play. And when you choose well, you keep more of your money working for you instead of working for the bank.

Reflection Pause

- ☐ Is your current bank paying you a meaningful rate on your savings, or just pennies?
- ☐ Have you added up how much you paid in bank fees last year - ATM, overdraft, maintenance?
- ☐ If your bank account is a bucket, is it sealed tight or quietly leaking?

TRADITIONAL VS. ONLINE BANKING

For generations, "going to the bank" meant exactly that - walking into a building, standing in line and speaking to a teller. Your bank was often chosen by geography: whichever branch was closest to your home or office. But today, that picture has changed. You can open an account on your phone in ten minutes. You can move money at 2 a.m. with a tap. Your "branch" might not even exist physically. Traditional banks and online banks now sit side by side and each has its strengths and trade-offs.

Take *Javier*, a teacher living in Phoenix. For years, he banked with a large traditional institution. His parents had accounts there, his first paycheck went there and his mortgage was linked there. But he noticed something odd: his savings account, holding nearly $30,000, was earning less than a dollar in interest each year. Meanwhile, his friend showed him her online bank statement - she had half the savings but was earning twenty times the interest.

Skeptical but curious, Javier opened an online savings account. Within three months, he saw the difference. Instead of pennies, he was earning real money in interest - enough to cover a couple of family dinners. He still kept his traditional account for everyday transactions and ATM access, but the bulk of his savings moved online. "It feels like my money is finally waking up," he said.

Javier's story is common. Traditional banks offer comfort and familiarity. Online banks offer efficiency and higher returns. The smart move often isn't choosing one or the other, but learning how to use both.

Traditional Banks: Familiar but Costly

Traditional banks give you what feels like stability. They have physical branches, face-to-face service and widespread ATM networks. If you like walking into a building and speaking to a human being, they deliver that. But they often come with trade-offs:

- Lower interest rates on savings.
- High fees in maintenance charges, overdraft fees, ATM surcharges.
- Slower adoption of digital-first features.

In many cases, you're paying for the "brick-and-mortar" experience, even if you rarely use it.

Online Banks: Efficient but Less Personal

Online banks flipped the model. With no branches to maintain, they pass savings on in the form of higher interest rates, no monthly fees and sleek apps. Many offer perks like early paycheck access or instant money transfers.

But they also have limitations:

- No branch to walk into when you want face-to-face service.
- ATM access may be limited or rely on partner networks.
- Customer service can feel distant when it's only chat or email.

For some, the convenience outweighs the drawbacks. For others, the lack of physical presence feels risky.

The Trade-Off Mindset

Here's the key: don't stick with a bank out of inertia. Many people do, simply because "I've always banked there." But loyalty to a bank rarely pays you back. Banks respond to competition, not sentiment. Your money deserves a home that works for you, not just one that's been around forever.

This shift isn't just in the U.S. Around the world, mobile-first banking is reshaping how people interact with money.

- In the U.K., challengers like Monzo and Revolut attract young customers with slick apps.
- In Brazil, Nubank has become one of the largest digital banks in the world.
- In Kenya, M-Pesa allows millions to send and receive money through mobile phones, bypassing banks entirely.
- In India, Paytm and other digital wallets bring banking to people who never had accounts before.

The future of banking isn't just online - it's mobile, instant and borderless.

So, should you go all-in with an online bank? Not necessarily. The smarter approach is often a blend. Use a traditional bank for the services where in-person access still matters - like mortgages, complex loans or cashier's checks. Use an online bank for higher-yield savings and no-fee accounts.

It's like having two tools in your financial toolbox. One is sturdy and familiar. The other is sharp and efficient. Traditional banks and online banks aren't enemies but are options. The right mix depends on your lifestyle, your comfort level and your goals. What matters is that you choose intentionally, instead of letting your money sit asleep in a low-interest account out of habit.

Reflection Pause

- ☐ Do you know what interest rate your savings account is earning right now? Is it closer to 0.01% or 4%?
- ☐ How often do you actually walk into a bank branch? Could you manage fine if your banking was mostly digital?
- ☐ What would your ideal setup look like—a blend of traditional stability and online efficiency, or leaning fully toward one side?

BEYOND BANKS: CREDIT UNIONS & FINTECH

When most people think of banking, they picture the big names: Chase, Wells Fargo, Bank of America, Citi. But they're not the only players in the game. Beyond the traditional banks sit two growing alternatives - **Credit Unions** and **FinTech companies** - each changing the way people interact with money.

Tanya, a nurse in Ohio, had always banked with one of the big institutions. She didn't question it as her parents did the same. But when she bought her first car, the dealer offered financing through a local credit union. The rate was 2% lower than what her big bank quoted. Curious, she joined the credit union, got the loan and later moved her checking account there too.

Her surprise? "It felt more personal," she said. "When I walked in, the staff knew my name. I wasn't just another account number." Tanya still kept a big-bank account for convenience, but her major loans and savings moved to the credit union – helping her save thousands in interest over time.

Credit Unions are member-owned financial cooperatives. Instead of being owned by shareholders, they're owned by the people who bank there. That means profits are often returned to members in the form of lower fees and better interest rates. They tend to be smaller, community-oriented and more customer-focused. The trade-off? They may have fewer branches, less flashy technology or smaller ATM networks. If traditional banks are like national chain supermarkets, credit unions are like local co-ops: closer to the community, sometimes less convenient, but often more aligned with your interests.

Then there's the new wave: **FinTech (financial technology)** companies. Apps like Chime, Venmo, Cash App, Wise and PayPal aren't "banks" in the traditional sense but they're where millions of people now move, store and even grow their money.

- **Chime** offers fee-free checking, early paycheck access and automatic savings features.
- **Venmo** and **Cash App** make peer-to-peer transfers effortless (splitting dinner, paying roommates).
- **Wise** helps people send money internationally at lower costs than banks.
- **PayPal** has become a global wallet, especially for freelancers and small businesses.

These services thrive on speed, convenience and user-friendly design. But they're not always as heavily regulated or insured as banks, which means you need to use them thoughtfully.

The Big Picture

What's happening here is a quiet revolution. For decades, banks had a near monopoly on how people accessed money. Now, credit unions challenge them with community-driven models and FinTech companies challenge them with speed and design. The power is shifting. So, the question again is: which tool works best for you in which scenario?

The Pros and Cons

- **Credit Unions**: Pro: better rates, member-first culture. Con: limited branches, sometimes clunky tech.
- **FinTech**: Pro: slick apps, low fees, global reach. Con: less stability, regulatory gray zones, sometimes weaker customer service.
- **Traditional Banks**: Pro: broad services, global access, trust built over decades. Con: higher fees, lower savings returns.

In reality, many people end up using a mix.

Banking no longer looks like one-size-fits-all. You're no longer limited to the nearest branch or the biggest logo. From community-driven credit unions to app-based FinTechs, you now have more choices than ever. The key is to stop drifting with what's familiar and start picking intentionally because every percentage saved in fees or gained in interest adds up to real money, real freedom and real progress toward your goals.

Reflection Pause

☐ Do you know if your local credit union offers better rates than your current bank?

☐ How many FinTech apps (like Venmo, Cash App, PayPal) do you already use without thinking of them as "banking"?

☐ Could you save money or stress by diversifying across traditional banks, credit unions and FinTech, instead of sticking with just one?

BANKING HABITS THAT BUILD WEALTH

Up to this point, we've looked at what banks do, the types of accounts they offer and the different flavors - traditional, online, credit unions and FinTech. But knowledge by itself doesn't build wealth. Habits do. And when it comes to banking, a few simple habits can make the difference between money that slips through your fingers and money that steadily grows.

Remember *Carter* (from Chapter 2) who had a high income, lavish lifestyle but felt broke at month-end. For him, everything went into one checking account. Bills, spending, savings - it was all jumbled together. At the end of the month, he had no idea where the money had gone (apart from the luxury spends).

We made a few tweaks:

- A separate high-yield savings account for his emergency fund.

- An automatic transfer on payday to his IRA.

- Bill pay set up so recurring expenses left his account without him touching them.

- A "luxury fund" checking account linked to his debit card, so monthly spending was capped.

Six months later, Carter said, "I haven't had to think about saving. It just happens. And for the first time, I am enjoying spending because I know it's already accounted for." His habits had changed, not his income.

Habit 1: Automate the Essentials

The less you rely on willpower, the stronger your financial system becomes. Automate bill payments for rent, utilities and subscriptions. Automate transfers to savings and investments on payday. Automate credit card payments so you never miss due dates.

When money moves automatically, you're less likely to forget, delay, or overspend. Automation builds consistency and consistency builds wealth.

Habit 2: Separate Your Accounts

Don't let all your money sit in one pot. Use separate accounts to give each dollar a job:
- Checking for daily expenses.
- Savings for emergencies.
- High-yield savings or money market for short-term goals.
- Investment accounts for long-term growth.

When you mix it all together, it feels like a big pile that's both endless and empty. When you separate it, you create clarity.

Why Habits Matter More Than Rates

People often obsess over whether their savings account pays 3.9% or 4.2%. That matters, but not nearly as much as building consistent habits. An extra 0.3% interest won't transform your finances if you're not saving at all. But a habit of saving 15% of your income, automated and separate, will change your life regardless of the exact rate.

Habit 3: Build and Protect an Emergency Fund

Banks give you easy access to your money, which makes them the perfect place for an emergency fund. Aim for your emergency funds to be parked in a high-yield savings account. This fund keeps you from relying on credit cards when life throws curveballs - job loss, car repairs, medical bills. An emergency fund is less about earning interest and more about buying peace of mind.

Habit 4: Audit Your Fees

Set a calendar reminder twice a year to review your bank statements. Look for overdraft charges, ATM fees or maintenance fees. If you're paying them regularly, it's a sign something needs to change - either in your habits or in your choice of bank.

Remember: every $35 overdraft fee is money that could have been growing in your savings instead of leaking out of your bucket.

Habit 5: Use Banking to Match Your Values

Money is emotional. If you value generosity, set up an automatic monthly donation. If you value travel, create a dedicated "travel fund" sub-account. If you value security, automate transfers to your emergency savings.

When your banking setup mirrors your values, it doesn't just organize your money - it motivates you. Every transfer feels like a step toward the life you want.

Wealth doesn't come from giant leaps. It comes from small, steady steps repeated over time. Banking habits are those steps. They're the plumbing fixtures that keep your financial water flowing in the right direction towards security, growth and peace of mind.

Like Carter, you don't need more income to feel in control. You need better systems. Because when your banking habits run smoothly in the background, your mind is free to focus on what really matters and living the life you want.

Reflection Pause

- ☐ Do you currently separate your money into different accounts, or does it all sit in one pot?
- ☐ If you automated just one transfer - say, $100 to savings every payday - how would that change your stress levels?
- ☐ Which banking habit would save you the most mental energy right now: automating bills, building an emergency fund or cutting fees?

MAKING BANKS WORK FOR YOU

We began this chapter with a simple idea: banks are the plumbing of your financial life. They move money quietly in the background: bringing it in, sending it out, storing it safely. When the pipes work, you barely notice them. When they leak or clog, you feel it immediately.

By now, you've seen the full picture:

- Banks safeguard your money and help it move.
- Different accounts serve different purposes - checking for flow, savings for safety, CDs and money markets for specific goals.

- Interest and fees are the rules of the bank's game and you can either play blindly or learn to play smart.
- Traditional banks, online banks, credit unions and FinTech apps all offer trade-offs. The trick is choosing the mix that fits your life.
- And most importantly, your habits and not the bank itself, determine whether your money grows or drains away.

The lesson is clear

Banks are not just holders of money. They are tools.

And like any tool, they can either work for you or against you.

Many people drift through banking passively. They open the first account offered, leave money where it sits, pay whatever fees come up and hope for the best. Over time, that passivity costs them thousands in lost interest, unnecessary charges and missed opportunities.

But when you take an active role towards choosing the right accounts, minimizing fees and automating your savings, you flip the script. Suddenly, the bank is working for you. The same paycheck, the same bills, but a very different outcome.

A Quick Recap with Carter

Remember Carter from the last section? His income didn't change. His bank didn't magically pay more. What changed was his system. Separate accounts. Automatic transfers. Bill pay. A luxury fund. Those small changes created clarity and control.

That's the essence of smart banking. It's not about chasing the "perfect" bank but also about building a system that reflects your values, protects your money and grows your wealth.

Think of your banking setup like your car. You don't just drive forever without checking the oil, the tires or the brakes. A quick check-up prevents bigger problems down the road.

The same goes for money. A banking check-up once or twice a year can catch leaks, reveal better opportunities and keep your financial system running smoothly.

Here's another truth: _banking is the foundation_, not the finish line. It's not where wealth is created, but it's where wealth begins. Get the plumbing right and your budgeting, saving, investing and giving all flow more easily. Ignore it and even strong income feels chaotic.

Banks aren't good or bad. They're pipes. They'll carry your money wherever you point them. If you ignore them, they'll leak, drip and sometimes flood. If you manage them well, they'll carry your money smoothly toward your goals.

This chapter wasn't about making you love banks. It's about making banks work for you. So don't let your bank quietly decide your financial future. Do the check-up. Choose your accounts. Automate your flows. And remember:

Money doesn't just need to be earned, it also needs to be directed.

Worksheet: My Banking Check-Up

Take 20 minutes. Be honest. This isn't about judging your past and maybe building a better system going forward.

1. **List Your Current Accounts**

    o Checking: ____
    o Savings: ____
    o Other (CDs, Money Market, Credit Union, FinTech):
    ____

2. **Check the Interest**

    o Checking interest rate: _______ %
    o Savings interest rate: _______ %
    o Could you move to a higher-yield account?   Yes / No

3. **Check the Fees**

    o Maintenance fees: $_______ per month
    o Overdraft fees last year: $_______
    o ATM fees last year: $_______
    o Are these acceptable, or can you eliminate them?

4. **Check the Access**

    o Do you have enough ATM access where you live?   Yes / No
    o Do you have online access that's easy to use?   Yes / No

5. **Check the Habits**

    o Do you automate savings on payday?   Yes / No
    o Do you have a separate emergency fund account?   Yes / No
    o Do you use banking to match your values?   Yes / No

6. **My Next Three Banking Actions**

    1. ____

    2. ____

    3. ____

5

Credit & Debt - The Good, the Bad and the Ugly

Do you still remember the first time you held a credit card in your hand? Most likely, it was shiny, had your name embossed on it and it felt like a badge of adulthood. When the cashier swiped it through the machine and handed back the card with a receipt, you may have felt exhilarated. You didn't hand over any cash, your wallet didn't feel lighter and your checking account still had the same balance. Yet, you walked out with your purchase. It would have been thrilling.

That thrill is what makes credit cards and credit in general, so tempting. They give you a sense of freedom, almost like having a superpower. You don't need to wait until payday to buy the shoes you've been eyeing, book a last-minute flight or go out for dinner with friends. A small plastic rectangle seems to say: *Go ahead, you deserve it. Pay later.*

But that's the thing: *later always comes.* The first bill arrives and suddenly, the magic trick isn't so magical. The numbers on that crisp white statement are no longer invisible. They stare back at you. Maybe it's manageable this month. But what about next month, when another bill comes and then another?

Credit doesn't feel like spending and further the phenomenon referred to as **The Illusion of Effortless Spending**. And that's the danger. When you hand over cash, you see the bills leave your hand. You feel the transaction. With credit, you swipe or tap and nothing seems to change. It's like waving a wand and having things appear. That illusion makes it far easier to overspend.

There's a reason restaurants and stores love when you pay with a card as you tend to spend more. Psychologists have shown that people will pay higher prices, add more items and even splurge on things they hadn't planned, simply because the act of swiping feels painless. The money isn't leaving *now*, so it feels less real.

A friend of mine, *Sophie*, once shared her story. In college, she signed up for her first credit card because a rep was giving away free pizza coupons for new applications. It seemed harmless - free pizza and a "just-in-case" card. But soon, that card became the way she bought books, clothes and late-night takeout. The minimum payment looked small, so she only paid that. A few hundred dollars turned into a thousand, then two. By the time she graduated, Sophie had racked up nearly $14,000 in debt – a significant portion of her first year's salary that she could comfortably handle. She told me, "It felt like the debt just snuck up on me, one swipe at a time". Her story isn't unusual. Many people's first taste of credit comes young, often without much guidance. And that taste can either teach you how to handle it wisely or leave you burned for years.

However, credit itself isn't the villain. In fact, credit can be incredibly useful. It builds your financial reputation (your credit score), unlocks opportunities like renting an apartment or buying a home and even provides perks like cashback, airline miles or fraud protection. Used wisely, it's a powerful tool.

But it's a double-edged sword. That same piece of plastic that earns you rewards can also sink you in debt if you treat it like free money. It's a lot like fire. In a fireplace, fire keeps you warm, cooks your food and lights your home. But if you let it out of control, it burns down the house. Credit is the same - it has to be contained, managed and respected.

Then, Why We're Drawn to It? There's also something deeper going on. Credit promises instant gratification. Humans aren't naturally wired for patience - we want the reward now, not later. Credit whispers, "Why wait? You can have it today." And in today's world, where everything is available at the click of a button, that whisper has turned into a roar. Buy now, pay later apps. One-click checkout. Credit offers in every inbox. It has never been easier to spend money you don't yet have.

That's what this chapter is about - credit and debt in all their forms. The good, the bad and the ugly. We'll talk about how credit, when used responsibly, can open doors and work for you. We'll also look at how debt, when left unchecked, can grow faster than you imagine, creating stress and financial chains. And we'll explore the habits and strategies that turn credit into a tool instead of a trap. By the end of this chapter, you'll see that the goal isn't to fear credit or avoid it completely. It's to understand it, respect it and master it. Because in the world we live in, credit is everywhere.

Credit begins as a promise: freedom now, payment later. But like every promise, it demands to be kept. Whether it becomes a blessing or a burden depends less on the card itself and more on the hand that holds it. The question isn't whether you'll encounter it but rather whether it will serve you or enslave you.

Reflection Pause

- ☐ Can you remember your very first experience with credit? How did it make you feel? excited, powerful, nervous, or maybe indifferent?
- ☐ When you swipe or tap today, do you actually feel like you've spent money, or does it still feel a little unreal until the bill comes?
- ☐ If credit is like fire, is your current use of it warming your home or burning down your kitchen?

THE GOOD: CREDIT AS A TOOL

When most people hear the word *credit*, their first thought is usually *spending*. The two are so closely linked in our minds that we forget credit, when used wisely, can be one of the most powerful tools in personal finance. Like a hammer, it can build or it can bruise but in skilled hands, it's mostly about building.

Credit is essentially <u>your financial reputation</u>. Every time you borrow and repay money, you're leaving behind a trail that tells lenders, landlords and even potential employers how trustworthy you are. That reputation, derived from the credit score, becomes your passport to opportunities.

Take *Nisha*, a young professional in Chicago. She paid her credit cards in full each month, never missing a due date. When she applied for a mortgage to buy her first condo, her excellent credit score earned her a lower interest rate. Over 30 years, that "good behavior" translated into saving tens of thousands of dollars in interest. All because she used credit as a tool, not a crutch.

Credit can also <u>act as a bridge</u> when timing doesn't line up. Imagine your paycheck comes Friday, but your utility bill is due Wednesday. A credit card gives you breathing room, keeping your cash flow smooth. It's not free money, but it can be a safety valve. Used carefully, this flexibility helps you avoid overdraft fees, late fees or scrambling to borrow money in a pinch.

Then there are <u>the perks</u>. Many credit cards offer cashback, travel points, or airline miles. Used responsibly i.e. meaning you pay your balance in full every month, these perks are like free bonuses.

Take *Daniel*, who travels frequently for work. By funneling his expenses through a rewards credit card and paying the bill off each month, he accumulates enough airline miles to cover personal vacations with his family. What could have been just ordinary spending turns into free flights, hotel upgrades and even airport lounge access.

Of course, rewards aren't worth it if they tempt you to overspend. But for disciplined users, they're a way of letting credit work for you.

Credit also comes with <u>built-in safety features</u>. If your debit card is stolen, the money disappears directly from your account and it can take time to resolve. With credit cards, fraudulent charges usually don't touch your actual money if you dispute the charges timely and the bank handles the mess.

This makes credit not just convenient, but safer for big purchases or online shopping. It's like having an extra lock on your financial front door.

Building Trust Over Time

The longer you use credit wisely, the more trust you build. That trust can lead to lower borrowing costs for big life goals like buying a home, starting a business or even refinancing student loans. Good credit says, "I can be trusted with money," and the system rewards that trust.

It's not glamorous. No one celebrates paying a bill on time. But those small, boring acts of responsibility accumulate into a reputation that pays off for decades.

At the fear of repeating myself, <u>Credit is like fire</u>. Handled carefully, it warms your home, cooks your meals and lights your nights. It's essential. But mishandled, it burns. Fire itself isn't good or bad but it's how you use it. Credit works the same way and doesn't have to be scary.

In fact, it can be one of your greatest allies if you respect it and use it wisely. The key is to treat it as a tool, not as income. When you do, credit works for you - opening doors, saving money and adding value to your life, instead of quietly draining it.

Reflection Pause

☐ When you think about your credit right now, does it feel like a door-opener or a weight?
☐ Are you currently using credit to your advantage (e.g. earning rewards, building history, protecting purchases) or just using it as a way to spend more?

THE BAD: CONSUMER DEBT TRAPS

If credit in its best form feels like fire warming your home, then consumer debt gone wrong is that same fire jumping the fireplace and catching the curtains. It spreads quietly, faster than you expect and soon you're in a mess you never thought possible.

The truth is, most people don't set out to get into debt trouble. Nobody wakes up and says, "I'd like to pay 25% interest for the next decade." Debt trouble sneaks up slowly, disguised as convenience, rewards or "just this once" decisions.

Take *Carlos*, a recent college grad working his first job in Dallas. He was proud of his new independence with his own apartment, a car and dinners with friends on the weekends. He had a credit card with a $5,000 limit and figured as long as he made the minimum payment, he was being responsible. That first month, his bill came: $1,200. The minimum payment was just $35. Easy. He paid it, no problem. The next month, another $1,000 in charges, plus the interest from last month. The balance grew. The minimum stayed "manageable," so he kept paying it. By the end of the year, Carlos had nearly maxed out the card. He had been faithfully making payments, but the balance barely moved. Interest piled on faster than his payments chipped away at it. What started as dinners, gadgets and a few weekend getaways had now become a $4,800 anchor dragging his finances down.

When he finally did the math, he realized if he kept paying the minimum, it would take him over 20 years to clear that debt and he would pay more than double the original balance in interest. The trap had closed. The **minimum payment trap**.

So, why does the trap work? Credit card companies are clever. They design the system to keep you hooked:

- **Minimum payments look small.** A $35 or $50 payment feels harmless compared to the $1,000 balance behind it. But that's just the hook. By paying just the minimum, you're covering mostly interest, not the debt itself.

- **Interest compounds against you.** Every month, you're charged interest on not just your original balance but also the unpaid interest from last month. It's compounding, but in reverse.

- **Spending feels painless.** As we discussed in the beginning of the chapter, swiping a card doesn't "feel" like spending, so it's easy to underestimate how much you owe until it's too late.

Buy Now, Pay Later – The New Trap

It's not just credit cards. "Buy now, pay later" services, where you can split purchases into four easy installments, have exploded in popularity. They look harmless. A $200 jacket becomes "just four payments of $50." No interest, no fees (as long as you don't miss).

But stack a few of those "harmless" installments together and suddenly you've got four or five payments hitting at once. Miss one and the late fees start. The psychological trick is the same: break down big costs into small, digestible bites so you underestimate the total. It's the new version of the minimum payment trap, wrapped in slick apps and cheerful marketing.

Debt isn't just numbers on a statement. It weighs on you. People in heavy consumer debt often describe feeling anxious, guilty, or ashamed. They avoid opening bills. They dread checking bank accounts. Some even stop answering phone calls, worried it's a collection agency.

It's like living with a background hum of stress that never turns off. Even if you're doing well in other areas of life, the debt nags at you. It makes the future feel smaller, not bigger.

Imagine you're rowing a boat toward your financial goals. Bad debt is like a leak in the bottom of that boat. You can row harder (read: increase your income) but as long as the leak is there, you're bailing water instead of moving forward. The leak doesn't just slow you down but can sink you if ignored long enough. That's why recognizing consumer debt traps early matters so much.

It's easy to judge others for falling into debt traps. But the truth is, the system is designed to encourage it.

- Ads push instant gratification.
- Stores offer "easy financing" at checkout.
- Credit limits get raised as soon as you approach them.

- Minimum payments are set low enough to look friendly, but high enough to keep you stuck.

In other words, the traps are everywhere. Falling into one doesn't make you weak. Staying in one without taking action is where the real damage happens.

Consumer debt traps are comparable to invisible quicksand. They don't look dangerous at first with a small payment here, a little installment there. But step too far in and suddenly you're stuck, sinking slowly, unsure how to get out.

The good news? Quick sand doesn't mean doom if you know how to stop, stabilize and climb out. That's what we'll tackle in the next sections: how to spot when debt is snowballing out of control and how to fight your way back to solid ground.

Reflection Pause

☐ Have you ever paid just the minimum on a credit card without realizing how little progress it made on the balance?

☐ Do you use "buy now, pay later" services and if so, do you know exactly how many active installments you're juggling?

☐ If your finances are a boat, is there a leak quietly draining your energy and momentum?

THE UGLY: HOW DEBT SNOWBALLS OUT OF CONTROL

If the "bad" side of credit is the trap, the "ugly" side is what happens when you can't get out and the trap tightens. This is where debt turns from a manageable inconvenience into a life-altering weight. It doesn't just nibble at your wallet anymore; it devours your peace of mind, your plans and sometimes even your relationships.

Lena was a marketing coordinator in Seattle. She had one credit card, used mostly for online shopping and travel. When a few unexpected car repairs came up, she put $2,000 on the card. She planned to pay it off in a couple of months. But then work slowed down, her hours were cut and she couldn't keep up. At first, she paid the minimum. Then she skipped a month. Then another. Late fees piled on. Interest kept compounding. By the time she faced the situation, that $2,000 balance had ballooned to over $6,500. All well-hidden within her card limit of $10,000, never once pausing her from spending more on the card.

Lena's story is the ugly face of debt: how something small grows out of control when left unchecked. Let's break down how the math of snowball happens but against you.

Suppose you carry a $5,000 balance on a credit card with a 20% interest rate (very common and on the lower end). You decide to pay only the minimum. Let's say, 2% of the balance or about $100.
- Month 1: $5,000 balance → $100 payment, $83 goes to interest, only $17 reduces the debt.
- Month 2: $4,983 balance → another $100 payment, another $80+ in interest.

At that rate, it could take over **20 years** to pay off that $5,000 and you'll end up paying nearly $10,000 in interest alone.

That's the ugly math.

Compounding, which is your best friend when investing, becomes your worst enemy when you're in debt.

Instead of snowballing your wealth upward, it snowballs your obligations downward.

The Emotional Spiral

The numbers are scary enough. But the emotional side is worse. Debt often leads to:
- *Avoidance: People stop opening bills or checking balances because it's too painful.*
- *Shame: They feel guilty for "letting it get this far."*
- *Anxiety: Constant worry about collectors, late payments or declining credit scores.*

- *Hopelessness*: *The belief that they'll never catch up, so why bother trying.*

This spiral can trap people for years. It's not just about owing money. It is also about how debt makes you feel small, powerless and stuck.

When balances go unpaid long enough, creditors may send accounts to collections. Suddenly, it's not just numbers on a statement. It's phone calls at dinner, letters in the mail, sometimes even lawsuits. This phase is where the "ugly" label really fits. Debt stops being invisible and becomes intrusive, affecting not just your finances but your daily peace.

On top of it, debt rarely stays isolated. Once you're stuck making high-interest payments, you have less cash for rent, food, healthcare and almost everything else. So people often turn to... more debt. Payday loans. Another credit card. Borrowing from friends. It's like using one shovel to dig yourself out of a hole while another shovel digs the hole deeper. The cycle feeds itself and the debt snowball rolls faster downhill.

Think of debt like building a house of cards. At first, it's stable enough where one card leans on another, balances hold. But add more layers or bump the table just slightly (a job loss, a medical bill, an unexpected expense) and the whole thing collapses. Ugly debt isn't just about the numbers; it's about fragility. When you're stretched too thin, even small shocks can send your financial life crashing down.

Here's the thing: ugly debt thrives in silence. The longer you ignore it, the stronger it grows. That's why one of the bravest steps someone can take is simply acknowledging the problem, pulling out all the statements, listing the balances, facing the truth and discussing with your loved ones. That first step doesn't fix everything, but it turns the lights on in the room. And once you see clearly, you can start finding a way out.

Debt, at its ugliest, is a snowball rolling downhill. Left alone, it gathers speed, grows in size and crushes whatever is in its path. The only way to stop it is to face it, grab it and push back before it flattens your future.

The good news? Just as compounding works against you in debt, it can work for you once you start paying it down consistently. In the next section, we'll draw the line between "good debt" that can build your future and "bad debt" that tears it down - because not all borrowing is created equal.

Reflection Pause

- ☐ Do you know exactly how much interest you're paying on your debts right now, or do you only look at the minimum due?
- ☐ Have you ever put off opening a bill or checking a balance because you didn't want to face the number?
- ☐ If debt is compounding against you, what's one step you could take this week to stop the snowball from growing bigger?

GOOD DEBT VS. BAD DEBT

Yes, there is Good Debt. Not all debt is created equal. Some types of borrowing can set you back years, while others can move you forward. The difference comes down to one question: *Does this debt build my future or does it rob it?* That's the heart of the distinction between good debt and bad debt.

Think of debt like food. Calories are calories, but some nourish your body while others just bloat it. A bowl of vegetables fuels you. A bag of chips fills you for the moment but leaves you sluggish later.

Debt works the same way. All debt carries a cost but some forms build long-term strength, while others give you a quick rush followed by regret. Let's take a look at some major types of debt and assess their "worthiness"

1. Mortgages

Buying a home with a mortgage can be an example of good debt. Housing is a basic need and over time, real estate often appreciates in value. Your payments gradually build equity (aka ownership) instead of disappearing into rent. Of course, a mortgage only counts as "good" if the home fits your budget. A too-big mortgage can quickly shift from being as asset to an anchor.

2. Student Loans

Education is another area where debt can be worthwhile. A reasonable student loan that leads to a higher-paying career is an investment in future earnings. A nurse, lawyer or engineer often wouldn't get there without some upfront borrowing. But again, context matters. Borrowing $150,000 for a degree that doesn't increase your earning potential isn't good debt. It is financial quicksand dressed in a graduation gown.

3. Business Loans

For entrepreneurs, business loans can fuel growth. Borrowing to expand a shop, invest in new equipment or hire staff can multiply revenue far beyond the loan's cost. The risk is real, but so is the potential payoff.

4. Car Loans (Usually)

Cars are tricky. They're necessary for many people but depreciate the moment you drive them off the lot. Taking a modest loan for reliable transportation can be justified. But buying a $60,000 luxury car on credit when your income can't support it? That's bad debt disguised as status.

5. Credit Cards

High-interest credit card balances are the classic example of bad debt. Buying clothes, gadgets, or vacations on borrowed money that accrues 20% interest is like paying double or triple for something fleeting. They give you the smiles only to chop off your legs the next second. Avoiding them are your best course of action.

6. Payday Loans

These are debt in their ugliest form. Tiny loans with astronomical rates. They trap people in cycles that are nearly impossible to escape.

Good Debt is usually when borrowing helps you build while Bad Debt is when borrowing drains.

The Grey Area

Some debts don't fall neatly into good or bad but depend on the circumstances. Car loans, personal loans, even certain credit card uses can be neutral if handled wisely. The key is asking: Is this debt helping me grow, or is it shrinking my future?

Priya, a first-generation college student, faced two borrowing decisions. One was a $25,000 student loan for a nursing program. The other was a $7,000 balance on her credit card from travel and shopping. The student loan, though daunting, launched her into a stable career with a salary that paid for itself many times over. That debt lifted her future. The credit card debt, meanwhile, dragged her down. Interest charges kept her balance high for years. The same person with two types of debt - one building, one draining. And the situation is not unique to Priya but a lot of my other clients.

Priya eventually paid off the card but she told me, "If I had understood the difference earlier, I would have felt less shame about my student loans and way more urgency about my credit card."

Before taking on debt, pause and ask the key questions:
1. Will this purchase or investment grow in value or shrink?
2. Will this debt increase my future income or stability?
3. Is the interest rate reasonable compared to the benefit I'll gain?
4. Am I borrowing for a want or a need?

If the answers lean toward growth, opportunity and value, it may be good debt. If they lean toward consumption, impulse and high cost, it's almost certainly bad.

Always remember, Debt is never free. It always takes something from you. But when chosen wisely, it can give back more than it costs. The challenge is to distinguish between the debts that feed your future and the ones that eat it alive.

Good debt builds. Bad debt drains. The choice is in your hands every time you sign a loan agreement, swipe a card or click "buy now, pay later." The key is not to fear debt, but to recognize its nature and only invite the kinds that strengthen your financial story.

Reflection Pause

- ☐ Do you currently carry debts that are building your future (like a home or education), or that are quietly draining it (like credit cards)?
- ☐ When you look at your monthly payments, how many are buying assets and how many are paying for things already long gone?
- ☐ If you labeled each debt you have right now as "nutrient" or "junk food," what would your plate look like?

STRATEGIES FOR MANAGING AND PAYING OFF DEBT

Once you've named your debts as good, bad or ugly, the next step is learning how to manage them. For the bad and ugly ones, this means not just paying the bills, but creating a plan to dig out and stay out. Because here's the truth: debt rarely disappears on its own. If anything, it grows when ignored.

But with the right strategies, even the heaviest debt burden can be tackled. It doesn't require winning the lottery or landing a huge raise. It requires a clear system, consistency and a mindset shift from "I'm stuck" to "I'm in control."

Alicia, a social worker in Denver, carried balances on six different credit cards. None of them were massive. A $500 here, $1,200 there, $3,000 on the biggest, but together, they weighed on her. She felt overwhelmed. She tried paying a little on each card, but it felt like she was running in place.

One day, she decided to try something different: the *Debt Snowball* method. She lined up her debts from smallest to largest balance. She kept making minimum payments on all but the smallest card, and she threw every extra dollar at that one. Before she realized, that $500 card was gone. That first victory felt incredible.

Encouraged, she rolled the payment she had been making on the $500 card into the next one. Then the next. Each card gone gave her more momentum. Within 18 months, Alicia had paid off every single credit card.

Her story shows the power of having a clear strategy. Let's look at the two most effective ones.

The Debt Snowball

The *Snowball* method focuses on psychology. You list your debts from smallest to largest balance, regardless of interest rate. You pay the minimums on all but smallest and attack that one with everything you can. When it's gone, you move to the next smallest, then the next. Each payoff gives you a "win," building momentum like a snowball rolling downhill, getting bigger and faster.

Why does it work? Because Humans are emotional beings. We need to feel progress. Small wins create motivation that spreadsheets alone can't.

The Debt Avalanche

The *Avalanche* method focuses on math. You list your debts by interest rate, from highest to lowest. You pay the minimums on all but the highest-interest debt and hammer that one first.

When it's gone, you move to the next-highest rate. This saves you the most money in the long run because you're eliminating the costliest debt first.

Why does it work? Because it's the most efficient path with fewer dollars lost to interest.

Let's also look at some other helpful strategies you can deploy to tackle debt faster:

1. **Automate Payments:** Set up automatic payments for at least the minimums to avoid late fees and protect your credit score.

2. **Negotiate Interest Rates:** Call your credit card company and ask for a lower rate. Sometimes, especially if you've been a long-time customer, they'll say yes.

3. **Balance Transfers:** Some cards offer 0% APR for a limited time on transferred balances. Used wisely, this can buy you breathing room to pay down debt faster. But beware, if you don't pay it off in time, the high interest kicks back in.

4. **Side Hustles and Extra Income:** Throwing extra money at debt accelerates progress. Freelance work, weekend jobs, selling unused items or other extra income options can help fuel the payoff plan.

5. **Emergency Fund First (Small One):** Before tackling debt aggressively, build a small emergency fund. Otherwise, every unexpected expense will send you back into debt.

Paying off debt is like running a marathon. If you try to sprint the first mile, you'll burn out. But if you pace yourself, celebrate each mile marker and keep going, you'll cross the finish line. There will be setbacks - a flat tire, a medical bill, a surprise expense. That doesn't mean you failed. It just means you keep running.

Debt can feel like an immovable mountain, but mountains are climbed one step at a time. The Snowball and Avalanche methods are just different paths up the same slope. What matters isn't which path you choose but it's that you start climbing and keep moving.

Alicia didn't become debt-free overnight. She built momentum, stuck with her plan and celebrated each small win. That's what transformed her story. And it's what can transform yours too.

Reflection Pause

- ☐ If you lined up your debts right now, which method would motivate you more? The Snowball (smallest balance first) or Avalanche (highest interest first)?
- ☐ Do you have at least a small emergency cushion, or are you still relying on credit cards for every surprise?
- ☐ What's one debt you could realistically wipe out in the next three months and how would that feel?

BUILDING A HEALTHY RELATIONSHIP WITH CREDIT

If earlier sections showed us the dangers of credit when misused, this one is about something more important: how to live with credit in a way that's healthy, sustainable and even beneficial. Because the truth is, avoiding credit altogether isn't realistic or wise in today's world. Credit is everywhere. The key is not running from it, but learning how to live with it responsibly.

Marcus, a software developer in Austin, learned this lesson the hard way. Fresh out of college, he treated his first credit card like an extension of his income. His logic was simple: "If the bank gave me a $5,000 limit, that must mean I can afford $5,000 worth of stuff." Within a year, Marcus was juggling balances across two cards, paying minimums and constantly stressed. After a late payment dinged his credit score, he couldn't qualify for the best rate on a car loan. That's when it clicked (and a lesson for all):

credit isn't free money; it is borrowed trust.

He shifted his approach. Instead of maxing out cards, he kept his balances low, using them for groceries and bills he already had the cash to cover. He set up autopay to clear the full balance every month. Slowly, his score climbed. Three years later, when he applied for a mortgage, the bank not only approved him but gave him a competitive interest rate. As Marcus puts it "Credit is like a dog. If you train it, it's loyal. If you let it run wild, it makes a mess."

Habit 1: Pay in Full, Always

The golden rule of credit: never carry a balance if you can avoid it. Paying in full each month means you enjoy the convenience, protection and rewards of credit cards without falling into the interest trap. If you treat your credit card like a debit card, with the discipline to only spend what you already have, you'll never fear the bill at the end of the month.

The Big Picture

Credit isn't just about borrowing. It influences many areas of life. Landlords may check it before renting. Employers in some industries review it before hiring. Insurance companies sometimes factor it into premiums. A strong credit profile can quietly save you money and open doors across your financial journey.

Habit 2: Keep Utilization Low

Your credit utilization, the percentage of your limit you actually use, matters. Using 10–30% of your available credit is seen as healthy. Maxing out cards regularly, even if you pay them off, signals risk to lenders. Think of it like driving. Just because your car's speedometer goes up to 140 mph doesn't mean you should be driving that fast. Just because your credit limit is $10,000 doesn't mean you should use all $10,000.

Habit 3: Protect Your Credit History

A long, consistent credit history is like a glowing resume. The longer you've had accounts open and managed responsibly, the more trustworthy you appear. Closing old accounts just because you don't use them can actually hurt your score. Let your credit age gracefully.

Habit 4: Use Credit for Convenience, Not Dependence

Credit works best when it's a tool for convenience and safety, not survival. Using it to book flights, rent cars, earn rewards or protect purchases is smart. Using it to cover everyday expenses you can't afford is dangerous. It's the difference between carrying an umbrella for unexpected rain and trying to build a roof with one.

Habit 5: Monitor and Maintain

Check credit reports at least once a year (they're free through a few sites in the U.S.). Look for errors, fraud or old accounts still showing up. Set up alerts with your bank to catch suspicious activity quickly. A healthy relationship with credit isn't "set it and forget it" but like tending a garden. Occasional care keeps things growing strong.

Credit is neither angel nor demon but a mirror. It reflects your habits back at you. Used wisely, it can protect you, reward you and open doors to opportunities. Used poorly, it can close those doors just as quickly.

Marcus learned this lesson after years of stress, but the turnaround wasn't magic. It was built on small, steady habits: paying in full, keeping balances low, respecting credit as borrowed trust. Those are habits anyone can adopt. A healthy relationship with credit isn't about fear. It's about confidence - the kind that comes from knowing the bill will be paid, the score will rise and the future will stay open.

Reflection Pause

☐ Do you currently pay your credit cards in full each month, or are you carrying balances that keep charging interest?

☐ How much of your available credit do you typically use and what does that signal about your habits?

☐ If your credit history is a story, what does it say about you: reliable, inconsistent, or just getting started?

MASTERING THE DOUBLE-EDGED SWORD

We've traveled a long way through the world of credit and debt. From thrill of the first swipe to traps of minimum payments, from the math of compounding interest against you to the habits that can make credit a lifelong ally, one truth has stood out: credit is a double-edged sword. In skilled hands, it builds trust, opens doors and even gives you rewards. In careless hands, it slices deep, draining your future, your peace and sometimes even your hope.

Back in first section, we compared credit to fire. It's worth repeating here. Fire isn't inherently good or bad. It depends on where you put it and how you use it. In a fireplace, it's warmth and comfort. Out of control, it's destruction. Credit is the same. It can help you buy a home, start a business or build a career. Or it can leave you stuck paying triple for dinners you barely remember. The difference is never the plastic in your wallet but it's the person holding it.

Facing the Truth

Many people avoid thinking about credit and debt because it feels overwhelming or shameful. But silence is what makes debt grow ugly. Facing it, laying out the balances, admitting the mistakes, naming the good and the bad, is the first step toward mastery.

When you pull everything into the light, you take back the power. You stop being the victim of a system and start being the strategist who uses it.

The healthiest approach to credit isn't fear and it isn't recklessness. It's respect. Respect credit as borrowed trust. Respect the cost of debt. Respect yourself enough to only use debt that builds your future. That mindset keeps you in the driver's seat. You decide when to use credit, how to use it and when to walk away.

On the other hand, Debt often feels like chains. But when you pay it down, when you stop feeding it, those same chains can become tools. A good credit score, once earned, gives you leverage. You borrow at lower costs. You get better opportunities. You're trusted more. It's not about never using credit again but about using it on your terms.

The "ugly" side of debt thrives on short-term thinking - spending now, dealing later. The "good" side of credit thrives on the long game - building history, protecting your score, planning for the future. That's the real shift this chapter invites you to make: stop thinking of credit as a moment-to-moment decision and start seeing it as part of your lifelong financial story.

Credit and debt are not enemies to fear or friends to embrace blindly. They are forces to be understood, respected and mastered. The banks, cards and scores are all playing their part. But the story of credit in your life is ultimately written by you.

Worksheet: My Credit & Debt Check-Up

Take 20–30 minutes. Be honest. No one else will see it but you.

1. **List Your Debts**
    o Card 1: Balance $_________ / Interest Rate _______ % / Minimum Payment $_______
    o Card 2: Balance $_________ / Interest Rate _______ % / Minimum Payment $_______
    o Loan (Car/Personal/Student): Balance $_________ / Interest Rate _______ % / Monthly Payment $_______
    o Mortgage: Balance $_________ / Interest Rate _______ % / Monthly Payment $_______

2. **Label Them**
    o Which debts are Good (building your future)?
    o Which are Bad (consumption, high cost)?
    o Which are Ugly (spiraling, overdue, or maxed out)?

3. **Choose Your Strategy**
    o Will you use the Snowball Method (smallest balance first) or the Avalanche Method (highest interest first)?
    o Which debt will you target first?

____

4. **Set One Credit Habit (Choose one to start this month.)**
    o I will pay in full each month.
    o I will lower my utilization below 30%.
    o I will review my credit report.
    o I will set up autopay.

5. **Step 5: Your Next Three Actions**
    o ____
    o ____
    o ____

6

Investing – Your Money Makes Friends

Picture this: you tuck a single dollar bill into your wallet. It sits there quietly, folded behind your credit card, waiting for the day you spend it. Maybe tomorrow it buys you a gumball from a machine. Maybe next week it helps cover a coffee. Either way, once it's spent, it's gone. That dollar lived a short, simple life.

Now imagine something different. Instead of spending that dollar, you give it a job. You place it in an account where it can grow. That dollar doesn't just sit still anymore - it goes out, mingles and starts making friends. Maybe it earns a little interest, so by the end of the year, it has one or two buddies hanging around. Over time, those new friends invite their own friends. Eventually, what started as one lonely dollar has turned into a bustling crowd of money working together on your behalf.

That is the essence of investing. It's your money - making friends - and those friends making more friends, while you go about your life. Saving is important, no doubt. But saving alone won't get you where you want to go. If you simply park your money in a jar, under a mattress or even in a low-interest savings account, inflation will quietly eat it away.

Think about your parents or grandparents. Maybe they used to say, "Back in my day, a dollar could buy a gallon of milk!" Today, that same dollar wouldn't even buy you a third of that gallon. Prices rise. Value shrinks. Money left idle loses strength.

Investing, on the other hand, flips the script. It allows your money not just to hold its value but to grow it. A dollar invested has the chance to become two, five, ten or more over time. And earlier you let your money make friends, bigger the party it can throw for you later in life.

Remember Carter from Chapter 2 and the thought of money like seeds. If you eat or trash all your seeds today, you'll feel satisfied for a moment but tomorrow you'll be hungry again. If you plant some of those seeds, you won't get fruit overnight, but give them time and they'll grow into trees. A single apple tree produces not just one apple, but many. Inside each apple are more seeds and if you plant those, you get more trees. Over decades, a whole orchard grows... Feeding you, your family and maybe even generations to come. That's what investing does. It turns today's fruits into tomorrow's orchard.

For many people, the first step into investing feels scary. The stock market seems like a casino. News headlines shout about crashes and bubbles. Friends brag about winning big or losing everything. It feels unpredictable and risky. Something like putting your hard-earned money into a machine that spits out random results.

But here's the truth: investing isn't about playing slot machines. It's about planting seeds and letting time do the heavy lifting. Yes, markets go up and down in the short term. But over the long term, patient investors who stay consistent tend to see their money multiply.

I once had a client, *Evelyn*, who was terrified of investing. She preferred keeping her money "safe" in a savings account. But when we compared how her $10,000 would grow in savings versus in a simple, diversified investment fund, the difference shocked her. In savings, after 20 years, she'd have maybe $12,000. In investments, with below average market growth, she could have over $40,000. Same starting point, wildly different outcomes. Evelyn realized that the real risk wasn't investing but rather in not investing.

Make no mistake, investing involves risk. But so does everything in life. Driving a car is risky. Starting a business is risky. Even doing nothing is risky because inflation is guaranteed to erode your money's value if it just sits there. The key isn't avoiding risk altogether. It's learning how to manage it. Diversify your investments, stay consistent and most importantly, give your money time to grow. The longer it stays invested, the more friends it makes.

Investing isn't about predicting the next hot stock. It's about giving your money the chance to build a network, to grow into something bigger than what you started with. One dollar alone can't do much. But one dollar making friends, over years and decades, can change your life.

Reflection Pause

- ☐ If you thought of each dollar in your account as either "lonely" (just sitting still) or "making friends" (invested and growing), how many of your dollars are truly at work?
- ☐ Do you see investing as gambling or as planting seeds that need patience to grow?
- ☐ What feels riskier to you: investing in a market that goes up and down or keeping money in savings where inflation steadily eats it away?

WHY INVEST AT ALL?

When people hear the word *investing*, they often think of Wall Street traders in suits, stock tickers flashing across screens or high-stakes bets that only "rich people" make. It feels distant, intimidating, something for "them" and not the regular folks. But nothing can be further from the truth. Investing isn't about being rich. It's about *becoming* secure. It's about giving your money a role in your life beyond sitting quietly in an account or vanishing through spending.

We've already talked about inflation nibbling away at savings, but let's go deeper and talk about *silent erosion of wealth*. The hidden cost of not investing is *opportunity cost*.

Imagine two friends, *Leo* and *Sam*. They both earn the same salary and save diligently. Leo tucks away $500 every month in a regular savings account. Sam invests that same $500 in a broad stock market fund. After 10 years, Leo feels proud as he saved $60,000, plus a little interest. But Sam? His account has grown to nearly $80,000–$90,000, depending on market performance. That's \$20,000–\$30,000 more from letting his money work for him and not from him working harder. The opportunity cost for Leo wasn't losing money. It was losing potential. By playing it safe, he gave up the chance for his money to multiply.

The Psychology of Safety vs. Growth

Why do people resist investing, even when the math is clear? Psychology. We are wired for survival, not wealth-building.

- ***Certainty feels good.*** *Putting money in savings feels safe because we know it will still be there tomorrow. Investing feels uncertain because markets go up and down.*
- ***Losses hurt more than gains help.*** *Psychologists call this "loss aversion." Losing \$100 feels twice as painful as gaining \$100 feels good. That's why people pull out of investments at the first sign of trouble.*
- ***The future feels abstract.*** *Spending money today gives us immediate pleasure. Investing for a future 20 or 30 years away feels distant, almost unreal.*

The irony? By avoiding short-term discomfort, we often invite long-term struggle.

Another reason people hesitate is because they misunderstand what investing really means. They hear "stock market" and picture roulette wheels. But investing isn't gambling. Gambling is based on chance. Investing is based on ownership.

When you buy a stock, you own a piece of a company. When that company grows by building better products, expanding into new markets or serving more customers, you share in its success. You're not betting on random numbers; you're partnering with human effort, innovation and progress.

Think of every product or service you love – your phone, your favorite clothing brand, the apps you use daily. Behind each of those is a company and investing allows you to ride along with their journey. And that's not a roll of the dice but being part of the world's growth.

Sometimes, the scariest thing isn't making the wrong choice but *not making a choice*. I once met a client, *Sophia*, who was so afraid of investing that she kept her entire savings in cash. Over 15 years, she diligently saved $100,000. But during that same time, stock market doubled. If she had invested even half of her savings in something simple and diversified, she could have had $150,000–$200,000. By avoiding the "risk" of investing, she took on the guaranteed risk of missing out.

This is what makes "not investing" the quietest, most dangerous trap. It doesn't feel like you're losing but in reality, every year you delay, you're leaving future dollars on the table.

Another real reason to invest is freedom. Investing allows you to exchange today's discipline for tomorrow's options. It's the art of saying, "I'll let my money work alongside me, so one day, I don't have to work as hard." It's also a partnership with time. Every dollar you invest becomes an employee you hire. The more employees you hire, the bigger the company of *your money* grows. One day, if you do it right, your money's company can cover your bills, fund your dreams and even support your family when you no longer can.

Remember, money that only saves is money that slowly slips away. Money that invests is money that multiplies, creating options, freedom and peace of mind. And investing isn't just for the wealthy. It is how ordinary people *become* wealthy or at least secure enough to live life on their terms. The question isn't, *"Should I invest?"* but rather *"Can I afford not to?"*

Reflection Pause

☐ How much of your money is "resting" (in savings, waiting) versus "working" (invested, growing)?

- ☐ When you think of investing, do you imagine gambling or do you see it as ownership in companies, homes or projects that create value?
- ☐ Which feels scarier: a market that dips and recovers, or a lifetime of money that never had the chance to grow?

THE POWER OF COMPOUNDING

If investing is your money, making friends; compounding is what happens when those friends start introducing *their* friends to the party. It's the ripple effect of quiet, patient growth that turns small beginnings into life-changing outcomes.

Back in Chapter 2, we brushed against compounding before. I can't emphasize enough the importance and magic of compounding, but now it's time to see it in full color. And to do that, let me tell you a story not of one person, but of three generations in a family.

Back in the 1970s, *Elena*, a schoolteacher, **saved** faithfully. She stashed away $100 a month in a savings account. Over 30 years, she saved more than $36,000. She was proud of her discipline. But here's the catch: her savings grew very little because interest rates barely kept pace with inflation. By the time she retired, her nest egg didn't stretch as far as she had hoped. Elena's effort wasn't wasted. She had something and that mattered. But her dollars never got the chance to make friends. They stayed lonely, growing slowly and cautiously.

Elena's daughter, *Marisol*, learned from her mother's example. She became a nurse and decided to do things differently. Instead of leaving her money idle, she **invested** $100 a month in a broad stock market fund. The difference was dramatic. Over 30 years, her contributions also totaled about $36,000. But with compounding, dividends reinvested and growth layered upon growth; her nest egg didn't just sit at $36,000. It grew to over $150,000. Same discipline. Same monthly amount. The difference was investing at work.

Now comes *Sofia*, Marisol's daughter. She saw her grandmother save and her mother invest. She decided to **start even earlier**. At just 22, with her first job, she began **investing** $100 a month, just like the women before her. But instead of stopping after 30 years, she stayed the course for 40. By the time she reached retirement age, Sofia's steady investing had blossomed into more than $350,000 - ten times what her grandmother had. And here's the wild part: Sofia didn't work harder, earn more, or save more than her mother or grandmother. She simply gave her money *more time* to compound.

Three women. Same family. Same monthly contribution. Different outcomes.

- Elena: $36,000 saved.
- Marisol: $150,000 invested.
- Sofia: $350,000 invested longer.

That's the power of compounding. It's not just about how much you save, but how early you start and how consistently you let time do its magic.

Compounding in Real Life

We often underestimate compounding because our brains aren't wired to think exponentially. We think in straight lines: add a little, get a little more. But compounding is like bending that line upward until it curves into a steep climb. That's why, in early years, it feels like nothing is happening. Your account grows slowly, almost boringly. But give it decades and the curve suddenly turns upward, and you look back astonished at how far it's come.

Think of planting bamboo. For years, nothing seems to happen above ground. Then one day, it shoots up several feet almost overnight. That's compounding. Quiet, invisible work that suddenly bursts into visible results.

The hardest part about compounding is waiting or **the patience problem**. We live in a culture of instant gratification - one-click orders, same-day delivery, streaming everything. But compounding doesn't play that game. It demands patience.

That's why so many people sabotage themselves. They pull money out too early. They chase quick wins, GameStop like stocks instead of letting steady growth do its work. They forget that real magic happens not in year 5 or 10, but in year 30 and beyond. It's not about timing the market but about *time in* the market.

Here's a beautiful twist: compounding isn't just a financial principle. It shows up everywhere in life be it learning (read a book a month for 10 years and you've consumed a library), health (exercise for 20 minutes a day multiplies energy, longevity and confidence) or relationships (small, consistent acts of kindness compound into deep trust over decades). The principle is universal: small, consistent actions, repeated over time, create results far greater than the sum of their parts.

Compounding is the quiet friend of investing. It doesn't shout, it doesn't brag and, in the beginning, it doesn't look impressive at all. But give it time and it becomes the loudest, most powerful force in your financial life. Elena's lonely dollars never made many friends. Marisol's dollars started inviting others. Sofia's dollars threw a party that grew into an empire. The difference wasn't discipline or intelligence but simply letting time compound their efforts. That's the invitation compounding extends to all of us: start today, stay patient and let tomorrow thank you for the friends you made.

Reflection Pause
- ☐ Think back: if you had invested even $50 a month starting 10 years ago, where would that money be today?
- ☐ What's stopping you from starting now? Even a small amount?
- ☐ Where else in your life (learning, health, relationships) have you seen compounding play out?

THE MAIN INVESTMENT VEHICLES

When you step into the world of investing, you'll quickly notice there are lots of vehicles on the road. Some are flashy sports cars, zipping around with excitement (and risk). Others are steady buses, moving slower but reliably. The trick isn't to drive every vehicle yourself. It is to understand which ones fit your journey.

For most people, the core investment building blocks are stocks, bonds, mutual funds and ETFs. Let's take them one by one, in plain language.

Stocks: Owning a Slice of the Pie

Imagine your favorite bakery. Let's say it's "Sweet Delights," the one that makes the cupcakes you can't resist. Now, what if you could own a small piece of that bakery? When the bakery sells more cupcakes and makes more profit, your slice is worth more. If the bakery struggles, your slice loses value.

That's what a stock is: ownership in a company. When you buy a stock, you're not just holding paper; you're owning a fraction of that business. If Apple, Amazon or Coca-Cola grows, you grow with it.

Why people like stocks:

- They offer the potential for high growth. Over long periods, stocks have outperformed most other investments.

- You can sometimes receive dividends, small profit-sharing payments from the company.

Why they're risky:

- Prices go up and down daily. Sometimes dramatically.

- If the company fails, your slice of the pie can crumble with it.

Analogy: Stocks are like roller coasters at an amusement park. Exciting, sometimes stomach-churning, but over time, the ride usually ends higher than where it started.

Bonds: Lending, Not Owning

Now imagine Sweet Delights bakery needs to buy a new oven but doesn't want to give away ownership. Instead, they borrow money from you. In exchange, they promise to pay you back later with a little interest.

That's a bond. Instead of owning part of a company, you're lending money to it (or to a government). Bonds are IOUs with a timeline. You give your money today and they promise to give it back with interest.

Why people like bonds:

- They're usually more stable than stocks.
- You know what you're promised (fixed interest, known timeline).
- Governments & reputed companies are often reliable borrowers.

Why they're risky:

- The company or government could default though less likely.
- Inflation can eat away at your interest. Earning 3% when prices rise 4% means you're actually losing ground.

Analogy: Bonds are like lending money to a friend who pays you back monthly with a little extra. Stocks are about sharing success. Bonds are about dependable repayment.

Mutual Funds: Team Effort Investing

Not everyone wants to pick stocks or bonds one by one. It's like going to a buffet and having to decide exactly which dishes to put on your plate. That's where mutual funds come in - they let you scoop a little of everything.

A mutual fund is a basket filled with lots of different stocks and/or bonds. Instead of buying shares of 20 individual companies, you buy into one fund that holds them all. A professional manager decides what goes into the basket and when to adjust it.

Why people like mutual funds:

- Instant diversification. Your money isn't tied to just one company.

- Someone else does the work of choosing investments.

- Great for people who don't want to micromanage.

<u>Why they're risky/limiting:</u>

- You pay management fees which can eat into returns.

- Some managers do better than others, so no guarantee your fund will beat the market.

- You don't control what's inside the basket.

Analogy: Mutual funds are like joining a community potluck. Everyone chips in and you get a full plate of variety without cooking each dish yourself.

ETFs: Mutual Funds with Flexibility

ETFs (Exchange-Traded Funds) are like mutual funds' younger, cooler cousin. They're also baskets of investments comprising stocks, bonds or both. However, they trade on the stock market like individual stocks.

This means you can buy and sell ETFs throughout the day at market prices, whereas mutual funds are priced only once a day. ETFs often track an index (like the S&P 500), so they're less about a manager picking winners and more about following the whole market.

<u>Why people like ETFs:</u>

- They usually have lower fees than mutual funds.

- Easy diversification. You can buy entire stock market in one ETF.

- Flexibility just like stocks - you can trade them anytime.

<u>Why they're risky/limiting:</u>

- They still go up and down with the market.

- Some niche ETFs focus on fads (like only holding "space exploration" companies) which can be risky.

Analogy: ETFs are like pre-packed meals at a grocery store - balanced, convenient, usually cheaper and you can grab them off the shelf whenever you want.

How They Work Together

Think of stocks, bonds, mutual funds and ETFs as instruments in an orchestra:
- *Stocks are the violins - loud, dominant, dramatic.*
- *Bonds are the steady drums - predictable, providing rhythm.*
- *Mutual funds are the conductor - choosing which instruments to highlight.*
- *ETFs are the sheet music - letting you follow the whole symphony at once.*

On their own, each can be powerful. Together, they create harmony. A portfolio that balances risk and reward.

Investing doesn't have to be complicated. At its core, you're choosing between owning, lending or pooling. Stocks let you own pieces of companies. Bonds let you lend. Mutual funds and ETFs let you pool with others.

Each vehicle has its role, its strengths and its weaknesses. The key isn't to drive just one but to understand them well enough to build a ride that carries you steadily toward your goals.

Reflection Pause

- ☐ If you had to describe your personality today, are you more like a stock (adventurous, high energy), a bond (steady, cautious) or an ETF/mutual fund (balanced, team-oriented)?
- ☐ When you imagine your investments, do you prefer picking specific "slices of pie" or do you feel safer holding a big basket?
- ☐ Which of these vehicles (stocks, bonds, mutual funds, ETFs) do you already use? Which feel intimidating or new?

RISK AND REWARD

Every investment carries a story of two characters - *Risk* and *Reward*. They're inseparable companions. Two sides of the same coin. You can't invite one into your portfolio without the other showing up too. The key is not to fear Risk but to understand how to live with it while letting Reward work for you.

Think of investing like visiting an amusement park. Some rides are gentle like a merry-go-round, safe and predictable. Others are thrilling like roller coasters with climbs, drops and turns that make your stomach flip. Both rides have their place. It just depends on how much excitement you can handle and how well you're buckled in.

Let's start with something simple: *there's no such thing as a risk-free investment*. Even keeping cash in a savings account carries risk i.e. inflation slowly erodes its value. Bonds carry risk that interest rates will change or a borrower could default. Stocks carry risk of volatility, where prices swing wildly. Risk is simply the possibility that the outcome will be different from what you expect - sometimes better, sometimes worse. Without risk, there's no growth. But without control, there's chaos.

In finance, risk and reward have a direct relationship. *Higher the potential return, higher the uncertainty you must accept*. It's like hiking a mountain. The higher you climb, the better the view but tougher the path. If you want the breathtaking panorama, you have to accept the occasional slip or rainstorm.

Safe, low-risk investments like government bonds, might offer steady but modest returns. Riskier ones like stocks, can grow faster, but also drop sharply at times. Understanding that tradeoff is the foundation of investing wisely.

Amira was a software designer who got her first big bonus. Eager to make her money grow, she dove into the stock market. She picked tech stocks she liked, watched YouTube gurus and saw quick early gains.

But when the market dipped, so did her enthusiasm. She panicked and sold several investments at a loss. A few months later, the same stocks rebounded and she missed out on the recovery. "I realized I wasn't losing because of the market" she told me. "I was losing because I didn't understand my own tolerance for risk."

After that experience, Amira built a more balanced portfolio:

- 60% in stocks for long-term growth,
- 30% in bonds for stability,
- 10% in cash for flexibility.

That mix wasn't exciting, but it was sustainable. The next time markets fell, she didn't panic. Her investments dipped but her plan didn't.

The Seatbelt of Diversification

Diversification is the seatbelt in your investment vehicle. It doesn't prevent every bump, but it keeps you from being thrown off the ride. Instead of putting all your money into one company or one type of asset, you spread it out across many. That way, if one company fails, another part can help balance the loss.

A simple example:

• If you only owned airline stocks during the pandemic, your portfolio would've plummeted.
• But if you also owned tech, healthcare and consumer goods, the pain would've been smaller. Some sectors went down, others went up.

Diversification doesn't eliminate risk; it manages it. It's like having different crops in your garden. If one fails due to weather, others can still thrive.

Know thyself. No two investors have the same comfort level with risk. Your *risk tolerance* usually depends on three things:

1. **Your Time Horizon:** The longer you plan to invest, the more risk you can take. A 25-year-old can ride out market ups and downs that a 60-year-old nearing retirement cannot.

2. **Your Financial Goals:** If you're investing for short-term goals (like buying a home in 2 years), you'll want safer, more stable options. If you're investing for retirement 25 years away, you can afford volatility.

3. **Your Emotional DNA:** Some people sleep fine when markets drop 20%. Others lose sleep over a 2% dip. The best portfolio isn't the one with highest returns - it's the one you can actually stick with.

And while it's easy to think of risk as something bad, risk isn't the enemy here. Risk is what allows for growth. Without it, the only guaranteed result is stagnation.

Think of fire again - it can burn you but it also cooks your food and keeps you warm. The key is control. Similarly, the goal of investing isn't to eliminate risk; it's to harness it intelligently.

Every investor faces the same tradeoff: you can't get higher returns without embracing some uncertainty. The secret isn't to fear the drops or chase the highs but to build a portfolio that lets you enjoy the ride without losing sleep.

Amira's journey wasn't about becoming fearless. It was about becoming *prepared*. Once she had her seatbelt i.e. diversification, balance and self-awareness, the roller coaster didn't scare her anymore.

Risk and reward will always travel together. The art of investing is learning how to let them dance without letting one lead you off the floor.

Reflection Pause

☐ When markets drop, do you feel anxious or do you see it as a chance to buy more while prices are low?

☐ Have you ever made an investment decision driven more by emotion than by plan like panic-selling or jumping into a trend?

☐ If you had to pick your "ride" in the investment amusement park, would you choose the merry-go-round (steady, slow), the roller coaster (exciting, volatile) or something in between?

COMMON INVESTING MISTAKES

Investing, at its heart, isn't just about numbers – it is about behavior. Markets move up and down but our emotions move faster. Most investing mistakes don't come from lack of knowledge. They come from overconfidence, impatience, fear and FOMO - the fear of missing out.

If you can recognize these traps early, you can sidestep decades of stress and lost money.

Let's start with *Jared's* story. Jared was an engineer in his late thirties who started investing right after the 2008 financial crisis. Everyone around him was panicking but he saw an opportunity. He bought a handful of index funds and individual stocks, determined to "buy low." For years, things went well. The market recovered, his portfolio grew and his confidence soared. He started following financial news obsessively, convinced he could "time" the next move.

Then came 2020. The pandemic hit. Markets plunged faster than anyone had ever seen. In two weeks, Jared saw nearly 30% of his portfolio evaporate. His stomach twisted every time he checked his account. After several sleepless nights, he sold most of his investments "just to stop the bleeding."

You can probably guess what happened next. Within months, the market rebounded. Faster than anyone expected. Jared watched from the sidelines as his portfolio recovered, but without him. He didn't lose because he picked bad investments. He lost because he panicked.

Mistake #1 – Timing the Market

Trying to predict short-term market movements is like trying to predict next week's weather in three different countries. You might get lucky, but you won't get it right consistently. Markets rise and fall every day, but historically, they have trended upward over the long term. The problem is that investors often pull money out right before the recovery begins.

Missing just a few of the market's best days can dramatically cut long-term returns. It's not about timing the market; it's about *time in* the market.

Discipline beats prediction.

Mistake #2 – Chasing Fads and "Hot Tips"

Every decade has its "sure thing." Dot-coms in the 2000s. Real estate in the mid-2000s. Crypto in the 2010s. AI stocks in the 2020s. There's always something everyone is rushing to buy. But when everyone's rushing in, prices are already inflated. The early movers profit; the crowd often gets burned.

Trends aren't inherently bad. Innovation drives markets forward but buying into hype without understanding what you're owning is gambling, not investing. If you ever find yourself investing because a friend made quick money or because a headline said "this time it's different," take a breath.

If it were truly a guaranteed win, it wouldn't need a commercial.

Mistake #3 – Ignoring Fees

Fees are the termites of investing. Tiny, almost invisible at first, but given enough time, they eat through your returns.

A 1% annual management fee might sound small, but over 30 years, it can reduce your returns by tens of thousands of dollars. That's why low-cost index funds and ETFs have become so popular. They keep more of your money working for you instead of paying someone else. Always check the *expense ratio* before investing in a fund.

Mistake #4 – Overreacting to News

Financial media thrives on drama. "MARKET CRASH!" "RECESSION LOOMS!" "STOCKS SOAR!". These headlines are designed to keep you watching, not to help you make good decisions. The daily noise often distracts people from their long-term goals. If you wouldn't change your entire diet because of one bad meal, don't change your investment strategy because of one bad day in the market.

Investing isn't a sprint. It's a marathon run over decades

Mistake #5 – Forgetting the Goal

Many people invest without a clear destination. They pick random funds or follow advice from relatives, but they never ask *why*. Are you investing for retirement? For a home? For your child's education? Your goal determines your time horizon, your risk tolerance and your strategy.

Without clarity, you're just throwing darts in the dark.

Mistake #6 – Impatience

The most underrated trait in investing isn't intelligence, IT IS PATIENCE. When markets rise, people want to make quick profits. When markets fall, they want to run. But real investing happens in years, not days. One of the greatest investors of all time, Mr. Warren Buffett, put it perfectly:

"The stock market is a device for transferring money from the impatient to the patient."

The impatient buy high, sell low and repeat. The patient buy reasonably, hold through storms and lets time reward them.

The Lesson from an 11-Year-Old Investor

Let's take a moment to talk about someone whose name has become almost synonymous with investing. Legendary Mr. Warren Buffett.

At just eleven years old, in 1942, he bought his very first stocks: three shares of Cities Service Preferred at $38.25 each, a total of about $114.75 - nearly his entire savings at the time. Not long after, the stock dropped to $27 a share, losing almost 30% of its value. Most people, adults included, would have panicked and sold at a loss.

But young Buffett didn't. He held on, waited patiently and when the price eventually climbed back up, he sold his shares at $40 each, earning a small profit of $5. That's where most stories would end. With discipline and a modest win. But here's the twist. Not long after he sold, the stock soared to over $200 a share.

He later joked that it was a good lesson not just about holding your nerve when prices fall, but also about thinking long-term. Had he held on, his small $114 investment could've grown almost fivefold. That early experience probably shaped Mr. Buffett's philosophy: the market rewards patience, not perfection. Even legends start small, make mistakes and learn to trust time.

So, remember, the market isn't your enemy. Your emotions are. You can't control when the next downturn comes or when the next bubble pops. But you can control *how you respond.*

The best investors aren't the smartest or the fastest but they're the calmest. They understand that wealth is built not in moments of excitement, but in years of quiet consistency. And avoiding mistakes isn't about perfection. It's about self-awareness. Because once you stop letting emotion drive your investments, you start letting logic build your future.

Reflection Pause

- ☐ Have you ever made an investment decision based on emotion (excitement, fear or FOMO)? What did it cost you?
- ☐ How much do you think you've paid in fees or hidden charges across your investments?

☐ What's one behavioral rule you could adopt (like "no selling for 48 hours after bad news") to protect yourself from your own emotions?

BUILDING INVESTING HABITS

If knowledge is the map, habits are the journey. You can read every book, watch every video and still not grow your wealth. Not unless you actually *build the habit* of investing.

The good news? Great investors aren't born with special instincts. They simply follow simple behaviors consistently. Wealth doesn't come from a lucky stock pick but comes from patience, routine and trust in time.

Aisha worked as a project manager in Portland. When she got her first full-time job, her HR department told her about the company's 401(k) plan and company match to her contributions up to 5%. She didn't know much about investing but she figured free money was too good to ignore. So, she started contributing 5% of every paycheck. She didn't think much about it afterward. It was automatic. The money left her account before she ever saw it.

Years went by. Her career advanced, her salary grew and she increased her contributions bit by bit. She never chased "hot" investments or timed the market. She didn't check her balance daily. She just stayed the course.

Twenty years later, she looked at her account and nearly fell off her chair. What began as small, invisible deductions from her paycheck had grown into a substantial portfolio - enough to give her freedom and peace of mind about retirement. Aisha didn't get rich overnight. She didn't gamble or obsess. She simply *made investing boring* and it quietly made her wealthy.

The Secret to Building Investing Habits: Automation

The easiest way to build an investing habit is to remove willpower from the equation. Don't make the decision every month. Make it once and automate it.

- *Automate contributions from your paycheck into your 401(k), IRA or brokerage account.*
- *Automate reinvestment of dividends.*
- *Automate portfolio rebalancing (many funds do this for you).*

When you automate, you save yourself from your own moods. You don't need to "feel like investing." You just do it quietly, every paycheck. Automation turns discipline into default.

Many people delay investing because they think they need a big amount to begin. But every portfolio, even the twelve-figure ones, started with the first $10, $50 or $114.75. It's not the amount that matters but the repetition. $100 a month for 30 years will outperform $10,000 invested once and forgotten.

When you start small, you also build comfort. You learn to handle market ups and downs in manageable doses, rather than emotional shocks. As your income grows, increase your contribution rate. A 1% annual bump can make a massive difference over time and you won't even feel it.

Separate Investing from Spending. One of the best habits you can develop is treating your investments like a bill. Just like rent or utilities, it's not optional. You don't wait to see what's left over at the end of the month but something you prioritize at the beginning. This mindset shift changes everything. Instead of thinking, *"I'll invest if I can,"* you start thinking, *"I'll spend what's left after I invest."* Over years, this single change can be the difference between financial freedom and financial frustration.

Keep It Simple Stupid (K.I.S.S.). You don't need ten different accounts or a dozen funds to succeed. Complexity creates confusion and confusion breeds inaction. Pick a simple plan, maybe one diversified index fund or ETF. Follow with regular contributions, rebalance once a year if really needed. And most important, don't panic when markets drop. That's it.

The hardest part is resisting the temptation to tinker. When in doubt, remember: "Simple and consistent beats clever and inconsistent."

Make Investing a Lifestyle, Not a Task. The best investors don't treat investing as a chore. They weave it into their life, the same way they brush their teeth or exercise. It's not dramatic but it's routine. They learn a little bit every year, adjust when life changes and stay the course through noise. Investing becomes something that happens quietly in the background while they focus on living. And here's the magic: once your money starts working for you, you stop worrying about it. That's when financial peace begins.

Aisha's story isn't about genius but about rhythm. Every paycheck, every month, every year, she kept the rhythm going. Over time, that rhythm compounded into freedom. That's the essence of successful investing: not chasing opportunity, but building habits that quietly create it.

When you automate, simplify and stay consistent, you transform investing from something intimidating into something inevitable. Let your future self be the one who reaps the rewards. Not because you made one big move, but because you kept showing up, one quiet, disciplined step at a time.

Reflection Pause

☐ Are your current investments automated or do they depend on you remembering to act each month?

☐ What's the smallest, simplest action you could take today to start or strengthen your investing habit?

☐ If you treated investing like paying your most important bill, how different would your financial life look in 10 years?

FROM SEEDS TO FORESTS - LET YOUR MONEY BUILD ITS OWN COMMUNITY

By now, you've met nearly every character in the story of investing - the lonely dollar that wanted to make friends, the impatient saver who feared risk, the calm investor who built habits and even the 11-year-old Mr. Warren Buffett learning patience the hard way.

The lesson that runs through all of them is simple but profound:

Investing isn't about chasing the next big thing. It's about building relationships between your money, time and patience.

When you invest, your money goes to work. It meets other dollars in companies, markets and funds. Together, they collaborate, multiply and grow stronger. You're not just accumulating numbers on a screen but cultivating a living ecosystem that, if tended well, can feed you for life.

The Patience Paradox

It's almost unfair how investing works. The beginning feels slow, painfully slow. You water the seeds and nothing seems to happen. Then one day, years later, the forest appears. Those who quit early never see the trees grow. Those who stay see abundance they couldn't have imagined at the start.

The paradox of investing is this: the less you interfere, the more it works. The less you chase, the more it rewards you. The less dramatic it feels, the more powerful it becomes.

The whole point of investing is to stop making your *time* the only thing that earns money. Your dollars can become teammates that never sleep, never tire and never ask for vacation days. Each invested dollar can produce more dollars, which then produce even more. Eventually, the income from your investments begins to cover your expenses, your goals, your dreams. That's when freedom begins - when your money's friends start working harder than you do. That's why the real measure of investing success isn't your balance. It's your **behavior**.

By now, you know a little something about the Investor's mindset:

- It's not about *when* you start --- it's about *staying started*.
- It's not about predicting markets --- it's about trusting time.
- It's not about chasing excitement --- it's about building habits.

The investors who win aren't those who get lucky; they're those who stay calm. They automate. They diversify. They ignore noise. They let their dollars make friends quietly, month after month. That's not glamorous but it's transformational.

Investing can also be considered the art of optimism. It's an act of believing that tomorrow will be better than today, that companies will grow, people will innovate and economies will adapt.

It's easy to think of money as something you spend or save. But the moment you invest, it becomes something more: a *partner*. It starts working for you. And the sooner you let your money make friends, the sooner you'll find yourself surrounded by allies. Dollars that earn, grow and multiply quietly while you live your life.

So, plant those seeds. Let them take root. And when the forest finally grows tall, remember: it all began with one lonely dollar that you decided to send out into the world.

Remember, Investing doesn't reward speed; it rewards *steadiness*. You don't have to outsmart the market but just outlast your own impulses.

Remember Aisha, the quiet investor who automated her savings and young Buffett, who learned that time is the greatest teacher. They didn't wait for the perfect moment; they created the perfect moment by starting early and staying patient.

Your turn starts now. Don't worry about perfection. Just begin.

Let your first invested dollar go out into the world and trust that it'll come back one day with friends.

Worksheet: My Investor Readiness Checklist

There are no right or wrong answers. And like previous exercises, be honest. No one else will see it but you.

Step 1: My Financial Goal(s)

☐ Retirement   ☐ Home down payment

☐ Children's education   ☐ Financial freedom/early retirement

☐ Other: ______________________________

Step 2: My Current Investing Habits

☐ I contribute automatically each month

☐ I diversify (own both stocks and bonds/funds)

☐ I reinvest dividends or returns

☐ I avoid panic decisions during market dips

☐ I review my portfolio annually

☐ I stay invested for the long term

Step 3: My Investment Mix (Approximate %)

Stocks: _______%   Bonds: _______%

ETFs/Index Funds: _______%   Cash/Other: _______%

Step 4: My Comfort with Risk

- o   I sleep well even when markets drop; I trust the process
- o   I get nervous but stay invested
- o   I panic and want to sell when prices fall

Step 5: My Next 3 Investing Actions

1. ____
2. ____
3. ____

Step 6: My One-Year Commitment

Write a single sentence promise to yourself:

"Over the next 12 months, I will _______ _______ _______ _____ _ _____ so my money keeps making friends even when I'm not watching."

7

Retirement - Future You's Paycheck

Imagine you're sitting on a porch, cup of tea or coffee in hand, watching the morning sun spill across your garden. You open the mailbox and find a letter - one written by your 65-year-old self. It begins like this:

"Dear Me,

Thank You.

Thank you for every paycheck you decided not to spend fully. For every investment you made when it didn't feel like much. For every time you chose 'later' over 'now.' Because of you, I can wake up today and do what I love - not what I have to. I can take trips when I want, spoil the grandkids a little and never check my bank app in fear. You gave me freedom. You gave me peace."

And as you read those words, you smile. Because it hits you - retirement isn't really about "stopping work." It's about giving *future you* the paycheck you'll still need when your working years end.

For many people, retirement feels like a faraway dream, something to think about "someday." But "someday" has a funny habit of sneaking up on us. We live busy lives. We pay bills, raise families, build careers. We tell ourselves we'll start saving *when things settle down*, not realizing that the sooner we begin, the lighter the load becomes later.

Retirement isn't a finish line; it's the next phase of financial independence.

It's not about age; it's about *options*. When you're retired, the bills don't stop showing up. Groceries, healthcare, travel - they all keep coming. The only difference is, your active paycheck doesn't. So you'll need a new one - a paycheck that comes from the work your money did for you. And that's the paycheck future you is counting on.

The "Two Yous"

It helps to think of your financial life as two people living side by side:
- ***Present You*** *who earns, spends and makes decisions today.*
- ***Future You*** *who depends entirely on the decisions decades from now.*

When you skip investing or delay saving, it's like borrowing from Future You's wallet. When you save and invest consistently, you're sending them income i.e. their future paycheck.

And the most powerful way to care for Future You isn't through massive one-time actions. It's through small, consistent contributions - a few dollars every payday that quietly grow into independence.

Our grandparents often retired with pensions and gold watches. The company took care of their future. Today, it's different. The responsibility has shifted. *We* are now the pension managers of our own lives. We decide how much to save, where to invest and how to make it last. That might sound daunting, but it's also empowering. You're not waiting for someone else to hand you security - you're building it brick by brick, dollar by dollar.

And thanks to technology, investing and planning have never been easier. With a few clicks, you can automate your savings, track your progress and literally watch Future You's paycheck grow.

Also, retirement doesn't mean quitting work. It means *having the choice* to stop working for money. Some people travel the world. Some start nonprofits. Some keep working part-time because they love what they do. The magic lies in the *choice*.

True retirement is when your investments, savings and passive income can pay for your needs; whether or not you decide to keep working. That's freedom. So, the goal isn't to escape work; it's to build *financial flexibility*. That's what your future paycheck buys you.

The Letter continues...

"...Remember how you used to think retirement was just about numbers? You were wrong. It's about time.

Time to be with people you love. Time to travel, learn, volunteer or rest without guilt. Time to live the way you always wanted because you gave yourself permission early.

I'm proud of you for not waiting until you had 'enough.' You started when you had something. That's what changed everything.

Love,
Future You."

It's a simple but powerful idea. You don't build a secure future all at once. You build it in moments of small discipline, one paycheck at a time. Retirement isn't a date on a calendar. It is a relationship between who you are today and who you'll be decades from now.

Every dollar you save and invest today is a promise kept to that future self. Every delay is a promise postponed. So, before we dive into the math, strategies, and accounts, remember this:

Retirement planning isn't about building a pile of money. It's about building a *bridge*. A bridge that connects your working years to your free years, paycheck by paycheck, step by step.

Reflection Pause
- ☐ If Future You could write you a letter today, would it be full of thanks or requests for help?
- ☐ How often do you think about the version of you who will depend on the decisions you're making right now?
- ☐ What would "freedom" look like for you at 60 or 70; and what steps could you take this year to make it real?

WHAT RETIREMENT REALLY MEANS

When you hear the word *retirement*, what comes to mind? For most people, it's an image of a gray-haired couple walking on the beach, a hammock under palm trees, maybe a golf course or a cozy morning coffee with no alarm clocks.

But that's the picture the financial industry has sold us for decades - not the *meaning* of retirement. Retirement isn't about *stopping work*. It's about *starting choice*. It's not an end. It's a shift from working because you have to, to working (or not) because you want to.

When you think about it, the goal isn't really to retire but to be *free*. Free to spend your days doing what fulfills you, whether that's consulting part-time, mentoring, gardening or traveling the world without checking your email every 10 minutes. For some, that freedom comes at 65. For others, it arrives at 45. For many, it comes not in one grand moment, but gradually over a series of small decisions that move you closer to independence each year.

The number in your bank account matters, but the real definition of retirement is this:

When your money works harder than you do, you're free.

Let me tell you about *Sanjay*, a client and friend I once worked with. Sanjay had spent nearly 30 years climbing the corporate ladder in a technology firm. He was disciplined, pragmatic and cautious - the kind of person who always paid off his credit cards and maxed his 401(k) contributions. When he turned 55, his company offered an early retirement package. His portfolio was in good shape, his mortgage was nearly paid off and his kids were grown. Everyone congratulated him... "You've made it! You're retired!"

But a few months later, Sanjay called, sounding uneasy. "I thought retirement would feel like freedom," he said, "but honestly, it feels like... emptiness." He wasn't struggling financially. He was struggling *emotionally*. The structure that had defined his life and filled his days (like meetings, teams and projects) was suddenly gone.

After some reflection, Sanjay realized he didn't miss the job as much as he missed *purpose*. So, he began teaching part-time at a local community college. It didn't pay much, but that wasn't the point. He found joy in sharing what he'd learned with younger engineers, mentoring them not just in technology but in career choices and life balance. One day, he told me something that stuck with me: "I didn't retire *from* something. I retired *into* something.". That's the key.

Retirement isn't about escape. It's about evolution.

The Emotional Shift

What if I tell you that money is the easy part of retirement. Math and planning can handle that. The harder part is the identity shift. For decades, your work defines your rhythm, your community, your purpose. When that's suddenly gone, people often face a quiet question: "Who am I now?"

That's why the happiest retirees aren't necessarily the wealthiest. They're the ones who planned not just financially, but emotionally. They replaced their 9-to-5 with new passions: volunteering, travel, art, mentoring, grandparenting or even starting small businesses. They kept learning, kept moving, kept growing.

There's no single right way to retire.

For some, it's early. Example the FIRE (Financial Independence, Retire Early) crowd, who aggressively save and invest to exit the workforce by 40. For others, it's more phased - gradually working fewer hours, consulting or freelancing into their 60s or 70s. And for many, it's traditional - full retirement around 65, after decades of steady contribution.

The "right" retirement is the one that fits *your* values, lifestyle and goals. It's deeply personal. Some want simplicity like a small home, travel once a year, books and peace. Others dream big with second homes, philanthropy, global adventures. Both are valid, as long as you plan accordingly. And here's something powerful to remember:

Retirement success isn't measured by how much you have. It's measured by how secure you feel.

Someone with a modest portfolio but low expenses and peace of mind may live more freely than someone with millions but constant anxiety. It's not about bragging rights. It's about breathing room.

So, ask yourself: what kind of life do you want your savings to buy? A quiet life? A meaningful one? A flexible one? Define that clearly, because the math comes later. First, you need the vision.

Remember that retirement is not a finish line but a bridge. It connects the working years you've built to the life you've always wanted. Sanjay's realization was powerful: he didn't retire *from* work; he retired *into* meaning. That's what we all are aiming for; not to stop living productively, but to start living *deliberately*. The rest of this chapter will help you build the financial side of the bridge and to make sure the freedom you crave has the paycheck it needs to stand strong.

Reflection Pause
- ☐ When you imagine retirement, what does "freedom" look like to you? Is it time, travel, purpose, peace or something else.
- ☐ Do you see retirement as an end to something or the beginning of something new?
- ☐ If you could choose a passion project today that you'd want to pursue later, what would it be?

THE MATH OF RETIREMENT: HOW MUCH IS ENOUGH?

Numbers can feel intimidating when you think about retirement. "How much do I need?" is one of the most common and most paralyzing, questions people ask.

The truth? You don't need a million dollars. You need a plan. And that plan starts by asking not *"How big should my nest egg be?"* but *"How much income will I need to pay Future Me?"*. Because retirement isn't about a lump sum sitting in your account. It's about creating a steady paycheck that arrives long after you've stopped working.

Maria and Jorge were both teachers in their mid-40s when they first came to me. They'd been saving for years but had no clear sense of what "enough" looked like. "I keep hearing about needing a million dollars," Jorge said. "But a million feels like Monopoly money. How do we even know what *our* number is?"

So we began with a simple exercise: instead of focusing on the total, focus on the *monthly*. "How much would you like coming in every month after retirement," I asked, "to live comfortably?". They thought about it: $6,000 per month, enough for bills, travel, hobbies and the occasional indulgence. And so we had a starting point. Not right, not wrong, but a start.

If you need $6,000 per month, that's $72,000 per year. Now, most financial planners use a rough rule called the **4% rule**. It suggests that if you withdraw 4% of your portfolio annually, it should last 25-30 years or long enough for most retirements. Or we can flip that rule around: If $72,000 is 4% of your portfolio, then your "enough" number is roughly: $72,000÷0.04 = $1.8 million

That means Maria and Jorge would need a retirement portfolio of about $1.8 million to safely withdraw $6,000 per month without running out too soon. Suddenly, "a million dollars" wasn't a random dream. It was math they could *see*.

Of course, that $6,000 doesn't all need to come from investments. Retirement income usually has multiple sources. Just like a stool with three legs:

1. **Employer or Government Support:** Social Security, pensions or any defined benefit plan. Suppose Maria and Jorge expect $2,000 combined from Social Security.

2. **Personal Investments:** Their 401(k)s, IRAs and brokerage accounts.

3. **Other Income:** Maybe a small rental property, side consulting or part-time teaching for fun.

If $2,000 comes from Social Security and another $1,000 from side income, they only need $3,000 per month from investments or $36,000 per year. Using the same 4% rule: $36,000÷0.04 = $900,000

Their "enough" number instantly drops from $1.8 million to $900,000. Same lifestyle, smaller goal because now the stool has three strong legs.

So, Why 4%? It's based on decades of research showing that if you invest primarily in a mix of stocks and bonds, a 4% annual withdrawal (adjusted for inflation each year) can last around 30 years. It's not perfect. Markets fluctuate and people live longer now but it's a practical starting point.

If you want to be more conservative, use 3.5%. If you're planning a shorter retirement or have strong passive income, you might lean toward 5%. The key isn't precision - it's direction.

And let's not forget **Inflation**. The quiet thief of retirement, just like Fees being the quiet thief of investing. A $6,000 lifestyle today might cost $9,000 in 20 years. That's why investing through retirement matters - your portfolio should keep earning even as you withdraw.

And **longevity** matters too. Many people underestimate how long they'll live. If you retire at 60, you could easily have 30 years ahead of you. That's *one-third of your life* still to fund. Planning for longer ensures you don't outlive your money and your peace of mind.

If math feels overwhelming, try this simple way to estimate:
1. Write down your current *monthly expenses.*
2. Remove expenses that might disappear (like mortgages or child-related costs).
3. Add new ones that might appear (travel, healthcare, hobbies).
4. Multiply that monthly amount by 12 × 25.

That's your rough target. Example: $5,000/month × 12 × 25 = $1.5 million. It's not exact science but it gets you in the right ballpark.

What Matters More Than the Number

The goal isn't to hit some magic figure. The goal is financial independence; it is reaching a point where work becomes optional. For some, that happens at $500,000 because they live simply and have rental income. For others, it might take $3 million because of lifestyle choices.

Your "enough" is deeply personal. It's not about matching a spreadsheet but rather about matching your values.

Ten years after that first conversation, Maria and Jorge had done something powerful: they automated their savings, increased contributions whenever they got raises and stayed invested through market ups and downs. They didn't chase trends. They didn't panic during downturns.

At 55, their accounts totaled over $1 million and growing. They were still teaching, still happy, but now they had something priceless: *clarity.* They knew what "enough" looked like. And that peace of mind was worth more than any number.

The math of retirement is meant to empower you, not scare you. When you turn a vague dream into a clear target, your financial future stops being abstract and starts becoming actionable. So don't obsess over the size of the number. Focus on the consistency of your actions. Because at the end of the day, Future You doesn't need a miracle. It just humbly asks for reliable paycheck built patiently, one month at a time.

Reflection Pause

☐ What would your ideal monthly income look like in retirement, one enough for bills and joy?

☐ If you had to guess, what percent of that could come from investments vs. pensions or other income?
☐ What's one small change you could make today, like automating a contribution, to bring that number closer?

THE THREE PILLARS OF RETIREMENT INCOME

When you picture a sturdy stool, what comes to mind? Three legs, evenly spaced, each carrying its share of the weight. If one leg weakens, the stool wobbles. If one breaks, you fall.

That's exactly how retirement income works. Financial independence isn't built on one stream of money. It's built on *multiple*, each with a different role, risk and rhythm. Together, they create balance.

Most people rely on three key sources, often called the **Three Pillars of Retirement Income**:
1. Government or employer support (like Social Security or pensions),
2. Personal savings and investments, and
3. Passive or part-time income.

Let's look at each and understand how they fit together to build Future You's paycheck.

Pillar 1 – Government or Employer Support

For most Americans, this starts with **Social Security**. You've been paying into it through payroll taxes your entire career and it quietly builds up credit toward monthly benefits in retirement. Think of it as the *foundation* leg of your stool: solid, predictable but not enough to live on alone.

The average Social Security benefit today is around $1,900 per month. It helps but is not designed to cover all your expenses. It's a safety net, not a full hammock.

If you're lucky enough to have a **pension**, that's a bonus. Pensions used to be common but they're increasingly rare outside government and union jobs. A pension pays you a fixed monthly amount for life, usually based on years of service and salary.

Example: A retired firefighter might receive $3,000 per month from their pension, plus $2,000 from Social Security – a respectable $5,000 total before even touching investments.

It's a powerful combination of stable and low-risk, but not one you can fully control. Social Security and pensions are determined by formulas and policy, not your effort. So you will need to build the other two pillars yourself.

Pillar 2 – Personal Savings and Investments

This is the pillar you have full control over - your **401(k), IRA, Roth IRA, brokerage accounts** and other investment vehicles we discuss in subsequent chapters. If Social Security is the foundation, this pillar is the **engine**. It generates growth and flexibility.

The idea is simple: you save and invest during your working years, let them grow and those investments later pay you through withdrawals, dividends or interest. This is where all earlier lessons of compounding, diversification and patience, come into play. Over decades, the growth in these accounts becomes the primary source of your retirement paycheck. For most modern retirees, *this pillar carries most weight.*

Let's revisit Maria and Jorge from the previous section. They expect $2,000 from Social Security, but they want $6,000 total. Their investments need to provide the remaining $4,000. That's where their IRAs and 401(k)s step in, turning their savings into income through careful withdrawals.

And the best part: this pillar grows even while you sleep. Unlike Social Security, which depends on laws and politics, your investments depend on time and discipline.

Pillar 3 – Passive or Part-Time Income

This pillar often gets overlooked, but can make a huge difference both financially and emotionally. Retirement doesn't have to mean "no work." It can mean *work on your own terms.* Many retirees earn part-time or passive income from things they enjoy:

- Renting out a basement suite, small property or vacation cabin.
- Consulting, teaching or coaching in their field of expertise.
- Turning hobbies like photography, writing or crafts, into small income streams.
- Investing in dividend stocks or real estate investment trusts (REITs).

It's not just about the money. For many, it keeps the mind sharp and the routine meaningful. The savings lasting longer is an added bonus.

Example: After retiring at 60, *Lisa* began offering piano lessons from the comfort of her home. She earns around $800 a month, which funds her travel budget without dipping into savings. "It's not work," she told me, "it's play that pays.".

That is the spirit of this third pillar. Something light, flexible and optional, but powerful when done right.

No single leg can carry your entire future. But together, they turn your retirement into something resilient, a stool that can handle life's uneven floors. The three pillars give you stability, growth and flexibility - a foundation, an engine and a cushion. Build all three and Future You won't just survive; they'll *thrive.*

How the Three Pillars Work Together

Each pillar has a distinct rhythm:

- **Social Security / Pensions** = *Stability.*
- **Investments / Savings** = *Growth.*
- **Passive / Part-Time Income** = *Flexibility.*

Together, they create a balanced retirement "ecosystem." When one leg wobbles, say, markets drop temporarily, the others keep you steady.

Let's visualize this balance:

Pillar	*Control Level*	*Risk*	*Purpose*
Government / Employer	*Low*	*Very Low*	*Base income, predictability*
Personal Investments	*High*	*Moderate*	*Growth, inflation protection*
Passive / Part-Time	*Medium*	*Low-Moderate*	*Lifestyle flexibility, purpose*

Because when the paychecks stop coming from your employer, these pillars will step in. They'll form the bridge that keeps your lifestyle steady, your choices free and your mornings peaceful.

Remember, Retirement income is about structure.

Reflection Pause

☐ Which of your three pillars is strongest today and which one needs the most attention?

☐ Are you relying too heavily on a single income source (like Social Security or one 401k)?

☐ What would a "third pillar" look like for you - something meaningful that earns lightly but brings joy?

RETIREMENT ACCOUNTS EXPLAINED SIMPLY

If the three pillars of retirement income are the foundation of your future, then retirement accounts are the *containers* that hold your money, jars where your future paychecks grow quietly over decades.

Unfortunately, these jars often come with confusing labels: 401(k), Roth IRA, Traditional IRA, SEP, 403(b)... The names sound complicated, but the idea behind them is surprisingly simple: they're just **buckets that give your money special tax advantages.**

Once you understand that, the rest is easy.

So, why do these accounts exist? Governments want people to save for their own retirement, so they created incentives. Legitimate and incentivized ways to reduce or defer taxes if you commit to setting money aside for your future.

You get rewarded in one of two ways:
1. **Save now, pay taxes later** (Traditional accounts)
2. **Pay taxes now, grow tax-free forever** (Roth accounts)

That's it. Every retirement plan you'll ever hear about is just one of these two tax timelines.

401(k) or The Workplace Powerhouse

The **401(k)** is the most common retirement plan in the U.S. and is typically offered through your employer. Think of it as your personal future-paycheck builder sitting inside your company's payroll system. Here's how it works:

- You choose to set aside a portion of each paycheck say, 3% before taxes.
- That money goes directly into your 401(k) account and gets invested (usually in mutual funds or target-date funds).
- You don't pay income tax on that amount today; you'll pay tax only when you withdraw it in retirement.

It's like planting a seed and letting it grow in a tax-sheltered greenhouse. You only pay tax when you finally harvest it.

Many companies match part of your contribution as part of the benefits package. For example, "We'll match 50% of the first 6% you contribute." That means if you earn $80,000 and contribute 6% ($4,800), your employer adds another $2,400, instantly boosting your savings by 50%. It's the easiest raise you'll ever get.

The other version of 401(k) is **Roth 401(k)**. They work the same way mechanically (same payroll deduction, same investment options, same employer match) but the _tax timing_ is different.

- In a **Traditional 401(k)**, you contribute *before* taxes. You get a tax break today, but you'll pay income tax when you withdraw the money in retirement.

- In a **Roth 401(k)**, you contribute *after* taxes. You don't get a tax break today, but all withdrawals, both your contributions *and* the growth, are **completely tax-free** later.

So, which is better? It depends on your future. If you think you'll be in a lower tax bracket when you retire, the Traditional 401(k) might make more sense. So defer taxes until later. If you think your income (and tax rate) will rise over time, the Roth 401(k) lets you lock in today's rates and enjoy tax-free money later.

Some employers even allow you to split contributions, i.e. part Traditional, part Roth, giving you both flexibility and diversification in your "tax future."

Think of it as choosing between two greenhouses:
- One gives you seeds today (tax savings now).
- The other gives you fruits tomorrow (tax-free harvest later).

Both grow plants - you just decide *when* you want to pay the gardener.

IRA or The Individual Route

If your employer doesn't offer a 401(k) or if you want to save beyond it, you can open an **Individual Retirement Account (IRA)** on your own through a bank, brokerage or investment app. An IRA works like a personal 401(k): you contribute money (currently up to $7,000 per year, or $8,000 if you're over 50) and your investments grow with tax benefits.

Similar to 401(k), IRA also has two main types: **Traditional IRA** and **Roth IRA**. And similar to 401(k), they differ only in *when* you pay taxes.

A Traditional IRA lets you contribute pre-tax money. You might get an immediate tax deduction for the amount you contribute. Your investments then grow tax-deferred, meaning you don't pay taxes each year on interest or gains. When you retire and withdraw, that money is taxed as ordinary income. This will work beautifully if you expect to earn less in retirement than you do now.

The **Roth IRA** flips the timeline, just like Roth 401(k). You contribute after-tax dollars, take no immediate deduction, but all future growth and withdrawals in retirement are completely tax-free. That means if you invest $6,000 today and it grows to $50,000 by the time you retire, you'll owe *zero* tax when you take it out. It's like paying for a ticket to the investment amusement park now and then riding all the attractions free for life.

The Roth is particularly powerful for younger investors, who have decades of compounding ahead.

Evelyn had worked for three different companies over twenty years. Each time she changed jobs, she left her 401(k) behind, figuring she'd "get to it later". By her early 50s, she had three separate retirement accounts, each with different logins, funds and forgotten passwords. The clutter made her feel disconnected from her own money.

One weekend, she finally decided to untangle it all. She rolled her old 401(k)s into a single Traditional IRA, which simplified her portfolio and gave her full control over her investments. When she finished, she looked at the consolidated total and said, half-smiling, "I thought I had crumbs in three jars. Turns out I had a whole loaf."

Evelyn didn't magically make more money that day, she just reconnected with it. And that sense of clarity gave her momentum to keep contributing regularly.

Catch-Up Contributions: A Boost for Late Starters

If you're over 50, both 401(k)s and IRAs allow extra "catch-up" contributions, a useful boost for late starters. It's the system's way of saying, "It's okay if you started late; here's a chance to sprint."

As of now:

- *401(k): You can add an extra $7,500 beyond normal $23,000 limit.*

- *IRA: You can add $1,000 extra beyond the $7,000 limit.*

Those extra dollars, invested wisely, can still make a big difference. It's never too late to start but it's always better to start today.

Because these accounts are meant for retirement, early withdrawals (before age 59½) usually come with penalties. And once you hit 72, Traditional accounts require Required Minimum Distributions (RMDs), meaning the IRS wants its deferred taxes back through yearly withdrawals. Roth IRAs, have no required withdrawals during your lifetime; another reason they're so beloved by long-term planners.

Remember, retirement accounts aren't mysterious. They're just containers, simple tools that let time and tax advantages work in your favor. The secret isn't knowing every rule but using them consistently. Automate contributions. Take the match. Consolidate when you move jobs. Each action adds a steady brick to Future You's paycheck.

Because decades from now, when the accounts start paying you every month, you'll realize something powerful: The jars you filled weren't just financial. They were promises --- promises you kept to yourself.

Reflection Pause

- ☐ Do you know where all your past 401(k)s and retirement accounts currently are?
- ☐ Are you missing out on free money from an employer match?
- ☐ Which tax strategy feels right for you: save taxes now (Traditional) or enjoy tax-free income later (Roth)?

BEYOND BORDERS – RETIREMENT ACCOUNTS AROUND THE WORLD

You might wonder if other countries have their own versions of 401(k)s and IRAs? The answer is Yes. Personal finance concepts remain the same across borders, just the containers change. Around the world, governments have built similar "containers" to help people save for the future, each with its own flavor and tax rules, but all sharing the same goal: encouraging long-term, disciplined saving.

In India, *the <u>Employees' Provident Fund (EPF)</u> works much like a 401(k). A portion of your salary is automatically set aside and your employer contributes too. It's mandatory for many salaried employees and provides both retirement savings and a safety net. Then there's the <u>Public Provident Fund (PPF)</u>, a voluntary, government-backed savings scheme open to everyone. It's known for tax-free returns and a long, 15-year maturity, making it one of the safest long-term "containers." For newer investors, <u>National Pension System (NPS)</u> blends both; a flexible, market-linked plan with partial tax breaks and choice of investment mix. Together, these create India's version of retirement buckets: some stable, some growth-oriented, all designed to help future you.*

The U.K. *offers <u>workplace pensions</u> that resemble U.S. 401(k)s where employers often match employee contributions and funds grow tax-deferred until withdrawal. In addition, there's the <u>Individual Savings Account (ISA)</u>, similar to a Roth IRA. You invest post-tax money and all growth and withdrawals are tax-free. ISAs come in different forms (cash, stocks & shares), making them flexible, tax-efficient containers for long-term goals.*

Japan's *iDeCo (individual-type defined contribution pension plan) mirrors a traditional IRA with pre-tax contributions, long-term lock-in and tax-deferred growth. Its counterpart, NISA (Nippon Individual Savings Account), is a lot like a Roth IRA where you invest after-tax money, but profits and withdrawals are tax-free. Japan's system encourages steady saving, often through employer payroll or local banks, helping individuals take charge of their future pensions.*

The names change, the tax rules differ, but the spirit remains the same. Every nation wants its citizens to plan for their later years and not rely solely on government pensions. Whether it's a 401(k) in the U.S., EPF in India, ISA in the U.K., or NISA in Japan; these are just local versions of the same simple idea:

Put your money in a protected container, let it grow over time and reward your patience with tax benefits.

No matter where you live or move, the habit matters more than the container. Systems may change; tax codes may differ but consistency and time speak the same financial language everywhere.

COMMON MISTAKES IN RETIREMENT PLANNING

Retirement planning looks simple on paper: save, invest and one day stop working, but in real life, it's full of emotional traps and quiet missteps. Most people don't fail because of math; they fail because of mindset. The good news? Every mistake here is fixable once you see it.

Mistake 1 – Starting Late

If compounding is the magic of investing, then *time* is its magician. The earlier you start, the easier the journey becomes. Many people delay saving for retirement because they think they'll "catch up later." But later has a way of arriving unannounced.

Remember Lena & James from The Snowball Effect (Chapter 2, Investing: The Growth). Put your snowball in motion sooner. Starting 10 years early, adds decades of growth. Remember that *you can't recover lost time, but you can start now.* Even a small contribution today is more powerful than a large one postponed.

Mistake 2 – Ignoring Inflation and Healthcare

Inflation is retirement's silent predator. A dollar today won't buy the same groceries twenty years from now. Many people plan their future budgets in today's prices and forget that costs rise especially healthcare.

Medical expenses often increase faster than regular inflation and even with Medicare or insurance, out-of-pocket costs can surprise retirees. Smart planners include healthcare in their projections or invest in tax-advantaged health accounts like HSAs while working. Treat medical planning as part of retirement planning, not separate from it.

Mistake 3 – Assuming You'll Spend Less

It's a myth that spending drops dramatically in retirement. Sure, commuting costs and work clothes disappear but new expenses replace them: travel, home projects, grandkids, hobbies, healthcare.

The first ten years of retirement often *increase* spending because you finally have the time to enjoy life. Plan realistically. Retirement should feel like freedom, not restriction. Budget for fun alongside essentials because you have earned it.

Mistake 4 – Chasing Yield and "Too-Good-to-Be-True" Schemes

Near retirement, fear of running out of money makes people chase "safe" high-return promises like annuities, obscure real-estate deals or the latest guaranteed-income product. If someone guarantees high returns with "no risk," walk away. If someone shows up before your retirement, promising fixed income with "no downside" but weren't there with you through the journey, be skeptical. You have done something right; right enough to make people come after your money.

In retirement, protecting your money is as important as growing it. Boring and steady beats exciting and risky when your paycheck depends on it. A rule of thumb: *if you don't fully understand how it makes money, don't invest in it.*

Mistake 5 – Panic During Market Dips

Retirees sometimes shift entirely into cash after one bad year, missing the rebound that follows. But your money will need to last thirty years, longer than most market downturns. A better approach: keep a few years of expenses in cash or bonds for stability and leave the rest invested for growth. That balance lets you ride out volatility without fear.

Remember Jared's story from Investing: he didn't lose because the market fell; he lost because he panicked.

Mistake 6 – Borrowing from the Future

Many people borrow from their 401(k)s thinking, "It's my money, I'll pay it back." Or you see those sneaky Insta reels, promoting how the interest you pay goes back into your account. Don't be influenced. Remember that those withdrawals hit twice: you lose growth while the money is gone and you repay with after-tax dollars, then pay tax again when you withdraw in retirement.

It's like digging a hole in your own garden. You can fill it back later but the plants that might've grown there are gone. Emergencies happen, but retirement accounts should be your *last* resort, not your first. Build an emergency fund outside instead.

Mistake 7 – Forgetting to Adjust

Health, family, housing and your life change. So does your definition of "enough." Your retirement plan should evolve too. Many people set a savings plan in their 30s and never revisit it. But tax laws, investment options and personal goals shift over time.

Revisit your plan at least once a year and ask yourself:
- Are your investments aligned with your current age and goals?
- Have contribution limits changed?
- Do you need more insurance or less?

Small updates keep your future paycheck healthy.

Mistake 8 – Not Planning for Longevity

We often underestimate how long we'll live. Today, many 65-year-olds will reach their 90s. That's potentially *thirty years* of retirement. Longevity is a blessing but it's also a budget challenge. If your plan stops at 80, you could outlive your savings.

A simple fix: design your withdrawals to last 30 years or more and consider income streams that don't run out like annuities, pensions or dividend portfolios.

Retirement mistakes aren't failures; they're feedback. You can recover from late starts, small balances or even wrong choices. What matters is awareness. Once you see the leaks in the bucket, you can patch them.

The biggest mistake isn't starting late but not starting at all.

Your future paycheck depends on what you do after reading this page. Every smart step you take today adds stability to the bridge between today and tomorrow. It could be upping your contribution, avoiding a hasty loan or rebalancing your investments. Because retirement isn't about perfection; it's about persistence. And persistence, more than anything else, pays Future You on time.

Reflection Pause
- ☐ Which of these mistakes feels closest to home for you right now?
- ☐ Have you ever delayed saving, thinking "I'll start next year"? What would Future You say about that?
- ☐ How confident are you that your plan accounts for inflation, healthcare and longevity?

BUILDING THE RETIREMENT HABIT TODAY

Retirement planning isn't something you do once but something you do *a little bit at a time, forever.* If the chapter on Investing taught you the habits of investing - automation, consistency and patience; this chapter is about applying those same habits with a *destination in mind*: **your future paycheck.**

Think of retirement habits as the *maintenance plan* for your financial engine. The investing habits you built keep the engine running while these habits make sure it's pointed in the right direction.

1. Treat Retirement Like a Monthly Bill

Every time your paycheck arrives, imagine Future You sending you an invoice: "Pay me first." Automating your 401(k) or IRA contribution is the easiest way to honor that invoice, even before rent, groceries or subscriptions get their share. It's not an expense; it's a transfer from your present comfort to your future independence.

2. Increase the Dial Slowly

Once a year or maybe every raise, bump your retirement savings by just 1%. You won't even feel it. But over 10 years, that small, quiet increase can double your savings rate. This "**1% Habit**" compounds like everything else.

3. Revisit, Don't Redesign

You don't need to rebuild your plan every year, just *review* it. Check if your contributions are on track, if your investment mix still matches your timeline and if you've accounted for life changes (a new home, child or job). A 30-minute check-up once a year can save you from decades of drift.

4. Borrow Motivation from Future You

If saving feels like sacrifice, flip the frame. You're not "giving up" money, you're *funding freedom.* Picture the version of you who no longer has to set alarms, who can spend a weekday afternoon with family, who travels without guilt. That person is real and counting on you to keep the habit alive.

Retirement habits aren't built through complexity. They are built through consistency. The principles that make investing work - automation, patience and time, will make retirement planning effortless. And earlier you turn these choices into habits, less they feel like sacrifices and more like *freedom deposits* in Future You's account.

Reflection Pause

☐ When was the last time you reviewed or increased your retirement contribution rate?

☐ Does your current saving pattern reflect what Future You deserves or what Present You finds convenient?

☐ If Future You sent you a thank-you note today, what would they thank you for?

THE PAYCHECK YOU'LL NEVER OUTGROW

Imagine your life twenty or thirty years from now. The alarm clock doesn't control your mornings. You work only if you *want* to, not because you *have to*. You can say yes to travel, family time or quiet hobbies without glancing at your account balance first.

That's not a fantasy. It is what financial independence feels like. And everything you've learned up to this chapter - budgeting, investing, credit and discipline - has been leading to this single moment: the point where your money starts sending you *paychecks* instead of the other way around.

Every contribution you've made so far - every 401(k) deposit, every IRA top-up, every dollar invested instead of spent - is a plank in the bridge connecting *Present You* to *Future You*. That bridge is sturdy because it's built on three things:

1. **Time** letting compounding work for you.
2. **Consistency** showing up even when progress feels invisible.
3. **Purpose** knowing what kind of life you're building toward.

You're not just funding retirement; you're *buying time*. The freedom to choose what fills your days is the ultimate return on investment.

The Real Goal of Retirement

Retirement isn't about stopping. It's about sustaining. Retirement isn't about surviving. It's about thriving. It's the point where your wealth becomes your worker, where every dollar you've trained over the years continues earning for you, quietly, relentlessly.

In the early chapters, we talked about your money making friends through investing. Now, with those friends, your money has formed a community; a team that works full-time to pay You.

The goal isn't to just retire rich. The goal is to retire ready and to have enough financial confidence that you can live life on your terms.

Let's return to that letter from *Future You* we read at the beginning of this chapter.

"Dear Me,
Because of you, I can rest without worry.
Because of you, I can work if I choose not because I must.
Because of you, my life fits me.
You didn't wait for perfect timing. You started when you could.
You treated my freedom like a bill to be paid and you paid it faithfully.
I don't live extravagantly but I live comfortably.
I laugh more, stress less and wake up grateful every day.
You didn't just save money. You bought peace.

With gratitude,
Future You"

Retirement isn't a destination; it's a *relationship* between these two versions of you. Every deposit, every review, every decision are all ways of staying in touch. In your working years, you earn money with your time. In retirement, your money earns *time* for you. The paycheck never really stops; it just changes sources. When you plan well, that paycheck becomes endless, a stream powered by the choices you made decades earlier.

And that's what this chapter has truly been about: giving *Future You* a stable, loving paycheck built not on luck, but on foresight, faith and a few good habits practiced consistently. Your future isn't something that just happens to you, rather it's something you *build*. Every dollar you save is a vote for freedom. Every habit you repeat is a promise you keep.

Someday, when *Future You* wakes up to another calm morning and smiles at the balance in their "paycheck," they won't think about math. They'll think about you, the version who cared enough to plan ahead.

Because in the end, retirement isn't about money. It's about trust. The trust between who you are today and who you'll be tomorrow.

Worksheet: My Retirement Readiness Checklist

Use this worksheet to see where you stand today and what steps will help Future You sleep peacefully tomorrow.

Step 1: Define Your Vision

In one sentence, describe what "retirement freedom" is to you:

____

Step 2: Know Your Monthly Target

Estimated monthly spending goal in retirement: $____________

Multiply by 12 × 25 = Estimated target nest egg: $____________

Step 3: Map Your Three Pillars

Income Source	Est. Monthly Income	Confidence Level (High/Med/Low)
Social Security / Pension	$__________	____
Investments (401k, IRA, etc.)	$__________	____
Passive / Part-time Income	$__________	____

Step 4: Check Your Habits

☐ I contribute automatically to a 401(k) or IRA

☐ I increase my contribution rate each year

☐ I've consolidated old accounts (or plan to)

☐ I review my retirement plan annually

☐ I've estimated healthcare costs and inflation impact

Step 5: Identify Gaps

Which of the three pillars needs strengthening?

____

What specific step can I take this year to strengthen it?

____

Step 6: Write Your Promise to Future You

"Over the next 12 months, I will _______________________________ so that Future Me continues to receive a steady paycheck for life."

8

Real Estate - The Roof That Builds Wealth

The day you hold the key to your first home is hard to forget. For *Maya and Daniel*, it came on a rainy Friday evening. They'd spent months touring listings, chasing loan pre-approvals and second-guessing every decision. When the realtor finally handed them the keys, it didn't look extraordinary. But as they stood under the porch light of their new home, rain misting over the driveway; they realized this wasn't just about a roof. It was about a *turning point*. "This is ours," Daniel whispered, half in disbelief. Maya smiled, still clutching the envelope of documents that listed numbers bigger than anything they'd ever signed for. They were homeowners now and beneath the excitement sat equal parts pride and a quiet panic.

For many, that first key is more than a milestone. It's a moment when adulthood feels tangible, when you've anchored yourself to a place, a neighborhood and a future. But it's also when you step into one of life's most powerful financial forces: **real estate.**

Owning a home isn't just about shelter. It's about *equity*. It's slow transformation of your monthly payments, what probably used to be rent, into ownership. It's watching your roof appreciate in value while you sleep. It's a form of wealth you can live in, touch and eventually pass down. Real estate is the bridge between emotional comfort and financial growth; a rare combination where money meets meaning.

When most people think of buying a house, they think of *security*. "No one can make me move." "I can paint walls any color I want." And while that's true, the deeper power lies beneath the foundation. Every mortgage payment is a quiet transfer from *liability to asset*. You start out owing a bank. Each month, a little more of that home becomes yours. Decade by decade, balance tips. By the time the loan is gone, you don't just own a structure, you own a piece of your net worth that worked for you while you lived in it. That's why real estate journey is often emotional: it starts as a home and ends as wealth.

Planting Bricks Instead of Seeds

In earlier chapters, we talked about planting seeds, small investments that grow through compounding. Real estate is similar but the seed is made of brick and wood. You plant money into a down payment. You water it with mortgage payments and maintenance. Over time, the property grows in value and in equity. You don't see the progress day to day. But ten or fifteen years later, you look up and realize your "living expense" has quietly become one of your biggest assets.

That's why real estate, done thoughtfully, becomes a form of long-term wealth creation that feels tangible. It's not a line graph on a screen. It's the place where your kids grow up, where family pictures hang, where comfort and compounding coexist.

The **Power of Leverage** is what makes real estate so unique: you can use other people's money, usually the bank's, to grow your own wealth.

Imagine buying a $400,000 home with a $80,000 down payment (20%). If the home value rises 3% a year, that's $12,000 in appreciation annually. But because you only invested $80,000 of your own money, that's effectively a 15% return on your cash before even counting loan paydown or tax benefits. That's the quiet magic of leverage. It accelerates growth on your contribution. It's like investing with a financial partner who covers the bill but lets you keep the upside.

Of course, leverage is a double-edged sword. If markets fall, the losses are magnified too. But when managed with care and patience, it's one of the most powerful engines for wealth creation available to everyday people.

When Maya and Daniel moved in, they didn't understand amortization tables or market cycles. They just knew they were done paying rent. But with each passing year, something else began to happen. Their mortgage balance dropped slowly, almost invisibly. The local market appreciated. Their home equity, the part they truly *owned*, grew without them noticing. Ten years later, they refinanced, pulling out some equity to pay for their child's college tuition. Their home hadn't just sheltered them but had *paid for their future.* That's when Daniel said something striking: "We thought we were just buying walls and a roof. Turns out, we were buying *momentum.*"

Real estate can be emotional, intimidating and incredibly rewarding. It's not about flipping houses or chasing quick profits but about building roots that grow value.

In the chapters ahead, we'll explore why real estate remains one of the most reliable ways to create long-term wealth, how to navigate the math behind it and how to avoid the traps that turn roofs into burdens. Because when done right, a home isn't just where your story unfolds but also the part that makes the story possible.

Reflection Pause

☐ What does "home" mean to you? Comfort, status or a stepping stone toward freedom?

☐ If you own, do you know how much of your monthly payment goes toward building equity?

☐ If you rent, what would need to change before you'd consider buying? Finances, stability or mindset?

WHY REAL ESTATE MATTERS

Everyone needs a roof. But not every roof builds wealth.

At its core, real estate sits at the intersection of two powerful human desires of **security** and **growth.** It gives you both a place to live and a way to quietly build financial independence. That's what makes it so different from any other asset class.

A stock certificate might show growth on paper. A crypto wallet might show promise on a screen. But a home? You can live in it, touch it, feel it. You can walk through your wealth every morning on your way to the kitchen. A roof that keeps out the rain, a door that locks at night, a place to call your own. And that's absolutely true.

But beneath that emotional surface lies a quiet financial machine. Every mortgage payment is part rent, part investment. The rent covers the cost of living; the investment builds your ownership share of the property a.k.a. equity. Over time, that equity becomes the silent partner in your financial journey. It's not flashy, it doesn't send monthly statements, but it grows through loan paydowns and appreciation. That's the beauty of real estate: it lets you build wealth *in the background* while life unfolds in the foreground.

Owning vs. Renting: The Psychological Shift

There's something deeply human about ownership. It creates stability, belonging and pride. The day you move from "someone else's property" to "my property" changes your mindset. Renters often think about monthly expenses; owners start thinking about value. You treat your home differently when you know improvements like a better kitchen, new paint or solar panels, increase something that's yours. That shift from spending to building is subtle, but powerful.

When you rent, you pay for use. When you own, you pay for growth. One is an expense line. The other is an investment.

Real estate builds wealth through three engines working quietly in tandem:

1. **Appreciation**: Property values generally rise over time with inflation, development and demand. Even modest annual growth compounds powerfully over decades.

2. **Amortization**: Each mortgage payment chips away at the loan balance. What starts as mostly interest slowly becomes mostly principal, meaning more of your payment builds equity.

3. **Leverage**: Real estate lets you use borrowed money to own appreciating assets. You might only invest 20% of the purchase price but benefit from 100% of the growth.

It's like owning a tree farm where you plant a few seeds (your down payment), but the forest grows on land much larger than you could afford alone.

Then, there is another kind of return that rarely shows up on spreadsheets: *peace.* Owning your home brings a sense of stability that's hard to quantify. You know where your kids will go to school. You know your rent won't suddenly rise with market swings. You start forming deeper roots in your neighborhood, your routines and your life. That emotional dividend is often what turns a house into a *home.*

Consider two friends *Laila* and *Marcus.* Laila rented for years in a growing city, enjoying flexibility and a modern apartment downtown. Marcus, meanwhile, bought a modest home farther out; a little older, a longer commute; but his own. Ten years later, Laila had invested in experiences, travel and a flexible lifestyle. Marcus had invested in paint, repairs and a rising property market. When they compared notes, Laila had wonderful memories but no home equity. Marcus had a home worth nearly double what he'd paid, a lower mortgage balance and an asset he could leverage for his next real-estate investment.

Neither choice was wrong. Both aligned with their goals at the time. But Marcus had built *ownership that grew while he slept,* while Laila chose a different path.

And that is why real estate matters. It's not about marble countertops or mortgage bragging rights. It's about financial structure and transforming one of life's biggest expenses into a wealth-building tool. It's about *stability today* and *freedom tomorrow.* It is also the only investment where you live in your asset and let it grow in value simultaneously. Your home gives you comfort *and* capital.

The Quiet Compounding Effect

Even if home prices only rise 2-3% per year, the effect over decades is stunning, especially when combined with slow paydown of your loan. Think of it as two compounding curves stacked on top of each other:

- *One from your home's value rising.*
- *One from your mortgage shrinking.*

They move in opposite directions and your wealth fills the space between them. That's why, historically, real estate has helped ordinary families build extraordinary wealth over time. Not through speculation, but through patience.

Real estate matters because it bridges the emotional and financial worlds. It blends your place of comfort and with power of compounding, all under the same roof. Every wall you paint, every payment you make, every improvement you plan are all investments in a larger story: your story of stability becoming strength and shelter becoming wealth. Because in the end, a house protects you from the weather and the future uncertainty.

Reflection Pause

☐ Is your home currently an expense or an asset in your mind?

☐ If you don't yet own, what small step could bring you closer? Is it saving for down payment, improving credit or something else?

HOW REAL ESTATE CREATES WEALTH

For most, buying real estate is the biggest financial move they'll ever make. But the quiet secret: you don't need to flip homes or buy ten properties to make it work. You just need to understand three silent engines that make real estate build wealth while you live your life.

1. Appreciation: The Value That Rises Quietly

Appreciation is the reason your parents' home, bought decades ago, now seems impossibly cheap. Over time, inflation, development and limited land push property values upward. Even modest appreciation can create significant wealth because real estate compounds *on entire value of the property*, not just what you paid upfront.

Example: If you bought a $400,000 home and it appreciated just 3% per year, it would be worth over $720,000 in 20 years *even if you never improved it*. And the appreciation on $400K started with 20% down payment or $80,000.

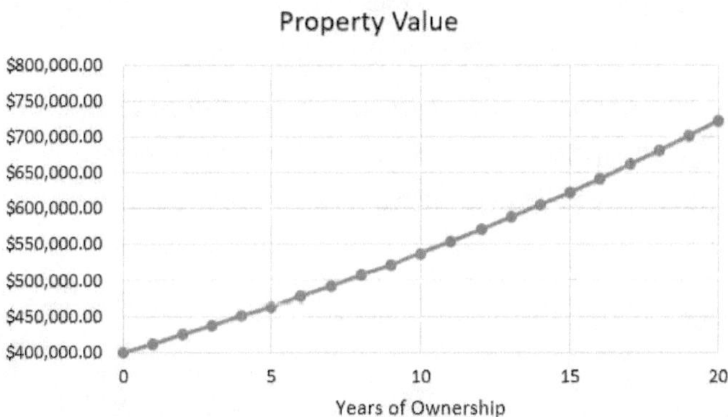

It's quiet, steady and largely invisible until one day, your home's value has doubled while your loan has halved.

2. Amortization: Ownership That Grows Every Month

When you make a mortgage payment, part goes to interest (the bank's earnings) and part goes to principal (your ownership). In early years, most of your payment goes toward interest. But as time passes, the split flips and more of your payment starts going toward *you*. Each month, you own a little more of your home. You're essentially paying rent *to yourself*.

Example: Let's say your $400,000 home has a $320,000 mortgage at 6% interest. After 10 years of steady payments, you might have paid down $70,000 of the loan OR $70,000 of *forced savings that you did for yourself*, whether markets rise or fall.

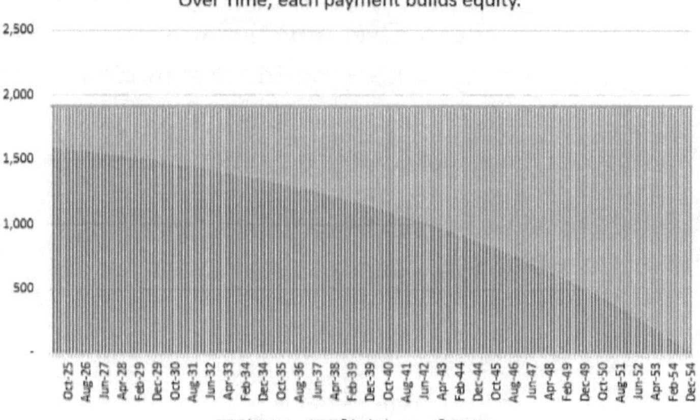

That's why homeownership often succeeds where manual saving fails. It automates discipline. Even if you skip investing one month, your mortgage payment keeps building wealth for you.

3. Leverage: Controlling More with Less

Leverage is what makes real estate special. It means you can use borrowed money to buy an appreciating asset which is much larger than what you could buy outright. Think of it like planting one tree and getting the growth of an entire grove.

Example: You buy a $400,000 home with $80,000 down payment (20%) and finance the rest. If property rises just 3% in a year ($12,000), your return isn't 3%. It's **15%** on your cash ($12,000 ÷ $80,000).

That's leverage in action. Using someone else's capital to multiply your own. But remember, leverage cuts both ways. If prices fall, losses are magnified too. And that's why real estate rewards *patience and prudence.* You don't win by flipping ladders. You win by climbing them slowly and safely.

When appreciation, amortization and leverage work together, the results are exponential. Let's put it all together:

Component	20-Year Effect on $400,000 home @ 6%
Appreciation (3% annual)	+$320,000 in value growth
Amortization (loan paydown)	+$160,000 in principal equity
Total Wealth Created	~$480,000 (excl. tax benefits)

And that's on a property you lived in. Not a rental, not a flip, just your home doing quiet math in the background.

The beauty of real estate wealth isn't just in the numbers but it's *dual use.* Unlike a stock portfolio sitting behind a login screen, your home gives you comfort, pride and stability *while* it quietly grows in the background. You get to live inside your investment — literally. Your wealth doesn't live in a vault; it lives in your daily life.

So, to summarize the three engines of Real Estate wealth

Engine	What It Means	How It Builds Wealth
Appreciation	Your property's value increases over time	Raises your net worth without new effort
Amortization	You gradually pay down your mortgage	Converts debt into ownership (equity)
Leverage	You use borrowed money to control a larger asset	Magnifies growth on your own investment

As you saw, Real estate creates wealth slowly, but surely like watching a tree grow. You don't see the change day to day, but you'll notice it when you look back a decade later. Because every month you live there, every payment you make, every year values rise. Your roof keeps working quietly to build your freedom. It's the one investment that gives you warmth today and wealth tomorrow or truly, *the roof that builds wealth.*

Reflection Pause
- ☐ When you make your next mortgage payment, how much of it is going toward you versus the bank?
- ☐ Have you calculated how much your home has appreciated since you bought it?
- ☐ If you don't own yet, what would your numbers look like with a 3% growth and modest loan paydown over time?

RENTING VS. OWNING: FINDING YOUR FIT

"Renting is throwing money away."
"Buying is always better."
You've probably heard both. And both can be wrong.

Real estate decisions aren't about slogans; they're about *fit*. What makes sense for one person might not make sense for another. The goal isn't to prove which path is superior but to understand what aligns with *your stage of life, goals and flexibility needs.*

Buying a home can feel like crossing a finish line. It's symbolic, maybe even a milestone of stability and pride. You can paint walls, grow a garden or knock out that oddly placed wall that's been annoying you since move-in day. Ownership also changes how you think about money. Rent feels temporary; a mortgage feels like progress. Each payment builds equity. A little bit more of that house becomes *yours*.

But let's pause here. Because homeownership also comes with *hidden costs* that renters never face. Property taxes, maintenance, repairs, insurance. The little leaks that quietly drain your cash flow.

Owning builds wealth *slowly*. Renting preserves *flexibility*. Both are valuable currencies at different times in life.

The Real Math Behind "Rent vs. Buy" is a bit more nuanced. When you rent, 100% of your payment goes to the landlord. When you own, a portion of your payment builds equity. That's true. But ownership also requires upfront costs like down payment, closing costs and ongoing maintenance. It's not free money; it's *forced savings*. To compare fairly, you need to look at both short-term affordability and long-term growth.

Example: Let's say you're deciding between renting a $2,000/month apartment or buying a $400,000 home with a $80,000 down payment. If you stay only 2-3 years, renting likely wins. You save liquidity, avoid transaction costs and retain mobility.

Cost	Renting	Owning (Year 1)
Monthly payment	$2,000 rent	$2,200 mortgage
Upfront cost	Security deposit: $2,000	Down payment + closing: ~$85,000
Annual property tax	—	~$4,000
Maintenance	—	~$2,000/year
Equity built (Year 1)	$0	~$6,000

But if you stay 7-10 years, ownership typically overtakes renting as appreciation and equity compound.

The Flexibility Premium vs The Stability Dividend

Renting gives something homeownership can't - mobility. If your job changes, your family grows or your life pivots, you can move without the friction of selling or market timing. For younger professionals, this flexibility is priceless. It allows you to chase opportunity or adventure without financial anchors. Think of renting as paying for freedom. You're not wasting money; but trading it to buy time and choice.

For families or anyone craving roots, homeownership offers something renting rarely can - continuity. You know your neighbors, your kids stay in the same school, your walls collect memories and not moving boxes. That stability is emotional wealth; a dividend that doesn't appear in spreadsheets. Even financially, homeownership acts as a hedge against inflation. Rents rise; a fixed-rate mortgage stays constant. So while your landlord's income increases each year, your cost of living stays stable and your equity grows.

Both sides are valuable - key is knowing which matters more right now.

So, when is Renting the Smarter Choice? Sometimes, the best real estate decision is to *wait*. Here are moments when renting might be the wiser move:

- You plan to move cities or change jobs in 2–3 years.
- You don't have a stable emergency fund yet.
- Local property prices are inflated relative to rents.
- You prefer financial liquidity or are still building credit.

Renting isn't a failure. It's a phase of financial strategy. The key is to use the rent-versus-buy gap wisely. Save aggressively for a down payment, improve credit and study markets.

And, when does Owning Become the Right Move? Ownership makes sense when:

- You're financially ready for maintenance, taxes and insurance.
- You plan to stay put for at least 5-7 years.
- Your housing cost ratio (mortgage + taxes + insurance) stays below 30–35% of income.
- You view home not as a trophy, but as a *tool for long-term wealth*.

That last one matters most. Your mindset decides whether your home becomes a wealth-builder or a weight.

Remember Laila and Marcus from earlier in the chapter? *Laila*, a data engineer, loved mobility. She rented stylish apartments, took contracts across states and invested his surplus income into index funds and ETFs. By 40, her investment portfolio rivaled many homeowners' equity and she could move wherever opportunity called.

Marcus, a nurse, bought a modest starter home at 28. He improved it gradually, refinanced smartly and rented out a room for extra income. By 40, he owned two properties, both appreciating steadily.

Different paths. Same outcome: *freedom*.

Real estate is personal. Don't let social media or family tradition decide your timing. Renting isn't "throwing money away". It is buying flexibility when you need it. Owning isn't "settling down". It is building roots that grow value. Both paths lead to freedom - one through *mobility*, the other through *equity*.

The secret is knowing which freedom matters most to you, right now.

Reflection Pause

- ☐ What are you optimizing for right now: freedom or roots?
- ☐ If you rent, are you saving what you could be building as equity?
- ☐ If you own, are you making your property work for you or just living in it?

BEYOND YOUR HOME: REAL ESTATE AS AN INVESTMENT VEHICLE

Buying your first home is usually about security. Buying your *next* property is usually about strategy. Once your roof is steady, it's natural to wonder: *Can real estate also become an income stream?* The short answer is, beyond doubt, yes. But the real question is *how*.

There are many ways to invest in real estate and not all of them require a hammer, a "For Rent" sign, or a landlord's patience. Broadly speaking, real estate investing takes two forms: active and passive.

In **active investing**, you buy and manage physical properties yourself. It's hands-on and full of moving parts: finding tenants, maintaining the property, handling repairs or overseeing renovations. You have full control over decisions but also full responsibility when something breaks at midnight. Examples include owning rental homes, flipping houses or running short-term vacation rentals.

Passive investing, on the other hand, lets you participate in the real estate market without becoming a landlord. Instead of owning and managing buildings directly, you invest through vehicles like REITs (Real Estate Investment Trusts), crowdfunding platforms or real estate funds. These give you exposure to property income and appreciation while someone else does the heavy lifting.

Think of it this way: Active investing is like running a restaurant. You handle the staff, the menu and the customers. Passive investing is like owning shares in that restaurant. You get a slice of the profits without washing the dishes.

Both paths can create wealth; they just require different types of energy. The more control you want, the more time and effort it takes. The more convenience you want, the more you rely on professional management. The goal isn't to choose one forever. Many successful investors start active, then gradually shift passive as their wealth (and free time) grows.

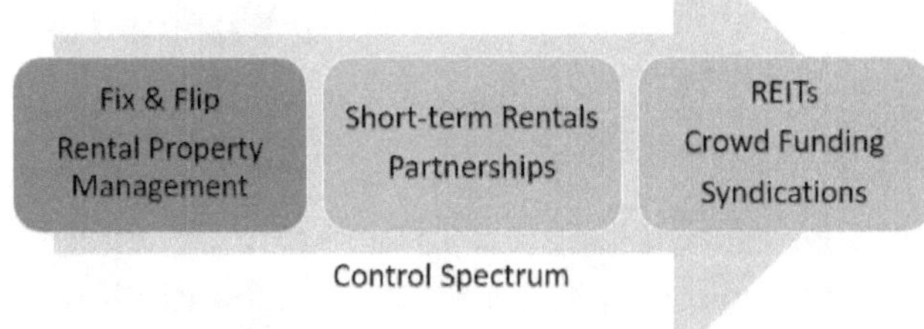

More control usually means more work

Active Investing: Turning Property into Income

Active investing is what most people picture when they think of real estate wealth: Owning a rental home, duplex, or condo that earns steady rent. The math behind it is simple and powerful.

Cash Flow = Rent – (Mortgage + Taxes + Insurance + Maintenance)

If that number is positive, your property pays you each month *and* grows in value over time.

Example: Suppose you buy a small rental home for $300,000 with 20% down ($60,000). You rent it out for $2,200/month. After paying $1,800 in expenses, you pocket $400/month in cash flow or $4,800 a year, while your tenants help pay down your mortgage. That's not just income but also a **self-reinforcing wealth loop**:
- Rent covers your costs,
- The loan shrinks every month,
- The property value rises over time.

Active investing also comes with real responsibilities:
- Finding and screening tenants.
- Handling repairs and maintenance (or hiring someone to).
- Managing vacancies and paperwork.

It's not passive income but *managed* income. That's why many investors hire property managers, usually for 8–10% of monthly rent, to handle the day-to-day operations. The key is to treat your rental like a *business*, not a hobby. Track income, expenses, maintenance and returns just like any other enterprise.

Passive Investing: Property Ownership Without the Headaches

For those who love idea of real estate but not the 2 a.m. "water heater broke" calls, passive real estate investing offers elegant alternatives.

<u>Real Estate Investment Trusts or REITs</u> are companies that own and operate income-generating properties such as shopping centers, apartments, warehouses, data centers, hospitals, etc. When you buy a REIT (like you would a stock), you're buying a share of a property portfolio. You receive dividends from rental income and your shares can appreciate as property values rise. They trade on the stock market, making them liquid and easy to diversify. It's real estate investing without the real estate drama.

<u>Real Estate Crowdfunding Platforms</u> are online platforms that now allow investors to pool money to buy or finance properties, from apartment complexes to commercial spaces; even, agricultural land. You can start with smaller amounts and gain access to deals that used to require deep pockets. Crowdfunding sits halfway between REITs and direct ownership; slightly riskier than REITs, but with more control and potential upside.

Balancing Real Estate Within Your Portfolio

*Owning property shouldn't mean ignoring other investments. The healthiest portfolios blend real estate with stocks, bonds and cash. This diversifies both risk and income type. Real estate adds **stability** (it's tangible, inflation-resistant) but it can also add **illiquidity** (hard to sell quickly). That's why combining it with more flexible assets creates balance along with long-term resilience.*

Remember Marcus, who bought his first home at 28 and rented out a room. Instead of letting it sit unused, he turned it into a studio rental. The rent from his tenant covered nearly half of his mortgage. He then went on to buy another home. Few years later, Marcus refinanced both homes at a lower rate and used the freed-up cash flow to start investing in REITs. His portfolio is now both *shelter* and *income engine.* Marcus said, "I'm not a landlord. I'm just letting my house work part-time."

Real estate investing isn't just for the wealthy or the bold. It's for anyone who wants their money to wear a hard hat and build something tangible. Whether you manage a duplex, rent a basement or hold REITs in your portfolio - you're letting your money buy more than returns. You're buying *stability, optionality and time.* Because the best kind of roof is one that shelters you and also *earns for you.*

Reflection Pause
- ☐ Would you rather own a single property you manage or invest in many properties through REITs or funds?
- ☐ How much "hands-on" involvement would you enjoy? Dealing with tenants or collecting dividends.
- ☐ What role could real estate play in balancing your overall portfolio?

THE RISKS AND REALITY CHECKS

Every type of wealth building carries a shadow. And in real estate, that shadow is risk. The good news? Most risks aren't hidden; they're simply ignored. The people who get burned are usually the ones who rushed in without reading the fine print or running the math twice.

Real estate is powerful, but it's not invincible. Knowing its weak spots helps you build smarter, sleep better and stay in the game longer.

Spot #1. The Temptation of Too Much Leverage.

Leverage is what makes real estate exciting. Controlling a large asset with a relatively small investment. But like a ladder, it helps you climb faster *only if you don't lean too far.* When investors borrow too aggressively, one small shake be it a job loss, a rate hike or a few months of vacancy, can send the whole structure wobbling.

You might hear people brag about buying five properties with 5 % down each. On paper, it looks brilliant. In practice, one bad year can drain every emergency fund they have. If your cash flow turns negative every time interest rates move a quarter percent, the house isn't an asset, it's a stress test.

Borrow enough to grow, not enough to lose sleep.

Spot #2. Liquidity: You Can't Sell a Bathroom

Unlike stocks, you can't sell 10 % of a house when you need cash. Real estate is *illiquid*. It takes time to find buyers, close deals and unlock equity. This isn't a flaw, it's a trade-off or maybe, even a feature. Illiquidity rewards patience but punishes impatience. It means you must keep enough cash elsewhere (read savings or short-term investments) to handle life's curveballs.

A property portfolio works best when it's supported by liquidity

Spot #3. The Maintenance Mirage

Many first-time investors underestimate maintenance. Roofs age, tenants move, HVAC units sigh their last breath right after warranty. A good rule: expect to spend 1–2 % of a property's value per year on upkeep. That's not pessimism, rather it's planning.

Successful investors don't hope nothing breaks; they budget knowing everything eventually will.

Spot #4. Vacancy and Market Cycles

Even great locations face empty months. Jobs shift, tenants relocate, economies slow. A vacancy doesn't just pause income but also magnifies every expense. That's why healthy cash flow matters more than chasing high appreciation.

Appreciation is a bonus; rent is survival.

Markets also move in cycles of booms, corrections and rebounds. If you buy assuming prices will *always* rise, you're not investing, you're speculating. The antidote is simple: buy properties that work at today's numbers, not tomorrow's hopes. If the rent covers costs and leaves a buffer now, appreciation will be icing later.

Spot #5. Emotional Attachment

Your home can be your heart; your investment should be your head. Many investors fall in love with property attributes like the view, the layout, the neighborhood. They sometimes ignore the spreadsheet screaming otherwise. Emotion belongs in the living room, not in the math. When you treat an investment property like a business, decisions become clearer. You repaint because it increases rent, not because you like the color.

Detachment doesn't make you cold; it makes you consistent.

Spot #6. The Illusion of Easy Money

Social media loves showing overnight flippers and "passive-income gurus." What it doesn't show is the months of renovations, the sleepless nights, the surprise tax bills. Real estate wealth is slow wealth - steady, tangible, earned through patience and persistence.

Real estate is real work; that's why it pays real rewards.

Spot #7. Taxes and Paperwork

Property ownership brings its share of forms and fine print like depreciation schedules, local regulations, insurance renewals, HOA rules. Ignoring these details can erase profits faster than a bad tenant. Keep records, know filing deadlines and get professional help when needed. The best investors I've met aren't the ones with the flashiest portfolios but the ones with the most organized spreadsheets.

A Balanced View of Risk

The goal isn't to avoid risk but to price it in. Think of every property as a small ecosystem: when one part fails, the others should keep it alive. That's why diversification matters. By city, by property type, by strategy. A vacancy in one unit shouldn't derail your entire plan. If we plotted risk on a curve, you'd see a simple truth:

- *Too little risk = slow growth.*
- *Too much risk = fast ruin.*
- *The sweet spot = controlled, educated leverage.*

Real estate rewards the patient, not the fearless. You don't have to predict the market; you just have to prepare for it. Cash reserves, modest leverage and disciplined management turn risks into routine. Because in the end, the best property investors aren't gamblers but guardians. They don't chase storms; they build roofs that last through them.

Reflection Pause

- ☐ What kind of risk keeps you awake at night? Debt, vacancy or uncertainty?
- ☐ Do you have a plan for repairs, vacancies, or market dips?
- ☐ If rent stopped for three months, could your property still survive?

BUILDING REAL ESTATE HABITS AND SYSTEMS

Real estate is built on systems. The people who thrive in this space don't always have the most money, the best timing or insider connections. They *do* have is consistency and a habit of treating every property like a small business and every dollar like an employee. They don't guess where the market is going. They build routines that make the market work *for them*.

1. Track Income and Expenses Like a Business

Whether you own one rental or five, create a small "Property Profit & Loss" summary. You don't need fancy software; a spreadsheet works fine. List every source of income (rent, parking, laundry, etc.) and every expense (mortgage, taxes, repairs, utilities, management). Update it monthly. When you can *see* where your money goes, you can spot leaks before they become floods.

A common rule among experienced landlords: know your property's monthly cash flow before you open the next one.

2. Build a Maintenance Fund

Every roof leaks eventually. The difference between panic and preparedness is a small reserve fund. Set aside 1–2% of the property's value per year in a maintenance account. For a $400,000 property, that's $4,000 - $8,000 annually. It sounds conservative until your HVAC dies in July or your water heater quits mid-shower. Investors who skip this step often end up funding repairs with credit cards or loans, which turns simple issues into financial stress. Maintenance isn't a surprise. It's a scheduled expense waiting for its turn.

3. Document Everything

Keep digital copies of leases, insurance policies, tax records, repair receipts and inspection reports. Create a single "property folder" in cloud storage (Google Drive, Dropbox, or similar). Add one page up front with your property snapshot (Address, Purchase price and date, Current loan balance, Monthly rent and key contacts (lender, manager, insurer) etc.). This small step saves hours later, especially when you refinance, sell or need to hand off management.

4. Automate Where Possible

Automation turns good habits into invisible ones. Online rent collection eliminates delays and excuses. Automatic transfers route a portion of rent to your maintenance fund each month. Calendar reminders schedule annual insurance reviews and property inspections. These small automations don't just save time but also remove emotion. You don't forget, delay or negotiate with yourself. The system simply runs. If your properties can pay their own bills, track their own performance and remind you when they need attention - congratulations, you've built a self-running machine.

The Mindset Shift: From Owner to Operator

Most people think buying a property is the finish line. In truth, it's the starting point. Owning real estate means becoming the operator of a tiny business. A business that has income (rent), expenses (taxes, repairs, insurance), customers (tenants) and a product (shelter).

*When you start treating your properties this way, your relationship with them changes. You stop reacting and start managing. You stop hoping and start measuring. Every investor I've worked with who found success shared the same trait: **they knew their numbers.** Not by memory, but through a simple, repeatable system.*

---

5. Review and Adjust Yearly

At least once a year, sit down and review your portfolio. Even if it's just one property. Ask three questions: What worked this year? What drained money or time unnecessarily? What opportunities exist to refinance, improve, or diversify?

Markets shift, interest rates change, tenants move. A yearly "property checkup" ensures your investments stay healthy. Think of it like an annual physical for your financial house.

6. Scale Slowly and Smartly

When one property runs smoothly, the temptation to buy another is strong. But growth should follow mastery, not momentum. Don't buy your second property until the first one runs with clean books, stable tenants and enough reserves for surprises. Scaling is exciting, but real estate is a marathon of management, not a sprint of acquisition. You don't want to own ten leaky roofs; you want to own two roofs that fund eight more.

When *Lena* bought her first condo in her late 20s, she didn't have grand ambitions. She just wanted to stop renting. But after five years, she realized her home had nearly $80,000 equity. She refinanced, used the equity to buy a small rental nearby and applied the same disciplined systems she'd used for her own home: organized files, clear tracking and automated payments.

By her mid-30s, Lena owned three properties. None were luxurious, but all were profitable. Her secret wasn't timing the market. It was treating each property like a business and letting time do the heavy lifting. When I asked her once to share the secret, she smiled and said, "Real estate doesn't reward busy people. It rewards organized ones."

Building wealth through real estate is about steady, repeatable habits. Small rituals like tracking, saving, automating and reviewing compound like the rent checks themselves. Because in real estate, fortune doesn't favor the fearless. It favors the *organized*.

The people who build lasting portfolios don't chase the markets but maintain the system. They don't pray for luck but prepare for longevity. That's the quiet rhythm of real estate wealth: calm, consistent, compounding - one roof at a time.

Reflection Pause

- ☐ What small system could you set up this month to make your property run more smoothly?
- ☐ If you couldn't access your property files for a week, would someone else be able to manage in your place?
- ☐ What would happen if an insurance claim or refinance required every document tomorrow?

THE ROOF THAT BUILDS WEALTH

Every home tells two stories. One is about shelter: the warmth of coming home, the smell of a familiar kitchen, the walls that hold laughter. The other is about wealth: the quiet financial engine running behind that comfort, turning each payment into progress. When you step back and look at your life's biggest expenses; housing, food and family; only one of them gives something back. That's what makes real estate special.

At start of this chapter, we met Maya and Daniel. Our anxious new homeowners holding their first key in rain. They didn't see an investment; they saw a commitment. But over the years, that key unlocked far more than a front door. It unlocked equity. It unlocked opportunity. It unlocked *freedom*. That's the story real estate writes over time. It starts with emotion and ends with empowerment. When done wisely, it's not about flipping houses or chasing trends. It's about using the same roof that protects your family to protect your financial future.

Real estate is continuity, not just numbers. It's something tangible you can pass on to future generations can stand on. A foundation. We often think of legacy as what we leave behind, but in truth, it's what we build *while we're still here.*

I've seen families gift homes to children, helping them skip years of rent and uncertainty. I've seen retirees sell one property and live comfortably off its proceeds for decades. And I've seen quiet landlords use rental income to support charities, communities and causes close to their hearts. Your home can outlive your career and even your lifetime, continuing to shelter, earn and serve.

But here's an honest truth: owning property isn't for everyone and it shouldn't consume everything. A house should serve your life, not define it. Balance matters. Liquidity, freedom and emotional peace are just as valuable as appreciation charts.

That's why the best financial plan isn't about *owning everything.* It's about *owning enough.* Enough to feel safe. Enough to feel free. Enough to pass something forward.

The House That Pays You Back

To Recap, in your early years, your home protects you. Later, it can empower you. With time, your mortgage shrinks, your equity grows and your property appreciates. Eventually, you realize you're living inside one of your smartest investments.

Every payment you made, every repair you funded, every repainting weekend were never just costs but also contributions. Even if you never buy another property, even if you never rent it out, your home can quietly transform into a retirement ally, a source of security and a piece of legacy.

We began this chapter with a simple truth - everyone needs a roof. But the real lesson is this: not all roofs are equal. Some just cover you from rain. Others build you a future. Real estate, done right, is one of the few investments that grows quietly while enriching your life daily. It's both the journey and the reward. Both the shelter and the strategy.

You don't need to own ten properties. You just need to own one with intention. Because that roof above your head? It's protection and participation. Participation in a lifelong project called wealth building.

At the end of the day, real estate also isn't about square footage. It's about *foundations*. In the financial kind, it is built through equity and appreciation. And in personal kind, it is built through love, care and consistency.

When you invest in your roof, you're also investing in your roots. And one day, those roots may become someone else's shelter. The roof that builds not just wealth, but legacy.

Worksheet – My Real Estate Readiness Checklist

Use this worksheet to reflect on where you are today and what steps could turn your roof into a wealth-building tool.

Step 1: My Current Home Base

- I currently: ☐ Rent ☐ Own ☐ Invest in Real Estate
- My home's estimated value: $___________
- My current mortgage balance: $___________
- Approximate equity (Value – Loan): $___________

Step 2: My Real Estate Goals

- Short-term (1–3 years): ____________________________________
- Medium-term (5–10 years): __________________________________
- Long-term (Legacy): ______________________________________

Step 3: Key Financial Indicators

- Monthly housing cost (mortgage + taxes + insurance): $__________
- % of income going toward housing: _______%
- Monthly savings/investment rate: _______%

Step 4: Maintenance & Protection

- Annual maintenance fund set aside? ☐ Yes ☐ No
- Home insurance reviewed this year? ☐ Yes ☐ No
- Property documents (deed, insurance, tax records) stored safely?
  ☐ Yes   ☐ No

Step 5: Next Steps

What's the one improvement or investment you'll make this year?

____

What's one new real estate habit you'll start?

____

Step 6: Legacy & Intent

If something happened to me tomorrow, would my family know what to do with this property?

  ☐ Yes   ☐ No

If no, what step will I take to fix that?

____

Part 3: Smart Money Moves

There's no such thing as bad weather - only inadequate gear.

— Adapted from Alfred Wainwright (via a wise colleague)

9

Insurance - Your Financial Seatbelt

It happened on a regular Friday evening. The kind where you leave work a bit early, thinking about weekend plans, maybe a family movie night. *John* kissed his wife *Avie* goodbye that morning, promised to pick up their daughter from her piano class and left for a quick client meeting. He never made it home. A speeding truck at an intersection changed everything in a blink.

The days that followed were a blur of shock, grief and impossible logistics filled with insurance claims, funeral arrangements and an empty chair at the dining table. John was only thirty-nine. He was the family's main earner, a careful planner but also someone who always thought he'd have "more time." Amid the chaos, one document quietly changed the course of Avie's life, a **term-life insurance policy** he had taken five years earlier.

John's policy was modest: a 20-year term plan with $1 million coverage. He paid around $45 per month, less than what the family spent on streaming subscriptions. At the time, he'd joked with Avie, "This is the one thing I hope we never use." In time of crisis, that same policy became their financial lifeline.

When the claim was settled, the payout did something extraordinary. It gave Avie *time.* It paid off their remaining $320,000 mortgage, ensuring she and their daughter could stay in their home. It covered college savings that John had just started building. And it took care of three to four years of household expenses, giving her breathing room to grieve, rebuild and find her footing again. Avie didn't have to sell the house, move back with parents or scramble for two jobs. She didn't have to uproot her daughter's life on top of already losing her father.

That policy didn't erase the tragedy. But it made sure grief didn't turn into financial devastation. Insurance didn't replace John. It replaced his *income*, his *protection*, his *promise.*

Most people think insurance is about money. It's not. It's about **preserving stability when life doesn't go according to plan.** Insurance isn't about accidents. It's about *avoiding financial ruin.*

We insure our cars, our home and now, even our phones. Yet many families go uninsured for their most valuable asset: the income that holds everything together.

We all carry invisible risks every day. A car crash. A medical emergency. A burst pipe. A broken phone. A storm. Most of the time, nothing happens and that's exactly why insurance feels like a waste. You pay and nothing goes wrong. You pay again, year over year and nothing goes wrong.

Then one day, something does. That's when insurance reveals its true purpose. It's not designed to make you rich. It's designed to make sure one disaster doesn't make you *poor.* In a way, insurance is like oxygen. Unnoticed until someone sucks out the air from the room.

People love growth. We celebrate investments, stocks, compounding. All the exciting parts of personal finance. But insurance doesn't excite anyone. It doesn't make headlines, isn't talked about in most personal finance books and it doesn't come with charts that rise up and to the right. That's why it's often overlooked. Yet ask anyone who's faced a sudden health emergency, a house fire, a death of a loved one or a lawsuit and you'll hear a common theme: "We thought we were fine... until we weren't."

You don't buy insurance because you expect bad things. You buy it because you know life doesn't ask for permission. It's your *financial seatbelt.* You don't wear it because you plan to crash. You wear it because you know the world isn't always predictable.

The Psychology of Protection

There's a reason people hesitate to buy insurance. It feels uncomfortable and forces you to imagine the unimaginable. But protection is an act of love, not fear. When you insure your life, you're saying to your family, "Even if I'm not here, I've still got you." You're turning money into time, pain into stability and loss into security.

John's story isn't rare. Every year, millions of families are held together by quiet, unglamorous insurance policies. Term life, health, disability or homeowners. Policies that stand like invisible walls between them and chaos.

The strange truth about insurance is that the *best* outcome is never using it. You pay your premiums, year after year and nothing happens. And that's perfect. But if the unthinkable does occur, it's the single line item in your budget that will matter most. It doesn't make you wealthier, but it protects what makes wealth possible: your home, your health, your family's future.

In this chapter, we'll strip insurance down to its simplest truth: protection. And take insurance out of the fine print and put it into plain English. We'll look at what it really is, which policies actually matter and how much coverage makes sense for your life stage. You'll learn what protection really means, which policies actually matter and how to strike the right balance between coverage and cost.

<u>Because wealth isn't just about what you *build*. It's also about what you *keep safe.*</u>

And while you can't control the next storm or accident, you can control whether it breaks your balance sheet or just becomes another story you survived. Because that's what Insurance really is: the calm you pay for, the protection you hope to never need and the promise that people you love will always have a roof, a future and time to heal.

Reflection Pause

- ☐ If something happened to you tomorrow, would your family have the financial space to grieve or the pressure to survive?
- ☐ Do you know your coverage and is it enough to replace your income for a few years?
- ☐ When you pay your premiums, do you see them as a cost or as an invisible promise to your loved ones?

WHAT INSURANCE REALLY IS (AND ISN'T)

The word *insurance* often makes people yawn. It sounds like paperwork, fine print and long phone calls. Not exactly the stuff of dreams where you see million-dollar buckets jingling with gold coins or the jackpot at casinos. But once you understand what it truly *does*, you start seeing it differently.

At its heart, insurance is about one simple idea: **transferring risk.** It means if something big and unexpected happens, you don't face it alone. You share that risk with a company that can afford to absorb it. You pay a little bit every month to make sure one disaster doesn't wipe out everything you've built. That's it. That's the whole concept. It's not about beating the odds; it's about protecting your future from the odds.

Imagine you're driving on a rainy day. You fasten your seatbelt. Once you wear it, you don't check every few miles whether it's "working". You simply wear it, drive confidently and go on with your day. That's what insurance does for your finances. It's the seatbelt that keeps a bad moment from becoming a financial catastrophe.

Or think of it like an umbrella. You carry it not to control the weather but to stop the rain from drenching you when it comes. And in life, the rain *will* come. Not every storm is avoidable, but being unprepared is always optional.

Many people misunderstand insurance because it doesn't *feel* like other financial tools. It doesn't give visible returns and it often feels like money disappearing into thin air. And that's why companies market "investment-linked" policies, blending insurance and savings. But this often creates confusion. Here's the truth:

Insurance protects. Investments grow.

The moment you try to make one behave like the other, both suffer. Insurance isn't meant to make you rich. It's meant to make sure a crisis doesn't make you *poor*. The goal isn't return on investment but the promise *of stability*.

A term-life policy doesn't pay dividends while you're alive but it gives your family the ability to keep living comfortably if you're gone. Health insurance won't double your money, but it keeps you from draining your savings during an emergency.

The Cost of Going Without

*Most bankruptcies in the U.S. stem from **medical bills, accidents or lost income**. All things that could have been mitigated by proper insurance. Without it, one event can undo years of financial discipline. A hospital stay can empty your emergency fund. A fire can erase your home equity. A lawsuit can threaten your savings.*

Insurance doesn't just save money but it also saves momentum. It ensures your financial journey keeps going even when life hits pause.

It's easy to see insurance as a stack of forms or a reluctant expense. But when you really think about it, it's a trade of **uncertainty for calm.** You're paying not for an event, but for *peace*. Peace that lets you focus on living, working and planning. All without fear that one twist of fate will undo your efforts. When you buy insurance, you're essentially saying, "I choose stability over surprise." You're taking responsibility not just for yourself, but for everyone who depends on you.

Insurance is a guardrail. You don't buy it hoping to "win." You buy it so you don't lose *everything*. It's the quiet agreement between your today and your tomorrow that no matter what happens, your life, your family and your finances will stay on the road. Because wealth without protection is like driving fast without brakes. It feels exciting until the eventual sharp turn.

Reflection Pause

- ☐ If insurance didn't exist, how much would you need saved to cover a worst-case event like medical emergency, home loss or major accident?
- ☐ Which type of risk could you handle comfortably and which could derail everything?
- ☐ When you think of insurance, do you see an expense or a promise to your future self?

THE BIG FOUR: HEALTH, LIFE, HOME AND AUTO

If you could only afford four types of protection, these would be it. Each one guards a pillar of your life: your *body, your income, your shelter and your mobility*. You might never need all of them at once, but when any one fails, your entire financial structure can tilt.

Let's break them down, not as products, but as promises.

1. Health Insurance – The Shield for Your Body

There's a reason health insurance sits at the top of every financial checklist - because a single hospital visit can cost more than a car and a prolonged illness can derail years of saving.

A broken leg? $10,000. An emergency surgery? $30,000–$50,000. A week in intensive care? Six figures, easily. Most people think health insurance is only about "coverage." It's not. It's about *access*.

It lets you make medical decisions based on need, not fear of bills. It gives you choices - which hospital, which treatment, which recovery plan. Even with premiums and deductibles, it's one of the few products that protects both your health *and* your financial stability.

If you're employed, check what your employer covers and where the gaps are. If you're self-employed, explore ACA marketplace plans or Health Savings Accounts (HSAs). But whatever you do, don't gamble your health on luck. No investment grows fast enough to outrun a hospital bill.

2.   Life Insurance – The Promise That Lives On

We often mistake life insurance as something for the old or wealthy. In truth, it's for anyone who loves someone who depends on them. If someone would suffer financially if you weren't here tomorrow, maybe your spouse, your child, an aging parent or your pets, you need life insurance.

The simplest and most effective kind is **term-life**. It's clean, affordable and focused. You pay a small premium for a fixed period (usually 20 to 30 years) and if you die during that term, your loved ones receive a lump sum. That payout is not about replacing *you*. It's about replacing the *income* that built your family's world. Think of it as a financial promise that your plans will continue, even if you can't.

A good rule of thumb: aim for coverage around 10–12 times your annual income, enough to pay off debts, cover education and maintain your family's lifestyle for several years.

Reflection moment: The premium for that peace of mind often costs less than dinner for two at a restaurant.

There are other types like whole life, universal, variable; but those blend insurance with investment and they often blur the line between protection and profit. For most people, term-life does the job beautifully. It's simple, direct and does exactly what it should: protect those who depend on your tomorrow.

3. Homeowners or Renters Insurance – Protecting Your Roof

For most families, the home is their biggest asset both emotionally and financially. But homes carry risk, too: fire, storms, theft, flooding or simply a burst pipe that decides to turn your living room into a pool. That's where Homeowners insurance comes in. It covers not just the physical structure, but also the contents like your furniture, electronics and sometimes even the cost of living elsewhere while repairs are made.

If you rent, don't skip protection. Renters insurance is inexpensive (often under $20 a month) and covers your personal belongings and liability even if your landlord's policy doesn't.

Here's what most people miss: insure your home for it's rebuild cost, not its market price. The market value includes land; the rebuild cost covers what you'd need if the structure were lost. And check your policy annually. Values, inflation and coverage limits shift faster than you think.

4. Auto Insurance – The Everyday Lifeline

If you drive, this isn't optional. It's law. But beyond legal compliance, auto insurance is what stands between a minor accident and a major financial setback. Even a small fender-bender can run thousands in repairs. A serious collision can involve injuries, lawsuits and months of downtime.

Auto insurance comes in three main buckets:
- **Liability coverage** pays for damage or injury you cause to others.
- **Collision coverage** covers damage to your own vehicle.
- **Comprehensive coverage** protects against theft, vandalism, weather or other non-collision events.

If your car is financed, lenders usually require both collision and comprehensive. Once paid off, you can adjust coverage but liability should always stay robust. Cheap policies often mean limited protection. The few dollars saved per month vanish quickly when you face a $20,000 claim.

Auto insurance doesn't just fix cars; it protects your freedom to move, work and live without financial paralysis after an accident.

How These Four Work Together

Each of these coverages protects a different dimension of your life:

- *Health insurance shields your body and income from medical shocks.*
- *Life insurance shields your family from losing financial stability.*
- *Home insurance shields your shelter from loss.*
- *Auto insurance shields your mobility and freedom that keeps everything else running.*

*They don't compete; they complement each other. Together, they form your **financial seatbelt system** keeping you safe no matter where the next impact comes from.*

You can think of these four as your financial "guardians". They're not glamorous and they don't post exciting returns, but they hold your life together when the world doesn't. Because the truth is simple: *no one plans to crash, get sick or lose their home but everyone plans to recover.* And recovery is a lot easier when protection was already in place.

Reflection Pause

☐ Which of these four protections do you currently have and which ones need review or strengthening?

☐ How often do you actually read your policy coverage or update it after major life changes?

☐ If something unexpected happened tomorrow how long could your finances stand on their own?

BEYOND THE BASICS: OFTEN-OVERLOOKED PROTECTIONS

By now, you've fastened your financial seatbelt with the Big Four. But like any good safety system, there are extra airbags hidden in the design. Protections most people never notice until they save the day. These aren't for everyone and they don't all deserve space in your budget. Still, it helps to know they exist, so when life throws a curveball, you're not caught wondering what you *could* have done.

Let's look at a few quiet guardians that rarely make headlines but often make the difference between an inconvenience and a crisis.

Disability Insurance - Your Income's Backup Plan

If your ability to earn money vanished tomorrow, what would you do? That question makes most people uncomfortable, which is exactly why they avoid thinking about it. Yet for many, a long illness or injury is far more likely than an early death. Disability insurance is simply *income insurance.* It replaces a portion of your paycheck if you can't work due to medical reasons.

When my client Julia, a physical therapist, slipped on icy stairs one winter and broke her wrist, she suddenly couldn't do the very thing that paid her bills. Her short-term disability coverage through work kicked in within weeks, covering 60 percent of her income until she healed. And that's the point. Disability insurance isn't about expecting disaster; it's about keeping the lights on while you recover. If your employer offers it, start there. If you're self-employed, a private long-term disability plan can be worth its weight in peace of mind.

Umbrella Insurance – The Hidden Hero

Think of umbrella insurance as the "extra layer" over everything else. It steps in when your regular liability limits on home or auto policies aren't enough. Say you accidentally cause a serious car accident or someone gets injured on your property. If the damages exceed your regular policy limit, the umbrella catches the rest, so your savings and future income stay safe.

For most people, a $1 million umbrella policy costs less than a weekend getaway. And like a real umbrella, you forget it's there until the day it keeps you dry in a storm you didn't see coming. You don't need it if you're just starting out with minimal assets. But once your savings, investments or property start adding up, it's one of the cheapest layers of serious protection you can buy.

Choosing What's Worth Protecting

Every policy, from the biggest to the smallest, is really an exercise in self-awareness. You're asking, "What could go wrong and would I be okay if it did?". Not everything deserves insurance. Some risks are small enough to absorb. Others could rewrite your story. The goal is to put cushions where the landings would hurt most.

When in doubt, insure what you can't replace: your income, your health, your roof and your ability to live without anxiety.

Travel Insurance – Peace in a Passport

We've all had that pre-trip excitement with tickets booked, bags packed, playlists ready, only to see the weather app explode with storm alerts. Travel insurance isn't about paranoia; it's about preserving joy. It reimburses you for canceled flights, lost luggage or medical issues abroad. Is it always necessary? Not really. For short domestic trips, probably not. But for international travel or expensive family vacations, it's worth considering.

I still remember a client whose honeymoon flight got canceled twice due to volcanic ash in Iceland. Something no spreadsheet could predict. Their travel insurance covered hotels, rebooking fees and half their sanity. Sometimes, peace of mind fits neatly inside your carry-on.

Pet, Gadget and Other "Micro-Protections"

Now we enter the world of optional add-ons - the kind that politely pop up at the checkout counter: *"Would you like to add insurance for just $12.99 a month?".* For most gadgets, answer is usually *no.* Extended warranties and device insurance often cost more than the repair or replacement itself. Still, if your work or lifestyle depends heavily on a specific device like a photographer's camera or a designer's laptop, a dedicated coverage plan can make sense.

Pet insurance, on the other hand, has quietly become more useful. Vet bills can rival hospital bills and a basic plan can cover surgeries or chronic conditions. If your pet is family (and let's be honest, they usually are), it's worth at least a look.

The key is to ask one simple question: "Would paying this premium save me from a true financial setback or just from mild inconvenience?". If it's the latter, skip it. Insurance should protect your *future*, not your *frustrations*.

Remember, Insurance doesn't have to be intimidating. It's simply the art of *choosing calm in advance*. A few smart layers - a disability plan, an umbrella policy, maybe travel coverage for that long-awaited vacation - can turn chaos into a speed bump instead of a roadblock. You don't need to protect against every drizzle. Just make sure you've packed an umbrella for the real storms.

Reflection Pause
- ☐ Which "smaller" risk in your life could cause the biggest headache? Your paycheck, a liability lawsuit or a canceled trip?
- ☐ Are there inexpensive add-ons, like umbrella policy or workplace disability, you've overlooked simply because they weren't urgent?
- ☐ If you trimmed unnecessary coverages, where could that money be redirected toward what truly matters?

HOW MUCH COVERAGE IS ENOUGH?

Here's a question that trips almost everyone: *How much insurance do I really need?* Too little and you're one bad day away from financial chaos. Too much and you're paying for peace of mind you'll never use. Finding the balance isn't about perfect precision but about **protection that fits your life**, like a seatbelt that's snug, not suffocating. Let's talk about what "enough" looks like. Not from a salesman's perspective, but from a practical one.

Health Insurance –Comfort Zone Between Premium and Panic

The biggest mistake people make with health insurance is chasing the *lowest monthly premium.* It looks cheaper upfront until you actually need care. Think of it like choosing a restaurant: the cheapest meal on the menu might leave you hungry later. Your goal isn't to minimize premiums; it's to minimize total cost, which includes what you pay *if* something goes wrong.

A simple rule:

- Choose the lowest deductible you can realistically afford out-of-pocket.
- Pair it with a Health Savings Account (HSA) if available, so you're saving for medical costs tax-free.
- Revisit your plan every year. Health, income and family needs all change faster than insurance portals do.

If you're healthy and rarely visit doctors, a high-deductible plan with an HSA can make sense. If you have ongoing prescriptions or family medical needs, paying a bit more in premiums for lower deductibles often pays off in calm and comfort. Because in health coverage, "enough" isn't about numbers but about *sleeping well at night.*

Life Insurance – The Income Multiplier Rule

For life insurance, the math is surprisingly simple. You want enough coverage to replace your income long enough for your family to rebuild their footing. The rough rule of thumb: 10–12 times your annual income. So, if you earn $100,000 a year, aim for $1 million to $1.2 million in coverage. That's typically enough to:

- Pay off your mortgage and debts
- Fund college or education goals
- Cover living expenses for 10–12 years
- Give your loved one's time; the most valuable currency of all

You don't need complicated investment-linked plans. A plain term-life policy, 20 or 30 years, depending on your life stage usually does the job perfectly. It's not about the payout; it's about the *promise.* A promise that your family's plans don't end where your life does.

Home Insurance – Rebuild, Don't Rebuy

Here's where many homeowners get it wrong: they insure their home for its market value instead of rebuild cost. The market price includes land which doesn't burn, flood or blow away. The rebuild cost is what it would actually take to replace the structure, materials and labor if disaster struck.

Ask your insurer to calculate the rebuild estimate each year. Construction costs rise faster than we realize. And while you're at it, review your deductible. Higher deductibles mean lower premiums but make sure you could comfortably cover that amount in cash. A home policy isn't about protecting your property value. It's about ensuring that if your roof disappears tomorrow, you still have a place to call home.

The "Enough" Mindset

You'll notice that every type of insurance boils down to one question: What would it take to make this event survivable, not comfortable?

That's the sweet spot. You don't need coverage for every inconvenience but just enough to prevent catastrophe. If your savings could handle the loss, skip the policy. If the loss would change your life, insure it. You're not trying to buy certainty. You're just paying to stay in control when uncertainty shows up.

Auto Insurance – Protection, Not Paperwork

Auto insurance feels straightforward until an accident reminds you how many moving parts it has. Here's an easy breakdown:
- **Liability coverage**: This is non-negotiable. It protects *other people* (and their property) if you cause an accident. Carry enough to protect your assets. $100,000/$300,000 minimum, more if you own property or investments.
- **Collision coverage**: Covers your car if you hit something. Drop it only when your car's value is too low to justify the premium.

- **Comprehensive coverage**: Protects against non-collision events like theft, weather, vandalism. Usually inexpensive and worth keeping.

In short: keep liability high, tweak the rest based on your car's age and value. If your car is essential to your livelihood, treat it like income insurance because every day without it can cost more than you expect.

The Layer Above – Umbrella and Disability

If you've built savings, own a home or have a growing investment portfolio, consider an umbrella policy. It extends your liability coverage beyond limits of auto and home insurance, often for just a few hundred dollars a year. Likewise, disability insurance deserves a quick revisit. If you rely on your paycheck (most do), make sure you have coverage that replaces at least 60% of your income if you can't work. Both of these aren't luxuries but stabilizers. They keep your progress from toppling when life shakes the table.

Insurance isn't about predicting the storm. It's about building a roof that's just strong enough to keep you safe. You need just enough *protective balance*. Enough to weather the unexpected but not so much that you forget to live in the present. Because at the end of the day, the best insurance policy is one that lets you focus less on fear and more on life.

Reflection Pause
- ☐ When was the last time you reviewed your coverage amounts or are they still based on a version of you from years ago?
- ☐ Could your family comfortably manage three months of expenses if your paycheck stopped?
- ☐ If you had to prioritize, which protection matters most right now? Is it health, life, home or income?

THE CALM YOU PAY FOR

When John took out that simple term-life policy years ago, he didn't think of it as "insurance." He thought of it as love on paper. A quiet promise that, come what may, his family would still have a roof, meals on the table and time to heal. That's really what insurance is: your love letter to the future. Not glamorous, not exciting, but deeply human. It says:

> _"If life takes an unexpected turn, my people will still be okay."_

You'll rarely see that on a brochure but that's the heart of it.

Every premium you pay buys a small piece of calm. It's not an expense but a transfer of fear. You hand over uncertainty to someone else and in return, you get to live your days without that quiet worry humming in the background. You can plan, work, travel, dream knowing that if something derails those plans, it won't derail your future.

And yes, you'll pay for years and might never file a claim. That's the sign of a peaceful life, not a loss. You wouldn't call seatbelts a waste because you didn't crash. You'd call them a wise precaution that let you drive with confidence. Insurance does just that, it lets you move forward _unafraid._

Insurance is a mindset. A way of saying: "I respect uncertainty, but I'm not ruled by it." It's one of the least talked-about parts of financial wellness because it's not exciting. There's no graph, no compound interest, no adrenaline rush. But it's what makes every other part _possible._ Without insurance, your savings are vulnerable. Your investments can vanish overnight. Your dreams depend on luck. And luck is a very bad strategy. When you have the right coverage, you can take bolder steps, chase new opportunities and live with more confidence. Because you're not just protecting against loss but also protecting your freedom to _keep living normally_ no matter what happens.

The Power of Reviewing Once a Year

Insurance is not a "set and forget" decision. Your life changes and so should your coverage. Maybe you bought a home, got married, switched jobs or had a child. Each milestone quietly shifts your risk. Make it a habit to review your protection every year to make sure everything still fits.

Just like you adjust your car mirrors before a long drive, adjust your coverage before every new chapter. Fifteen minutes of review once a year can save you years of regret later.

You'll never time the market perfectly. You'll never eliminate all risk. But you can build a financial life that bends without breaking. And that's where insurance gives you *financial resilience*. It's the invisible foundation beneath your wealth, the quiet constant beneath your dreams. You don't buy it because you expect disaster. You buy it so that, when disaster happens, it doesn't get to rewrite your story. And that's worth every premium, every policy and every ounce of peace it brings.

Money grows with smart choices. Wealth lasts with safe ones. Insurance is simply the quiet discipline that makes sure the wealth you build and the people you build it for (including you), stay protected long enough to enjoy it. Because the goal isn't to live fearlessly. It's to live *fear-free*.

Worksheet – My Protection Snapshot

Use this quick exercise to assess where you. It's not about buying more but knowing what *really* matters for your life stage.

Step 1: My Current Coverage

Type of Insurance	Do I Have It? (Y/N)	Coverage Amount / Details	Next Review Date
Health Insurance			
Life Insurance			
Homeowner/Renters			
Auto Insurance			
Disability Insurance			
Umbrella / Liability			
Other(Pet,Travel, etc.)			

Step 2: My Protection Priorities

Rank each area below from 1 (most important) to 5 (least urgent):

☐ Health   ☐ Life   ☐ Home   ☐ Auto   ☐ Income   ☐ Other

What's my biggest coverage gap right now?

____

If something happened tomorrow, which policy would I miss most?

____

Step 3: My Next Actions

One small step I can take this month to improve my protection:

____

One policy I will review, adjust or cancel this quarter:

____

One person I'll discuss insurance with (spouse, parent, advisor):

____

Step 4: The Peace Test

Close your eyes and imagine this: If your car broke down, your house flooded or you were suddenly out of work for six months, would your life keep going with a manageable detour or come to a stop?

If your answer brings peace, you're doing well. If it brings anxiety, that's your next to-do.

10

Wills & Trusts - Protecting What You Leave Behind

The Letter You Don't Want to Write (But should)

When *Maira's* father passed away, she found herself sitting on the living room floor surrounded by unopened envelopes, account statements and sticky notes that only made sense to him. There were bank accounts she didn't know existed, policies with no listed beneficiaries and a small rental property no one in the family even remembered he owned. Grief of losing him was heavy enough but confusion that followed made it even harder. A few months after the funeral, Maira said something that stuck "He spent his whole life protecting us but when he left, we didn't know how to protect what he built." Her father wasn't careless. He was, in fact, thoughtful but just *unfinished*. Like most people, he'd always meant to "get to it next weekend."

Writing a will feels like sitting down to write a letter you never want anyone to read. It forces you to imagine a day you're not here and no one likes that conversation. So, we postpone it. We convince ourselves we're too young, too healthy or too busy. But the truth is, a will isn't about death. It's about *direction*. It's the letter that tells your family, *"Here's what matters. Here's how to handle it. Here's how I've taken care of you, even from beyond the room"*. A will is not a document of endings. It's a document of *continuity*.

Let's also talk about *David* and *Jonathan*. Their parents passed away within months of each other. Both were doing well, had similar-sized estates, owned homes and both had children of their own. But the aftermath could not have been more different.

David's parents had left a clear will. Everything was written down: which child would handle the finances, how the property would be divided, even how sentimental items like jewelry, photographs and heirlooms would be shared. The process was calm, respectful and quick. David felt like they were still guiding him.

Jonathan's parents, however, had left no will. Only conversations that no one fully remembered. Within weeks, family dinners turned into arguments. Every document required signatures, witnesses and waiting periods. Bank accounts were frozen, bills were unpaid and trust - not the legal, but the emotional one - began to erode. Was Jonathan fighting about money? Or was he fighting *uncertainty*.

Estate planning often sounds like something reserved for people with mansions, companies or multiple properties. But the truth is, *anyone with responsibilities needs a plan.* If you have a family, a house, savings or even a favorite guitar you want someone specific to have, you have an estate. A will isn't about the size of what you leave behind; it's about the clarity of what happens next. Without one, your loved ones don't just lose you but also lose time, money and peace trying to interpret your intentions.

More Than Money

What you leave behind isn't just cash or property - it's meaning. Your will can carry your values, not just your valuables. Some people include small "letters of wishes" or "legacy notes", personal messages, life lessons or even simple requests like "keep the Sunday lunches going." These things often matter more than numbers. Because in the end, your true legacy isn't just what you owned but it is also what you stood for.

A will, at its core, is a final act of care. It tells your family that you thought of them practically, not just emotionally. It spares them the endless "what would they have wanted?" debates and lets them focus on what truly matters: healing.

When *Daniel*, a retired teacher, finally finished his will, he remarked, "I used to think writing a will meant preparing for death. But now I see it's a gift for the living." And that's the mindset shift we all need. Estate planning isn't about control but a way to keep protecting your family, even when you can't be there physically to guide them.

In this chapter, we'll take will, trusts and estate plans, something often seen as complicated or intimidating and break it down to the human level. You'll understand what happens if you don't leave a plan. How wills and trusts actually work and how to start one without expensive lawyers. And, most importantly, how to talk about it with your family in a way that feels natural, not grim.

Because writing a will is about *continuity*, not about finality. It's not the end of your story but how you make sure your story continues the way you meant it to.

Reflection Pause
- ☐ If something unexpected happened tomorrow, would your loved ones know where to begin?
- ☐ Are there important conversations you've been putting off because they feel uncomfortable?
- ☐ What one thing could you organize this week to make things easier for your family later? Could be a list, a note or a password. Anything...

WHAT HAPPENS IF YOU DON'T HAVE A PLAN

When someone passes away without a will, the world doesn't stop out of sympathy. But legally, everything pauses. Accounts freeze. Property titles stall. Everyone who loved the person is left juggling grief and paperwork. And while the emotional loss feels personal, the administrative mess that follows can feel painfully public between court filings, probate hearings and state rules deciding what happens next.

When a person dies *intestate*, the legal word for "without a will", their assets don't automatically transfer to family members. They go into **probate**, a court-supervised process to decide who gets what. That process can take months, sometimes years. And during that time, family members can't easily sell, access or even maintain assets.

A home can't be sold until the court approves it. Bank accounts stay locked. Even paying property taxes or utilities can become a bureaucratic maze. The worst part? The court doesn't know your family, it only knows and follows the law.

A few years ago, a friend shared how his aunt, *Rosa*, passed away without leaving a will. She wasn't super-rich. A retired schoolteacher with a house, a car and some decent savings. But what she didn't have was clarity. Her two children, *Elena* and *Marco*, both loved her deeply. Yet, within weeks of her passing, grief turned into arguments. Questions like who would manage the house or how should the savings be split? What about the jewelry she'd promised Elena years ago during a casual conversation? Without written instructions, everything became interpretation, subjective. And interpretation breeds tension.

They spent more than a year in probate court. Legal fees ate into their inheritance and emotional distance replaced their once-close bond. Marco ultimately sighed and remarked, "Mom would be heartbroken to see us like this.". She probably would've been because no parent imagines or wants their absence turning into a conflict.

The hidden cost of *not* having a plan often goes unnoticed until it's too late.

- **Financial Cost:** Probate fees, legal representation and court costs can consume 5-10% of the estate's value, sometimes much more. Money that could've gone to your loved ones.

- **Emotional Cost:** Family members may argue, sometimes permanently fracturing relationships.

- **Time Cost:** Probate can last from 6 months to several years, depending on the complexity and cooperation of heirs.

Most people think estate planning is for the rich. In reality, the smaller your estate, the more you need a plan. Because smaller estates have fewer buffers and delays hit harder.

But who decides without a Will? If there's no will, the **state** decides who inherits. Not based on love, but on legal hierarchy. Each state has its own order: spouse, children, parents, siblings and so on. And the law doesn't account for blended families, long-time partners, stepchildren or close friends.

If you live with someone but never married, they might receive *nothing.* If you promised a sentimental item to a niece or grandchild, that promise has no standing. A will, no matter how simple, ensures *your wishes* guide the outcome, not the state formulas.

The Paperwork Avalanche

After a loved one dies, the survivors often face a mountain of tasks with closing accounts, transferring titles, locating insurance, notifying agencies, filing claims and paying final taxes. Without a plan, this becomes detective work. Most families spend months just figuring out where everything is, sometimes discovering assets or debts years later.

Having a will and organized documents transforms that chaos into clarity. It's like leaving a clean desk instead of a puzzle.

And the best part: You don't need a lawyer to make a start. Even a handwritten list of assets, passwords and key contacts helps. But a signed, witnessed will ensures your intentions hold legal weight. And earlier you do it, better because life doesn't wait for the "right time."

Estate planning is one of those tasks that rewards early action and punishes delay. As one financial planner once said to me, "Writing a will doesn't make you old. It makes you responsible."

Life doesn't give advance notice but it gives us the chance to prepare. A will isn't about death or money. It's about direction and love. It ensures your family doesn't have to make hard choices while still in pain. And clarity, when you're gone, is the greatest comfort you can give. When everything is written down, grief has space to breathe. Families can mourn without fighting, act without guessing and heal without chaos.

Reflection Pause
- ☐ If something happened to you tomorrow, would your loved ones know where to find your important documents or passwords?
- ☐ Do the people you trust know what you'd want done with your assets or personal items?
- ☐ What small step could you take this week to make things easier later? Think... writing a list, naming an executor, talking to your family or something else?

WILLS, TRUSTS AND THE TOOLS OF CLARITY

When people hear the word *estate*, they often picture rolling lawns, fountains and marble gates. Something belonging to the ultra-rich, wealthy or titled. In truth, every one of us has an estate. It's everything you own, everything you owe and everything you care about. The car you drive, savings account you've built, home you live in and even that old watch you plan to pass down someday are all part of *your* estate. And decisions about what happens to these things, after you're gone or unable to decide for yourself, form the heart of estate planning.

It sounds complex because words like *executor*, *probate*, *trustee* feel heavy and technical. But once you strip away the jargon, it's really about one simple idea: making sure your voice continues to speak when you no longer can.

A Will: The Map You Leave Behind

Think of a Will as a map. It doesn't change the terrain; it simply shows your loved ones where everything is and what direction to go. It tells people you trust, your executor, how you want your assets distributed, who should take care of your children and even how you wish to be remembered in the small details that never make it into legal forms.

Without that map, your family stands at a crossroads with no clear signposts. The Will ensures that your intentions and not their assumptions, guide the journey. It can be as straightforward or as detailed as you like. You could name who inherits your home or savings, or simply note that everything be divided equally among your children. You can name guardians for your kids (especially important) or appoint a trusted friend to handle the sale of your business.

A Will can also include instructions that don't involve money at all. Perhaps you want certain personal items, like your mother's ring or your collection of travel journals, to go to people who will truly cherish them. These may seem small but they are often the details that carry the deepest emotional weight.

A good Will removes confusion. A great one carries warmth.

A Trust: The Autopilot for Your Wishes

If Will is a map, a Trust is like an autopilot system. A set of instructions that keeps running automatically, managing and distributing your assets exactly the way you designed, even after you're gone.

A Trust holds your assets under the care of a trustee (someone you appoint), who manages them for the benefit of your chosen people; your beneficiaries. Unlike a Will, a Trust doesn't usually go through probate, meaning your loved ones can access what they need without waiting months for the legal process to unfold.

Trusts also offer privacy. While Wills become part of public record, Trusts remain confidential. For many families, that privacy isn't about secrecy but also about dignity.

There are different kinds of Trusts, but most people start with what's called a **Revocable Living Trust**. "Revocable" because you can change it anytime and "Living" because it takes effect while you're still alive. You can move assets like your home, your accounts, your investments etc. into the Trust and still manage them as usual. When you pass, the trustee simply continues according to your plan. It's particularly useful if you have property in multiple states, children from different marriages or simply want to make the transition smoother for your family.

A Trust is not a sign of wealth but a sign of foresight. It keeps the gears of your legacy turning quietly, even while life moves on.

Clarity Toolkit

Together, a Will, a Trust, a Living Will and a Power of Attorney are tools that help you create what I like to call a clarity toolkit. Each one serves a slightly different purpose but they all work toward the same goal: protecting your loved ones from confusion and conflict.

You don't need to have all of them at once. Start simple. Write a will. Preferably add a medical directive. As life grows more complex, like another property or a side business, you can layer on a Trust.

Estate planning isn't a one-time event; it's a living document, just like your financial plan. As your story evolves, so should your instructions. The goal is direction, not perfection.

The Living Will: Decisions of Dignity

Then there's a tool that doesn't deal with money at all. A Living Will or advance directive. This is the document that outlines your wishes for medical care if you can't express them yourself. It might include things like life support, organ donation or other end-of-life choices.

It's not an easy subject to discuss, but it's one of the most profound gifts you can give your family. In the absence of clear instruction, loved ones are often left to guess. And guessing under emotional stress can leave lifelong scars. A Living Will spares them that burden. It says, "This is what I want. You don't have to decide for me." It gives you dignity and gives them peace.

Power of Attorney: The Voice That Speaks When You Can't

Alongside your Will or Trust, you should also consider naming a Power of Attorney i.e. someone legally authorized to make decisions if you become unable to do so.

There are two kinds. A *financial power of attorney* can pay your bills, manage your accounts or handle transactions on your behalf. A *medical power of attorney* (sometimes called a healthcare proxy) can make treatment decisions if you're unable to communicate them.

It's not about surrendering control; it's about ensuring continuity. Life can surprise us with an illness, an accident, even a temporary recovery period after surgery. A power of attorney keeps your life running while you focus on healing.

Choose someone responsible, organized and emotionally grounded. It's less about who loves you most and more about who can carry responsibility when emotions run high.

A Will and a Trust need not only divide wealth. They can carry wisdom too. They ensure that what you built in life continues with purpose, order and care. The irony is that while these documents are written in legal language, their essence is emotional. They are about compassion, clarity and continuity; the three qualities that outlast any signature or seal. When done right, they don't feel like paperwork. They feel like peace.

Reflection Pause
- ☐ Do your loved ones know who to call or where to look if something happens to you tomorrow?
- ☐ Have you chosen someone who can make calm, thoughtful decisions on your behalf both financially or medically?
- ☐ When was the last time you updated the documents you think you already have?

Making It Real (Without a Lawyer's Bill)

By now, the idea of writing a will or setting up a trust might feel less mysterious and more doable. Still, most people hesitate to take the first step because they assume it means calling a lawyer, scheduling long meetings and paying fees that rival a small vacation. The truth is, for most families, getting started doesn't need to be expensive or complicated. It just needs a bit of *intentionality*.

Estate planning, at its core, is about organization and communication. Not legal perfection at the first pass. The key is to make your wishes clear enough that, if you weren't around to explain them, your loved ones could still follow along as if you were sitting right beside them.

So, Start with What You Already Know. The best place to begin is not at a lawyer's office but at your kitchen table. Pull out a notebook or open a spreadsheet and start by answering three simple questions:

1. **What do I own?** Write down your assets like house, car, savings, investments, retirement accounts, life insurance, business interests and yes, even digital assets like crypto wallets or online businesses.

2. **Who do I trust?** Note names of people you would rely on to handle things responsibly. Maybe your spouse, sibling, adult child or a close friend. These are your potential executors or trustees.

3. **Who do I love?** List the people (or causes) you want to benefit. Your spouse or children, maybe also a friend who supported you, a charity or a place that shaped you.

This simple list forms the skeleton of your estate plan. Your *inventory of intention*. You've already done 60% of the work.

There is a hidden shortcut to estate planning. **Naming your beneficiaries.** One of the easiest and most overlooked estate-planning tools that doesn't require a lawyer at all. You can name beneficiaries directly on many of your accounts like bank accounts, retirement funds and insurance policies; and those assets pass automatically, outside of probate.

They're called **"Payable on Death"** (**POD**) or **"Transfer on Death"** (**TOD**) designations and they're powerful. A single signature (or online form submission) can ensure that your savings go directly to the people you choose, without any court delay. This small step often prevents the biggest headaches. I once worked with a family where the father had done nothing more than update his 401(k) and life insurance beneficiaries every few years. When he passed, those assets transferred seamlessly with no legal fees, no probate, no stress.

If you do only one thing after reading this chapter, make it this: review and update your beneficiaries. It's a five-minute act with decades of impact.

To start, prefer clarity over complexity. Begin by writing a simple Will. Once you've listed your assets and beneficiaries, it's time to put your intentions into writing. You don't need thick binders or fancy language. A **Simple Will**, typed, printed, signed and witnessed according to your state's requirements, is legally valid in most cases. Several reputable online platforms now offer guided templates for a small fee. They walk you through each question in plain English and generate a compliant document for your state.

Start with what's true today. You can always update it later. In fact, you *should* update it every few years or after major life events (a new house, child or marriage). A "good enough" will now is infinitely better than a perfect one that never gets written.

If your situation is straightforward; think one family, one home and typical assets; these templates are often sufficient. But if you have a business, blended family or property in multiple countries, it's worth getting professional advice to structure things properly. Important part being, **start**.

And in today's online world, one of the newest frontiers in estate planning is the **digital vault**. Secure online services where you can store important documents, passwords and instructions for your loved ones. Imagine a place where your family can find everything they'll need: your will, insurance details, bank info, even the code to your safe. Many digital vaults also allow you to upload personal letters, photos and videos so that your voice is preserved in the cloud. It's part legal tool, part love letter.

For many, that digital space becomes an emotional bridge. Your family doesn't just receive assets but also receive your words, your guidance and your presence in a moment when they need it most.

The Value of Professional Guidance

Of course, professional help is invaluable. Hiring an estate lawyer can save relationships later. They help you navigate the complex legal web in accordance with your state and country laws to make sure that your every wish has a home. If you own multiple properties, have a family business or anticipate any potential disputes, hiring an estate lawyer can also save time and money. Think of it like tax filing: if your finances are simple, online tools work great. If they're complex, a professional makes sure you don't miss something critical.

When you do hire a lawyer, don't approach it with intimidation. Treat it as collaboration. You bring your story; they bring structure. You don't need to understand every clause, just make sure to share every wish.

There's a quiet illusion that estate planning can wait until you're older or wealthier. But every year, I see families blindsided because they assumed they had more time. Not because they were unloving. Your plan doesn't need to be complicated to be effective. A handwritten letter, a named beneficiary or a notarized will can spare your family enormous pain. I often tell clients: start small, start today and start with love. You can always refine later. The first version doesn't need to be perfect; it just needs to exist.

Estate planning isn't an event you check off; it's a story you edit as life unfolds. It's less about control and more about care in a tangible form of love written in ink and intention. You don't have to wait for the "right" moment or "right" income level to begin. Start with one document, one signature, one small act of clarity. Because the most important part of protecting your legacy is simply *starting*.

Reflection Pause

☐ Have you listed your assets and named who should receive them, even informally?

☐ Do your accounts and policies have up-to-date beneficiaries?

☐ If someone opened your laptop tomorrow, could they find what they'd need to take care of your affairs?

TALKING ABOUT IT WITHOUT TEARS

For most families, *mortality* is the hardest topic to discuss, not money. The idea of talking about wills or inheritance feels morbid, as if saying the words might somehow invite the event. So, we avoid it. We joke, deflect and say, "We'll figure it out later." But silence doesn't protect anyone. It only leaves them unprepared.

The truth is, conversations about legacy are not about death. They're about *love, respect and continuity*. They're about making sure that the people you care about can live with clarity and confidence when you're not around to guide them. When done right, these conversations don't bring tears but relief.

I once met a couple, *Michael* and *Elena*, who decided to host what they called a "Legacy Dinner." Their children were in their twenties. Busy, independent and at that age where anything serious from parents feels like a lecture. They didn't make it one. They ordered pizza, opened a bottle of wine and said simply, "We want to talk about what we've set up, so no one's ever left guessing.". They explained where the will was kept, who the executor was and how each of their children would receive a share of the estate. They talked about smaller things too like the charity they'd support, who would keep the family dog if something happened and even what songs they'd want played at their memorials.

There were moments of laughter and a few quiet pauses, but by the end of the evening, the kids felt grateful. They saw it as *thoughtful*.

Michael recollected, "I thought it would be awkward. Instead, it felt like we'd lifted a silent weight off everyone's shoulders."

Compare that with another story, one I often call "Weight of the Unspoken" and seen too often. A parent passes away, leaving behind no written instructions, only vague conversations and assumptions. The children, each grieving in their own way, interpret those memories differently. "They wanted me to keep the house." "No, they said they wanted to sell it and split the money." Soon, the arguments aren't even about money, they're about *memory*. Each person is trying to honor what they believe their parent wanted and because no one can confirm it, everyone ends up hurt. It's a reminder that silence often causes more pain than any difficult conversation ever could.

How to Begin the Conversation

You don't need a grand announcement. Start small, start gently. You might say something like: "I've been organizing our finances lately, and I realized I want to make sure everything's clear for you, just in case."

Or, "We're doing our will this month. It's not about expecting anything to happen, it's just about keeping things simple and transparent."

By framing it around practicality and love, you take away the sting. You're not talking about endings; you're talking about continuity. If the topic feels too heavy for a family setting, start with one person and share your intention; could be your spouse, sibling or a close friend. Once you say it out loud, the rest becomes easier.

A powerful estate plan doesn't only distribute wealth; it also carries emotion, values and guidance. That's where something called a **"legacy letter"** or **"ethical will"** comes in. Unlike a legal will, a legacy letter isn't about who gets what. It's about what you've learned, loved and want remembered. It might include stories from your childhood or lessons about mistakes you made and what they taught you. Words of encouragement for your children or grandchildren and the hopes you have for your family's future could also very well be part of the letter. Some people record videos or voice notes, leaving a message their loved ones can replay in moments of doubt or nostalgia. These personal touches turn estate planning into something profoundly human. Your family won't just inherit *assets* also inherit *you*.

Every family also has its delicate corners and sensitive situations. Maybe you're planning to leave unequal shares or maybe you're supporting a child with special needs, or leaving a portion to charity. These can be emotional topics, but honesty, handled gently, always beats surprise. The key is transparency without drama. Instead of saying, "I'm giving more to your brother," you might explain, "Your brother will inherit a bit more because he'll have ongoing medical costs. It's not about fairness, it's about care."

When people understand your reasoning, they may not always agree, but they'll respect the thought behind it. And even if you're unsure how to bring it up, remember that estate planning doesn't start and end with the legal documents. Sometimes, a single heartfelt conversation can prevent years of misunderstanding later.

Talking openly about your plans also teaches your children or younger family members what responsible planning looks like. They see you handling life with foresight and grace and they're more likely to do the same. One of the greatest gifts you can give isn't the money you leave behind, but the example you set of *how* to handle it.

Death ends a life but not a relationship. Conversations like these keep your connection alive long after you're gone. Estate planning is about peace as much as about wealth. It's not about who gets what but about ensuring the people you love never have to wonder what you wanted. When you replace silence with clarity and fear with honesty, you give your family something far more valuable than inheritance: you give them *understanding*.

When the next generation views estate planning not as a morbid task, but as a natural expression of care, you've changed the family culture for good.

The Gift of Clarity

Most of us spend our whole lives building homes, careers, memories and meaning. Yet few of us take the time to decide what happens to all of it when we're gone. We buy insurance to protect what we have, investments to grow what we earn and retirement accounts to secure our future. But there's one final act of stewardship that's often overlooked: protecting what we *leave behind.*

Estate planning isn't about anticipating death; it's about *extending love beyond it.* It's how you say, "I've taken care of you, even for the days when I can't be here."

A well-written will or trust doesn't make headlines. There's no applause, no visible reward. But when it matters most, it's the single act that holds a family together. **The Quietest, Most Powerful Gift.** It ensures that your spouse isn't buried under confusion, that your children don't have to fight over decisions and that the things you worked for continue to bring comfort rather than conflict. It's a deeply personal act of love, written not in emotion but in foresight.

In a world obsessed with accumulation, it's easy to forget that *true wealth isn't just what we build but also what we pass on with peace.* Many people delay writing a will because they think they need to have everything figured out. But a will, like life itself, is a work in progress. You can always update it. The most important thing is to start. A simple, clear plan beats a sophisticated one that never gets written.

It's okay if your first draft feels incomplete. That's what revisiting it every few years is for. You don't need to plan forever. You just need to plan *enough*. Because clarity, even partial clarity, is a gift.

Legacy is about the money you leave AND meaning that money carries. It's about memories, lessons and love that continue to ripple through generations. A will or trust doesn't freeze your story; it keeps it flowing in the right direction. It's a continuation, not farewell. Because the truth is, when you plan well, you don't just leave things behind. You leave *peace*.

Peace Test

Close your eyes for a moment and imagine this: if something happened tomorrow, would your family know where to find everything? Would they know what to do, who to call, how to move forward?
If your answer brings calm, you're in good shape. If it brings anxiety, that's your cue. Start with one step this week. Clarity is not built in a day. It's built one decision at a time. And the moment you take that first step, you've already given your family the most valuable gifts of all:
Peace in a time of pain and direction in a time of doubt.

Worksheet – My Legacy Starter Kit

Use this or similar worksheet to begin your legacy planning in a calm, structured way. You don't need to fill it all at once, just start. Each small step today saves loved one's hours of uncertainty later.

Step 1: My Key People

Role	Name & Contact	Notes
Executor / Trustee		
Financial Power of Attorney		
Medical Power of Attorney		
Guardian for Minor Children		
Alternate / Backup Person		

Step 2: My Important Assets

Asset Type	Location / Institution	~Value / Account #	Beneficiary (if appl.)
Home / Property			
Bank Accounts			
Investments (Stocks, Funds, Crypto)			
Retirement Accounts (401k, IRA, Pension)			
Life Insurance Policy			
Vehicles			
Other Assets (Art, Collectibles, Business, etc.)			

Step 3: My Wishes and Instructions

Area	My Preference / Notes
Distribution of Assets	
Charitable Giving	
Care of Pets / Dependents	
Funeral / Memorial Preferences	
Personal Letters / Legacy Notes	

Step 4: My Digital Life

DO NOT WRITE DOWN ANY PASSWORDS OR PRIVATE KEYS HERE.

Account / Platform	Stored Where?	Who Has Access?
Email / Cloud Accounts		
Password Manager		
Social media		
Digital Vault / Document Storage		
Cryptocurrency / Digital Assets		

Step 5: My Legacy Notes

Jot down messages or reflections for your loved ones, the things you'd want them to remember most. *(If you don't feel like it, you can expand this into a full legacy letter later. Just start with points)*

- What lessons shaped my life?
- What advice would I give to my children or younger self?
- What values do I hope continue through our family?

Step 6: My Next Actions

Action Item	Due Date	Done?
List all my assets and passwords		
Add / Update beneficiaries on accounts		
Draft my first will or use an online template		
Schedule a review with an estate lawyer (if needed)		
Store documents safely / share location with executor		

Part 4: Beyond the Basics

"A ship in harbor is safe, but that's not what ships are built for
and a solid foundation isn't built just to keep you at the dock."
— *Adapted from John A. Shedd*

11

Cryptos, Collectibles and Cool Alternatives - The Shiny Side of Wealth

It started with a notification. "Bitcoin hits $60,000!"

Brian stared at the screen, heart racing. He'd first heard of Bitcoin back when it was a few hundred dollars but dismissed it as "digital Monopoly money." Now, he did the math. If he'd invested $1,000 back then, he'd have more than half a million dollars. The thought made him dizzy.

That night, he opened a crypto exchange account, watched a few YouTube videos and decided he wasn't going to miss *this* wave. Within a week, he'd put in $5,000. Not a huge sum, but enough to feel the thrill. For a while, everything went up. His portfolio doubled in two months. He told his friends they were crazy not to invest. He even started calculating how soon he could buy a Tesla with his gains.

Then, as quickly as it rose, the market crashed. Bitcoin dropped by 50%. Then 60%. Then 70%. Brian kept refreshing the app, watching his profits vanish. The same channels that had cheered him on now spoke of panic and "crypto winters". He hadn't just lost money but also his *confidence*. What hurt more wasn't the loss itself, but the realization that he hadn't really understood what he'd bought.

The Gold Rush Mindset is a "real" thing. Every generation has its gold rush. For our grandparents, it might've been land. For our parents, stocks or mutual funds. For us, it's Bitcoin, NFTs, startups, collectibles and the dream of being "early" to something the world will one day worship.

There's something intoxicating about the idea of spotting the next big thing before everyone else. It scratches two human itches at once: *curiosity* and *ego*. We tell ourselves it's about opportunity.

But often, it's about emotion. That surge of dopamine when the chart spikes upward, that private little thrill of being "in the know". The danger isn't in curiosity; it's in the chase. Because shiny things in finance are like fireworks; dazzling when they light up but quick to fade and dangerous if you hold them too long.

So, why do we chase the new? We live in a time where innovation feels like acceleration. Every few months, a new buzzword arrives. Crypto, Web3, metaverse, AI coins, digital art, fractional investing. Each promises revolution. And some of them *are* revolutionary. But there's a repeatable pattern here. Earlier you are, wilder the ride.

Most people don't enter these markets as pioneers; they join as spectators who show up after the party has already begun. They see others celebrating their gains and assume they're late to the next inevitable fortune. What they don't see is that early success stories rarely tell the whole story which includes sleepless nights, research, conviction and sometimes just luck.

In finance, everyone remembers the person who turned $1,000 into $100,000. No one remembers the thousand who quietly lost $900 along the way.

The Paradox of "Cool Money"

There's a fascinating paradox in modern wealth: more "modern" the opportunity, older the emotion behind it. Tulip mania of 1600s, railway boom of 1800s, dot-com bubble of 1990s. Every century has its version of people believing "this time, it's different".

And in some ways, it is different. Bitcoin's technology is groundbreaking. NFTs have changed how digital ownership works. Collectibles have become global investments through online platforms.

Part of the charm of alternative investments is the story they carry, or **Allure of the Unknown**. Stocks and bonds feel dull; Bitcoin feels futuristic. A mutual fund statement won't start a dinner conversation but a piece of digital art that sold for millions will. That allure of "cool" can make even most disciplined saver feel like they're missing out. The headlines scream of overnight millionaires. Social media celebrates "next big thing". Insta 10-second reels will make you believe you are too late.

The more rational part of our brain whispers *"Stay balanced"* but emotional part says *"What if this really is future?"*. And sometimes, it is. That's what makes it tricky. Same forces that make these innovations risky also make them transformative. Goal, then again, isn't to avoid them. It is to understand them before joining them.

Curiosity is good. It's how we learn, how we grow and how we adapt to changing times. Problem isn't curiosity here, it's impatience. Because **Curiosity Becomes Wisdom.**

A curious investor studies before buying. An impatient one buys before understanding. Curious investor asks, "What problem does this solve?" while impatient one asks, "How much can I make this month?". Brian's story isn't about greed; it's about timing and understanding. He wasn't wrong to explore Bitcoin; he was just too eager to skip the learning part.

And that's what this chapter is about. Understanding *why* behind the shiny things, so we can explore them with curiosity instead of chasing them with fear or FOMO. In the chapter ahead, we'll take a calm, plain-language look at the world of alternatives. Cryptocurrencies, NFTs, art, collectibles and even side hustles. We'll explore what makes them exciting, what makes them risky and how to enjoy their potential *without letting them derail your financial base.*

Because the goal isn't to avoid the shiny things, it's to keep them in their place. Because when you know the difference between *innovation* and *impulse*, you gain the rarest asset of all

Financial Peace in a Noisy World.

Reflection Pause

☐ Have you ever bought something, a stock, coin, collectible or even gadget, because everyone else seemed to?

☐ Did it make you feel smart, excited or anxious?

☐ What if the next "big thing" wasn't a product, but a mindset? Mindset with the ability to explore new ideas without losing your foundation.

Bitcoin and the New Meaning of Money

When Bitcoin first appeared in 2009, most people didn't take it seriously. It sounded like something out of a science-fiction forum. Digital coins mined by computers, owned by no government, created under a pseudonym and existing only on the internet. But underneath the jargon was a simple and radical idea:

What if we could build money that runs on math instead of middlemen?

To understand why Bitcoin matters, we need to revisit what money has always been - a story of trust.

In Chapter 1, we talked about how money began as barter, then evolved into shells, metal and paper. Each stage replacing trust between people with trust in something *bigger*: a government, a central bank, a collective promise. For centuries, we've accepted that when we hold a $10 bill, it's valuable not because of the paper but because the system behind it says so. That system of banks, treasuries and regulators is built and runs on faith.

Then came 2008.

The global financial crisis shattered that faith for many. Banks failed, bailouts multiplied and people realized that even guardians of money could stumble. Out of that disillusionment emerged a white paper from an anonymous figure named Satoshi Nakamoto, proposing Bitcoin - a *peer-to-peer electronic cash system* that wouldn't rely on any single authority. In essence, Bitcoin asked humanity a bold question: "Can we create trust without trusted institutions?"

The technology behind Bitcoin, called blockchain, is easier to grasp if you imagine it as a shared notebook. A notebook that everyone can read, verify and contribute to, but no one can *secretly* erase or alter.

Every time someone sends or receives Bitcoin, that transaction is recorded on this notebook and thousands of computers around the world check and agree that it's valid. Once written, it can't be undone. No single person or government owns the notebook. The rules are written in code and enforced by consensus. That's what gives Bitcoin its strange power. It replaces human trust with mathematical proof. It's as if, instead of trusting a bank clerk to update your account, you and a million others watched the ledger update together, instantly and transparently.

Digital Gold, Not Digital Cash

In its early days, people imagined Bitcoin would be used for everyday payments. Digital money for buying coffee or groceries. But its design; limited supply and slow transaction times; makes it more like digital gold than digital cash. Only 21 million Bitcoins can ever exist. That scarcity gives it an appeal similar to gold: it can't be printed, diluted or inflated away by policy. Investors see it as a hedge against currency devaluation, especially in countries where inflation erodes savings. Others view it as a long-term store of value in a digital age.

Still, calling it "gold" doesn't mean it's stable. Gold glitters steadily over centuries; Bitcoin dances to a drumbeat of volatility. Its price can double or halve in months, reminding everyone that the line between innovation and speculation is thin.

The promise of Bitcoin lies in freedom from borders, intermediaries and inflation. The peril lies in misunderstanding it as a get-rich-quick ticket rather than a long-term technology shift. It has democratized access to wealth creation for many but also opened doors to scams, lost passwords and dramatic booms and busts. Its energy consumption has sparked debates about sustainability, while its pseudonymous nature has raised questions about regulation. Bitcoin's greatest achievement so far may not be becoming world's main currency but in showing the world that *currencies evolve.*

If you step back, Bitcoin is less a rebellion and more a reflection; **a mirror to the System**; of sorts. It didn't appear because people hated money; it appeared because they wanted to rebuild trust in it. In that sense, Bitcoin is the next conversation in the same story. Gold anchored value in scarcity. Paper anchored it in institutions. Bitcoin anchors it in transparency and code.

Each stage asks the same human question: *How can we trust something we can't touch?* And whether Bitcoin becomes "future of money" or just a stepping-stone, it has already forced us to think harder about what money really means and who gets to define it.

So, why does this matter to You? You don't need to buy Bitcoin to benefit from its lessons. Its true value may lie in what it teaches about *ownership and control.* When you hold Bitcoin, you hold it directly; no bank, no account manager, no intermediary. That's liberating but also demanding. Lose your password and coins are gone forever. The responsibility is entirely yours. That mirrors a larger truth about modern finance: greater freedom always comes with greater responsibility.

Bitcoin isn't a guarantee of wealth; it's an invitation to understand. It is still young and unpredictable; just like every form of money that came before it. It may or may not replace currencies, but it has already changed conversations about trust, transparency and power of collective agreement. In the end, Bitcoin isn't just a new kind of money. It's a reminder that money itself is an evolving story. One that, like humanity, keeps finding new ways to express faith.

Reflection Pause

☐ What do you trust more? The code, institutions or people?

☐ If money is ultimately about shared belief, what does Bitcoin tell us about the future of belief itself?

☐ Would you feel freer holding your own keys or safer letting someone else guard them?

NFTs, Art and World of Digital Ownership

In March 2021, a digital artwork sold for $69 million. It wasn't a sculpture, painting or photograph. It was a collage of 5,000 digital images stitched together by an artist known as Beeple, sold through a technology most people had barely heard of: an NFT.

For months, world was stunned. How could something you couldn't even touch cost more than a mansion? Answer AND confusion, both lie in how our idea of ownership is evolving.

Ownership has always meant control. If you own a house, your name's on the deed. If you own a car, you hold the title. If you own a painting, it hangs on your wall. But what does it mean to "own" something that lives entirely online? A song, a meme, a virtual sneaker or a piece of art that anyone can screenshot? That's where **NFTs or *non-fungible tokens***, come in.

Explained simply, think of an NFT as a **digital certificate of authenticity**. A way to prove that your version of something is *the* original, even in a world full of copies. Each NFT is recorded on a blockchain, same kind of public ledger that powers Bitcoin, which means it's traceable, verifiable and tamper-proof.

Let's say an artist uploads a digital painting and "mints" it as an NFT. That process creates a unique token linked to that artwork. Think of it as a signature etched into internet forever. Anyone can view the image, but only the token holder owns the *authentic* version. It's like having Mona Lisa in your living room while rest of the world hangs posters of it.

So, what problem is it solving? **It empowers Creators**. How? For decades, artists struggled with middlemen like galleries, publishers and agents, who took large cuts and controlled distribution. NFTs flipped that model. Suddenly, a musician could sell a song directly to fans, a digital artist could sell to collectors worldwide and even writers or game designers could earn royalties *every time* their work resold. Imagine Picasso earning a small share every time his paintings changed hands. That's what blockchain allows: automatic, programmable royalties. For many creators, this isn't just innovation; it is liberation. They could finally earn what their work was worth, directly from those who valued it most.

But like every revolution, NFT world came with noise; that too plenty of it. Soon, everyone from celebrities to corporations jumped in. Profile pictures of cartoon apes sold for hundreds of thousands of dollars. Speculators flooded the market, flipping NFTs like trading cards. For a while, it felt like digital Wild West. Fortunes made and lost overnight. And then came the crash. Market cooled, hype faded and most of those speculative tokens became digital ghosts: unsold, untraded or forgotten.

But the technology and idea didn't die. Because beneath the frenzy is a new way to define and transfer ownership in digital world.

Ownership in the Physical World: Collectibles and Meaning

If NFTs made headlines for digital art, collectibles have told a quieter version of the same story for centuries. A first-edition comic book, a vintage watch or a rare baseball card have their value in meaning and scarcity more than utility.

When someone buys an old coin, they're not buying metal. They buy history. When someone invests in art, they're not buying paint but emotion. It's the same reason collectors of all kinds - from vinyl records to collectible limited-edition plates - treat their possessions like portals to time, memory or craftsmanship.

The difference is, NFTs made that same emotional exchange digital and global. You no longer need a gallery or vault to own something valuable. You can hold it on your phone.

The challenge and beauty of both, art and NFTs is their worth can't be calculated the way you calculate stock returns. They blend emotion and economics in a way that logic alone can't measure. Or Art meets Finance.

A painting that moves you might not rise in price. A pixel that goes viral might. Both are valid in their own worlds. That's why investing in collectibles, digital or physical, requires a different mindset. You don't just ask, *"What will this be worth?"*; you ask, *"Why does this matter?"*

When meaning drives value, the reward is financial and emotional. And NFTs were just the first step. The same technology could soon be used for:
- Property titles: Proof of home ownership stored on blockchain.
- Event tickets: Verified and resale-proof.
- Digital identity: A secure passport for online life.
- Fractional art investing: Owning 1% of a masterpiece.

Imagine a world where you can own part of a Monet or a piece of real estate in another country with a few clicks. The implications go far beyond collectibles. They touch how we define trust, trade and proof itself.

So, we now come to what I refer to as **The Collector's Balance**. Whether it's NFTs or fine art, rule is the same: curiosity is good but foundation comes first. You build your base with savings and investments; you explore the shiny side with care and proportion. Think of your financial life as a gallery with 90% structure, 10% play. Your traditional assets keep the lights on; your collectibles add color to the walls. The goal isn't to avoid beauty or novelty but to enjoy them *without betting the house on them.*

NFTs and collectibles remind us that money isn't just math but also emotion, story and identity. Whether you collect rare art or digital tokens, what you're really collecting is a piece of the world that speaks to you. The key is not to silence that voice but rather it in harmony with your financial foundation. Because ...

the goal of wealth isn't just to own things of value but also to value the things you own

---

Reflection Pause

☐ What kind of "art" or collectible do you connect with emotionally? Music, visuals, design or storytelling?

☐ Would you still value it if no one else did?

☐ How much of your portfolio today reflects meaning versus momentum?

Side Hustles and Passion Projects

If cryptocurrencies and collectibles are shiny *assets* of new age, side hustles are its shiny *engines*. Unlike coins or art that you buy, a side hustle is something you *build*. It's an alternative investment where the main currency is YOU, not money.

A side hustle isn't just about earning extra cash (though that's always nice). It's about *diversifying your identity*. When your only income stream comes from your job, your financial stability depends entirely on your employer's decisions. But when you have something of your own, however small, you start shifting from employee to entrepreneur, from dependent to independent. That small online shop, blog or weekend gig might not make you rich, but it gives you something priceless: confidence.

And confidence, in personal finance, compounds faster than interest.

Not every side hustle needs to be wildly profitable. Some are worthwhile simply because they blend joy and learning. A friend of mine, Andy, loved baking. On weekends, he'd experiment with recipes, post photos online and sell cupcakes to neighbors. He didn't quit his job but just turned his hobby into a mini business that earned enough to fund his family vacations each year.

His return wasn't just financial; it was emotional. It gave him energy, community and purpose beyond his 9-to-5. And that's the essence of what I call **Return on Enjoyment (RoE);** measure of satisfaction per dollar or hour spent. A side hustle with a high RoE feeds your creativity even if it doesn't pay your bills (yet). And sometimes, that passion plants seed for something much bigger later.

The Shift from Ownership to Creation
In earlier generations, wealth came from possessions. Could be land, gold or shares in a company. Today, a growing number of people are realizing that wealth can also come from what you create:
- *A YouTube channel that earns through ads.*
- *A small Etsy shop selling handmade crafts.*
- *A newsletter, a podcast or a photography business.*
- *Consulting, coaching or teaching skills you already have.*

The internet has made it possible for anyone with a laptop and curiosity to create something real; something that grows, even while you sleep. It's not about quitting your job tomorrow. It's about unlocking optionality and freedom to shape income around what you enjoy.

We live in a world where one income stream feels increasingly fragile. Layoffs, recessions, automation, artificial intelligence continually remind us that job security isn't guaranteed. But *skill security* is.

A healthy financial life today often includes multiple "mini portfolios":
- **A main job** for stability.
- **Investments** for growth.
- **A side hustle** for autonomy.

Each serves a different purpose. One pays bills, one builds wealth and one builds identity. It's the third one, side hustle, that often sparks most joy because it's chosen, not imposed.

It is often good to remember that not every passion is a business. And not every business should come from passion. The sweet spot lies where the two overlap. Ask yourself:

1. What do I love doing enough to do for free?
2. What do people already ask me for help with?
3. What could I teach or offer that creates value for someone else?

When your answers to all three intersect, you've found something powerful - a hobby with market potential. Or the Japanese secret to a joyful life a.k.a. **ikigai; concept meaning "a reason for being".**

It could be photography, tutoring, digital art, language coaching, travel planning or even writing a book on personal finance (ahem). The key is small, consistent steps. You don't need a business plan, just proof that someone values what you offer.

Of course, side hustles have their dark side too. Social media glorifies "hustle culture" or idea that if you're not monetizing every waking hour, you're wasting time. Reels about social media millionaires in a year, selling courses *in the link below*.

That's nonsense, with a capital N. A true side hustle adds to your life; it doesn't consume it. It should energize, not exhaust. It should feel like *creating something that reflects you*, not *escaping from something that drains you*. The goal isn't to work 18 hours a day. It's to build a few hours a week of creative ownership. A stark reminder that your worth isn't defined solely by a paycheck.

The beauty of side hustles is that they can evolve into long-term assets, digital or otherwise. A blog becomes a brand. A skill-sharing workshop turns to an online course. A handmade craft store becomes a small e-commerce business. A podcast turns into a revenue stream.

And even if none of those happen, skills you build around marketing, sales, storytelling, customer empathy make you more valuable in your main career. That's why I tell clients: a side hustle is never wasted effort. Even if returns aren't financial yet, they're *educational equity*.

Side hustles remind us that financial independence isn't just about having money but also about *creating value on your own terms*. When your skills earn for you, your confidence grows. When your passions sustain you, your life expands.

And when you combine both, your money starts working for you and *you* start working for yourself. Because at the end of the day, freedom doesn't begin when you stop working. It begins when you start *choosing* what to work on.

Reflection Pause

- ☐ If you had five free hours a week, what would you love to build, share or teach?
- ☐ Would you still enjoy it if it earned nothing at first?
- ☐ What's one small idea that keeps resurfacing and you keep pushing aside because "now's not the time"?

Keeping the Shiny Things in Their Place

Shiny things are exciting because they speak to possibility. Bitcoin promises a new kind of money. NFTs promise a new kind of ownership. Side hustles promise a new kind of freedom. Each one carries a spark and sparks are wonderful, as long as they land on stone, not dry grass.

What we're really guarding against here isn't asset itself. It's **spillover** or the moment curiosity overruns the foundation you built. The solution isn't avoidance; it's **proportion**. You make room for new ideas without letting them crowd out essentials.

Think of your finances like a well-designed home. You have structural walls (emergency fund, core investments, insurance), living spaces (goals you use and enjoy) and accent lighting (alternatives that add interest and character). Lighting matters because it sets the mood. But you never swap a load-bearing wall for a chandelier.

The Calm Portfolio: Core, Explore and Play

A helpful way is to place shiny things is a three-bucket view:
- ***Core (70-80%)** – The boring heroes: cash reserves, stock/bond funds, retirement accounts. This is the part that lets you sleep.*
- ***Explore (10-20%)** – Thoughtful alternatives: Bitcoin or top cryptos you understand, a few pieces of art or collectibles with provenance, a small angel bet or a modest stake in a side venture.*
- ***Play (0-10%)** – Permission to experiment: the sandbox for ideas that are fun, speculative or unproven. If it goes to zero, your life doesn't change.*

This isn't a rule as much as a rhythm. Some years you'll dial Explore down. In seasons of abundance, you might nudge it up. The point is intent, not perfection.

Follow the pre-flight checklist for any shiny thing before money leaves your account. Ask these four quiet questions:
1. **Can I explain it simply?** If you can't describe how it works and how you could lose money in five sentences; you don't own an asset; you're holding a mystery.
2. **What's my maximum pain?** Set a loss limit before you buy (dollar or %). If it hits that line, you step away. Curiosity doesn't require captivity.
3. **Where does this live?** With crypto: which exchange, which wallet, which backup? With collectibles: where stored, insured and documented? With a side hustle: where does time come from and what stops it from consuming weekends?
4. **What's the exit?** Price target, timeframe or milestone. "I'll just see what happens" is not a plan; it's a weather report.

Write the answers down. Your future self will thank you when emotions get loud.

Here are some ready guardrails for Crypto, Collectibles and Side Hustles but principles may apply to other *shiny objects* in your life or the near future

Crypto Guardrails - Freedom with Responsibility

Remember that crypto is ownership without a help desk. It's liberating and unforgiving. Keep the freedom while adding the guardrails.

- **Custody:** Start on a reputable exchange, then learn self-custody slowly. If you move to a hardware wallet, practice small first, back up your seed phrase offline and tell a trusted person how to access it if needed.
- **Concentration:** Avoid turning Explore into All-In. If price moves tempt you to "average up" endlessly, cap your total crypto allocation in advance and honor it.
- **Noise diet:** Price feeds FOMO. Purpose feeds patience. Check your thesis more than your app.

Remember: volatility is the toll you pay to cross the crypto bridge. Only cross with luggage you can afford to carry back.

Collectibles Guardrails - Story, Scarcity and Proof:

Collectibles blend heart and numbers. Honor both.

- **Provenance over popularity:** Documentation, signatures, certificates, condition reports. A quiet, well-documented piece often beats a trendy one with echoes for paperwork.
- **Liquidity lens:** Ask, "How would I sell this?" Know the likely venue (auction house, specialist marketplace, dealer) and typical fees. Slow markets aren't flaws; they're features needing cash flow planned around them.
- **Preservation plan:** Proper storage, climate considerations and insurance riders where needed. Cost to care is part of price to own.

If you'd love the piece even if it never appreciated, you're buying art. If you'd hate it without a price chart, you're buying a headline.

Guardrails for Side Hustles: Build, Don't Burn

Side hustles expand identity until they shrink your life.

- **Time budget:** Assign a fixed weekly slot (e.g., 4-6 hours). If demand grows, expand <u>after</u> three consistent months. Not after one hot weekend.
- **Profit clarity:** Track simple P&L: revenue, direct costs, tools/ads and your time value. A joyful break-even can be perfect; a "profitable" grind may not be.
- **Seasonal sprints:** Work in projects, not forever-marathons. Launch a 4-week test, review, rest, then choose whether to continue. Momentum likes intervals.

The goal isn't more hustle. It's more agency. You're not escaping your life; you're shaping it.

The Antidote to FOMO: A Personal Policy

Write a one-page <u>Investment Policy for Alternatives</u> in human language and zero jargon. Include:
- **My why:** Curiosity, learning, access to potential upside, joy of collecting, creative outlet.
- **My caps:** Explore = __%, Play = __%, single-bet limit = __%.
- **My process:** Research steps, cooling-off period (e.g., wait 48 hours before any new buy), and a second opinion rule ("run it by X").
- **My red flags:** Debt-funded bets, anonymous promoters, guaranteed returns, complex things I can't explain, purchases fueled by envy or urgency.

Policies turn willpower into autopilot. You don't need to be stronger tomorrow if you're clearer today.

Money has seasons and so do we. In some seasons, you'll crave novelty. In others, you'll seek calm. It's okay to shift emphasis without betraying your plan. Pause buys during stressful life events. Increase cash when you feel stretched. Take a curiosity sabbatical if the noise gets loud. Discipline is not rigidity but responsive consistency.

Shiny things aren't the enemy of a good plan but more like its accent color. When your foundation is sturdy, the edges become a playground rather than a cliff. You say yes with joy and no without fear. You try, learn, adjust and keep your balance.

Remember that the real flex isn't owning every new thing. It's owning your framework along with quiet confidence that lets you participate in future without mortgaging your present. You don't have to choose between safety and curiosity. You get both in their rightful place.

Reflection Pause

- ☐ If your Explore and Play buckets vanished tomorrow, would your Core still carry your life with calm?
- ☐ Which guardrail (custody, provenance, time budget, policy) do you need most right now?
- ☐ Are you exploring from strength or trying to repair boredom with risk?

Curious, Not Captive

If core of personal finance is steadiness, edges are where curiosity lives. Bitcoin challenged what money means. NFTs asked whether ownership can exist without touch. Side hustles reminded us that wealth isn't only what you hold but also what you create. Each one is a doorway. Walk through with awareness and you'll find learning, joy and sometimes outsized returns. Rush through and you'll find noise, hype and sleepless nights.

The trick is not to mute curiosity but to give it boundaries. You've already built the boring, beautiful parts with an emergency fund, broad-market investments, real-estate, insurance and estate plans. Those are your load-bearing walls. Alternatives are the accent lights. They add mood, color and character but don't hold up the house.

You've also seen the pattern now: every era has a gold rush. Tulips, railways, dot-coms, crypto seasons. All different Halloween costumes with the same human heartbeat underneath. Our job isn't to predict every cycle. It's to stay principled through them. Principles like:

- *never risk what you need for what you want;*
- *only buy what you understand;*
- *set your exit before your entry;*
- *document where things live; and*
- *let time, not Insta, set your pace.*

When you explore from strength, you're not gambling. You're learning in public with training wheels on. A capped allocation means a mistake is a lesson, not a life event. A written policy turns "maybe" into "measured." And a simple habit like pausing 48 hours before any exciting buy, can save you from a hundred tiny regrets.

This chapter isn't an invitation to avoid the shiny things. It's permission to enjoy them without becoming owned by them. Curiosity is fuel; caution is the seatbelt. Worn together, they take you farther. **Own your framework** in a calm, written way to say yes to the future without mortgaging present. Keep core sturdy, edges playful and let curiosity make you wiser, not busier.

Peace Test

Close your eyes. Imagine your Explore bets flat for a year. Did you still sleep well, still invest in Core, still enjoy your life? If yes, you're exploring from strength. If no, shrink the sandbox until calm returns.

Worksheet – My Alternative Playbook

Use this worksheet to keep your shiny side shiny (and small). *Fill it out once, revisit yearly.*

1) My Why (two sentences, human words)

• Why I'm exploring alternatives (learning, asymmetric upside, supporting creators, joy, income variety):

____

• What "success" looks like (calm + consistency, not just profit):

____

2) Due Diligence Checklist (initial box before any purchase)

☐ I can explain in five sentences, including how I could lose money.

☐ I've read one bull and one bear view.

☐ I've set a maximum position size (_% or $__).

☐ I've written an exit plan (price, thesis break or timebox).

☐ I'll wait 48 hours before confirming the buy.

☐ I know where it lives (wallet, vault) and how my family can find it.

☐ I can answer: "If this goes to zero, does my life change?"

3) Personal Policy for Alternatives (sign it)

My caps: Explore ____ %/$ | Play ____ %/$ | Single bet max ____ %/$

Red flags: debt-funded bets; anonymous promoters; guaranteed returns; "limited time"; can't explain; embarrassed to tell a friend.

Cooling-off rule: I wait _____ hours before any new buy.

Second opinion: I run ideas by _____________________ (person).

Review cadence: Yearly check-in date: __ / __ / __

4) Rebalance Ritual (10 minutes, once a quarter)

1. Check allocations vs caps.

2. Skim gains above target from Explore/Play back to Core.

3. Archive wins & lessons (one paragraph each).

4. Re-read your "Why." If it still feels true, proceed. If not, shrink exposure.

12

Financial Independence - Not Just for Millionaires

On a Tuesday that looked like any other, Denise's alarm went off and… nothing happened. Not because she had overslept and not because the battery died. She silenced it, rolled onto her back and stared at the ceiling fan she'd ignored for ten years of rushed mornings. It wasn't the fan that felt different. It was the *math*.

Two weeks earlier, she and her partner had finished a quiet ritual at the kitchen table: a net worth snapshot, a simple spending review, the annual "are we still on track?" check they jokingly called their "coffee board meeting." They never announced it on social media. They didn't frame it as a countdown to retirement. They were simply checking whether the life they wanted still aligned with the life they were living. That night, numbers whispered something they hadn't heard before.

If they kept spending roughly what they spent last year and if the portfolio did nothing heroic, they could cover an entire year of expenses without a paycheck. Not forever. Not a grand Exit. But a year. A year to test a new city. A year to work four days instead of five. A year to write the book she kept promising herself she'd start "when things calm down." Freedom didn't arrive with fireworks but as *options*.

So, on that random Tuesday, the alarm clock lost its authority. Denise still had a job she liked. Teams depended on her. Calendar still had boxes in it. But for the first time since she graduated, she didn't feel *summoned*. She felt invited. She got up, made coffee and watched the light move across the counter like she had time to notice it.

She wasn't a millionaire. She wasn't "done." She and her partner had simply spent five years widening the gap between what came in and what flowed out, then letting the difference compound. They called it their **cup-of-coffee plan** because the rules fit on a napkin:

- One cup to talk about the month - what felt good, what felt wasteful, what could be lighter next time.
- One cup to nudge the system - bump the 401(k) by 1%, automate a small transfer to a brokerage account, adjust the grocery budget back to reality.
- One cup to daydream - if we had one extra day each week, what would we do with it?

It wasn't glamorous. Rather, it was simple and stubborn. When raises came, they split them: half for life, half for freedom. When their friends upgraded to bigger everything, they upgraded selectively. They still traveled, but with a plan instead of a tab. They still ate out, but not because the fridge was a stranger. Little by little, monthly costs that didn't add joy were shaved down and money that added joy was funded first.

Financial independence didn't crash into their lives like a lottery ticket. It seeped in through routines. It looked like a fully funded emergency cushion. It sounded like "no" was allowed when work asked for more weekends. It felt like knowing they could pause, not because the world told them to but because they decided to.

That Tuesday, Denise opened her laptop and wrote an email she'd been editing in her head for months. She didn't quit. She asked for a pilot: four nine-hour days, same output, one quieter day for deep work and the writing project she wanted to test. Her manager surprised her by saying yes. "Try it for a quarter. Show me it works." The freedom wasn't the schedule; it was the confidence to ask without fear because the math softened the risk.

At lunch, she walked to a café with a notebook. She priced a perfect Tuesday. Not an Instagram-perfect day but *her* day. A long walk. A few hours of focused writing. A call with her parents without multitasking. Dinner at home because she liked cooking when she wasn't rushing. It didn't require a yacht. It required fewer auto-renewed expenses, mindless upgrades and more deliberate "yeses."

Across town, another version of Tuesday was playing out. Same profession, bigger title, bigger salary. Alex earned more than Denise but every raise had gone straight into life with a nicer lease, nicer car, nicer food and nicer everything. The numbers looked glamorous on paper and tight in practice. When the company hinted at a reorg, Alex felt stuck. It wasn't about pride. It was math again, monthly math that required everything to keep moving at full speed.

Neither person was right or wrong. They were simply living the consequences of different equations.

That's the quiet truth of **Financial Independence**: it isn't a number on a screen; it's the feeling that tomorrow is negotiable. For some, that will eventually mean work becomes optional. Investments and cash flows cover a simple, satisfying life and a job becomes something you choose for meaning, not money. For many, especially in early or middle chapters, FI shows up as a ladder of small freedoms: a six-month cushion, a paid-off car, a flexible role, a part-time year after a stressful stretch, courage to switch industries without fear of the first paycheck gap.

We've all been sold the idea that freedom arrives only after **big**. Big exits, big balances, big declarations. The cup-of-coffee plan says freedom arrives after **small**. Small gaps, small trims, small systems, repeated until your days bend toward the life you meant to live.

That evening, Denise and her partner sat back at the kitchen table. No champagne. Just tea. They wrote three sentences on a sticky note:
1. **Perfect Tuesday costs:** $X per year.
2. **FI number (today):** 25 × that annual spend.
3. **This quarter's nudge:** +1% to savings, +1 hour to the weekly writing block, +1 conversation we've been avoiding.

They stuck the note on the inside of a cabinet door. Every time they reached for coffee beans, they reached for their future too.

Over the next months, not much changed on the outside. They still showed up at work. They still laughed with friends. They still had days that went sideways. But underneath, something fundamental had shifted: the alarm clock was no longer a command. It was a choice. And choice, more than any headline or market chart, is what financial independence feels like early on.

You don't have to be a millionaire to find that feeling. You have to be a designer of spending that reflects your values, of income that slowly widens and of investments that quietly carry the difference. One cup of coffee at a time.

Reflection Pause

- ☐ If you didn't need your next paycheck to keep the lights on for six months, what would you ask for at work this quarter?
- ☐ What does your perfect Tuesday actually cost and which two expenses in your week don't earn their keep?
- ☐ What is your next +1% nudge (to savings, to income or to time) that would move freedom from "someday" to "sooner"?

FIRE, Decoded (Plain-English, No Hype)

Financial Independence, Retire Early a.k.a. *FIRE* sounds dramatic until you translate it into one sentence: **when the income from your savings and investments can comfortably cover your annual living costs, work becomes optional.** Optional doesn't mean you'll never work again. It means you can choose *why* you work and *what* you work on. It could be for joy, impact or variety. And not because the bills demand it. Underneath the numerous blog posts and acronyms is a surprisingly gentle equation:

$$\textit{Financial Independence Number} \approx 25 \times \textit{Annual Spending}$$

Why 25? It's a back-of-the-napkin way to reverse a 4% starting withdrawal rate. If your invested nest egg can support withdrawing about 4% in the first year (and then adjusting that dollar amount for inflation thereafter), you're in the neighborhood where the portfolio can historically support decades of spending. It's a rule of thumb, not a commandment. A place to start conversation, not to end it.

If your annual spending is $60,000, your rough FI number is $1.5 million (60,000 × 25). If it's $40,000, the target drops to $1 million. Notice what changed: not the market, not your salary, but your spending. That's the quiet power of FIRE thinking - lowering *permanent* expenses doesn't just help this month; it shrinks your lifetime target. Trim $100/month for good (the subscription you don't use, the second lease you don't need) and you've lowered your FI target by about $30,000 ($1,200 × 25). One small item, one big timeline shift.

But before we get lost in arithmetic, let's ground this in what FI isn't. FI isn't monastic minimalism. It isn't a race to a finish line where joy is suspended until a magical date. It isn't quitting in a blaze of glory and then counting pennies in fear. The healthiest version looks like life design: you build a calm base; add the work you enjoy and carry enough buffer to flex when markets or moods wobble.

Think of FIRE like a family of cousins, not a single template:

- **Lean FIRE.** You aim a simple lifestyle, low fixed costs and a very high savings rate. Tradeoff is less margin for surprise but a faster timeline. A person content with $30–40k/year (depending on location) hits FI on a much smaller number.

- **Regular (or "Baseline") FIRE.** A balanced, comfortable spend that reflects *enoughness* without bloat. Many households live here once housing and transport are right-sized.

- **Fat FIRE.** Higher spending with extra buffers for travel, dining, gifts and spontaneity. Target is larger, timeline longer but the lifestyle looks similar before and after FI.

- **Coast FI.** You save aggressively early, reach an invested base, which if left alone, is on track to fully fund retirement by itself. Then you "coast," lowering your savings rate (sometimes to zero) while you spend your 30s or 40s on career experiments, caregiving or more play.

- **Barista FI.** You cover most of your costs from investments and use part-time work to bridge the rest (often chosen for health insurance or social connection). Optionality without the all-or-nothing leap.

These flavors aren't ranks; they're strategies. The right one is the version you'll actually live with.

Now, about that famous 4%. It comes from research looking at historical portfolios and asking, "What withdrawal rate could a retiree have started with and not run out of money over 30+ years?" The nuance matters: your mix of stocks and bonds, your fees, taxes and the order of market returns all influence the answer. In strong decades, you could have taken more. In tough ones, less. That's why many modern planners use guardrails instead of a fixed dollar raise every year. For example, start around 4%, but if markets fall early, dial back spending to 3.5% for a year or two; if markets soar, let spending float up a bit. Small adjustments remove a lot of anxiety.

The piece that most people miss? *Income is not the north star; savings rate is.* Two households both earning $150,000 can have wildly different timelines. If one saves 15% and the other saves 40% (by right-sizing housing, cars and recurring lifestyle creep), the second household's FI date moves forward by *years*, not months. That's because a high savings rate does three things at once: it piles up capital faster, builds the muscle of living on less and lowers the target itself by cementing a calmer lifestyle.

FI Rungs – Bringing your "forever" to Now

You don't need to hold your breath until "forever." Most FI journeys unfold in **rungs**:
- *30 days of expenses in cash gives breathing room.*
- *3 - 6 months savings provides true stability.*
- *Coast point is when invested base can fund traditional retirement without new contributions.*
- *Work optionality is touched with enough savings that you can switch to part-time, take a sabbatical or change careers with minimal fear.*
- *Full FI is reached when your portfolio and passive flows cover your annual spend.*

Notice how work optionality arrives before "never work again." That's the part that changes the texture of your days quickly. It's also why FI is "not just for millionaires." Many people find that a modest buffer, a sane spending level and deliberate work choices create the lived feeling of independence years before a spreadsheet says "100%."

What accelerates the path? The three levers of Spend, Earn & Invest.

- **Spend:** Anchor the big three (housing, transport, food), then treat recurring fixed costs as the boss fight. Trimming here moves the date; trimming only lattes mostly moves your mood.
- **Earn:** Negotiate, skill-stack, switch teams when it makes sense and let side income be aligned income. Something you don't dread. Even a temporary 12–24 month "sprint" at a higher savings rate can pull FI dramatically closer.
- **Invest:** Keep it boring and broad. Automate contributions to low-cost, diversified funds. Place assets tax-smart and give yourself gift of time in the market instead of time *trying to outsmart* the market.

Along the way, <u>design for resilience</u>. Markets don't care about our plans; they care about their cycles. The risk that bites early retirees hardest is sequence of returns, bad markets right after you start withdrawing. Two defenses help: keep a cash buffer (6–24 months of spending, depending on comfort) and keep flexibility (willingness to trim spending or pick up enjoyable income for a season). A part-time role you like is not failure; it's engineering.

Healthcare, taxes and family obligations often feel like deal breakers until you replace fear with a plan. Marketplace insurance, HSAs, part-time roles with benefits and tax-diversified accounts (a mix of Traditional, Roth and taxable) give you multiple dials to turn. For mortgages, pay down or invest isn't a moral question but a math-plus-sleep question. If peace spikes when you prepay, measure that too.

Above all, **keep FI human**. The point isn't to win a spreadsheet; it's to shape a Tuesday you love and then multiply it. Some will choose Lean to arrive sooner; others will choose Fat to arrive familiar. Many will choose Coast or Barista to arrive *happier*. All are valid if they're chosen on purpose.

So yes, FIRE can be reduced to a neat equation. But the real engine is a weekly cup of coffee: check the gap between income and needs, nudge one habit and ask one joyful question: *If I had more freedom next quarter, what would I do with it?* Do that long enough and one day the alarm clock loses its edge not because money shouted "You're done," but because your life quietly answered, "I'm free to choose."

Reflection Pause

☐ Using today's spending, what's your FI number? How does it change if you permanently trim one fixed expense?

☐ Which FI flavor feels most *you* right now (Lean, Regular, Fat, Coast or Barista) and why? Or None?

☐ What single lever (spend, earn, invest) could you nudge +1% this quarter to move your FI date meaningfully sooner?

Designing the Life You Want; One Cup at a Time

Financial independence sounds like a finish line, but it's really an interior design project for your days. Before we talk numbers, we talk *shape*: what does a great Tuesday look like? Not the postcard version but rather the one that actually fits your personality, your relationships, your energy. FI works best when it's built from the inside out: design the day, price the day and then, fund the day.

Start with a pen and 20 quiet minutes. **Write the story of a perfect normal day.** Not a vacation. Not a day of fireworks. A day that would make you exhale. When do you wake up? Who are you with? What kind of work, if any, fills your focus blocks? Where do you move your body? When do you eat, talk, read, switch off? This sketch is your blueprint. Money is just the scaffolding.

Now, *price your Tuesday*. The exercise is disarming because most joy is cheaper than we fear and most stress is more expensive than we admit. Line by line, estimate what supports that day for a whole year:

- Housing that matches your rhythm
- Food that feels good
- Transport that doesn't drain
- Health & movement
- Tools of craft or play (camera, guitar, library card or hiking gear)
- Generosity & community (the causes you want to say "yes" to)
- A small mischief budget (because spontaneity)

Add it up. That number is more honest than any rule of thumb because it's yours. We'll still use the "×25" FI shorthand later, but now that shorthand points to a life you actually want, not a vague standard of "comfortable."

Next comes the ritual that turns intention into drift-proof behavior: the **Koffee Method**. Once a week (or every other week), sit down with your favorite drink for 30 minutes. Even same chair, same notebook, same low-stakes vibe and have three mini-conversations:

1. **Look back (five minutes).** What expenses delighted you? Which ones felt like background noise? Circle one recurring cost that didn't earn its keep.

2. **Nudge the system (fifteen minutes).** Make one small change: bump a contribution by 1%, cancel a zombie subscription, automate $100 from checking to brokerage the day after payday, book the cheaper recurring refill you kept forgetting.

3. **Design forward (ten minutes).** Choose a micro-experiment for the next week: try a work-from-café half-day, block a no-meeting morning, test walking errands instead of driving, invite a neighbor for a potluck. Your life is a product you get to iterate.

Small moves, repeated, beat heroic resolutions that burn out by Thursday. The Koffee Method works because it shrinks FI from "someday" to "this week."

To keep momentum, think in **freedom ladders**; a set of reachable rungs that make independence *felt* long before spreadsheets declare victory:

- **Rung 1: 30 days of cushion.** One month of expenses in cash, which turn emergencies into annoyances.

- **Rung 2: 3 - 6 months in reserves.** Real stability, helping with fewer frantic choices.

- **Rung 3: Coast point.** Your invested base, if you stopped contributing, would still grow to fund traditional retirement by 60 - 65. This unlocks parenting seasons, sabbaticals or career pivots without derailing the long game.

- **Rung 4: Optionality at work.** Enough savings that you can ask for four days a week, switch teams or try consulting without bargaining with fear.

- **Rung 5: Full FI.** Investments and cash flows cover your annual spend; work is a choice.

You don't wait on the bottom rung until you can leap to the top. You climb, rest, look around and choose the next rung that matters. Many people discover that Rung 4 changes life the most. Optionality isn't zero work; it's *chosen* work.

Return on Enjoyment (RoE)

Alongside ladders, add a compass: Return on Enjoyment (RoE). Not every expense needs to be minimized; it needs to be understood. Ask of each recurring cost: Does this increase quality of my ordinary days? High RoE stays. Low RoE gets rethought. Fancy coffee that bookends your writing block? High RoE. Premium cable half-watch while doomscrolling? Probably low. A gym you love and actually visit? High. A second car for few short overlapping errands a week? Maybe not.

Here's where it gets powerful: trimming a low-RoE fixed cost often makes a bigger difference than swatting at random "bad" habits. Permanent reductions pull your FI date forward because they lower this *year's spend and your lifetime target. A $120/month bundle you won't miss erased is ~$36,000 less needed for FI (×25) and that extra monthly cash can go directly to the engine that funds your perfect Tuesday.*

Along with pricing your Tuesday, the design should also include *place*. If your perfect day includes long walks and community, but your neighborhood fights you at every step, consider geo-experiments. Spend a month working remotely in a cheaper, walkable city. Run the full cost-of-living math (rent, groceries, transport, taxes) AND run the RoE math (well-being, time reclaimed, health). Many families find that a modest shift in location buys years of FI timeline *and* better days now. That's not a mandate to move. It's permission to test.

In your Tuesday's, don't neglect *time design*. Money gets all the attention but your energy sets the limits. Use your Koffee session to draw a week that honors your best hours: two protected focus blocks, a no-meetings morning, an evening with phones in a drawer, one dinner with friends or a blank Saturday afternoon. Then treat money as the supporting actor: budget for childcare swaps, for the co-working pass, for the cooking class that makes home dinners feel like an upgrade. Remember that FI is really a time story long; before it's a net worth story.

And because life changes, bake in review and forgiveness. Your Tuesday will evolve. Promotions, kids, aging parents, health - they'll bend your blueprint. The Koffee Method isn't a contract; it's a conversation. If a month goes off the rails, the ritual invites you back without shame. If a year goes beautifully, the ritual keeps complacency from drifting your lifestyle upward without consent.

A quick example. Mateo sketches his day: morning run, deep work till noon, lunch with his partner twice a week, guitar in the evening, a weekend hike. He prices it: a smaller apartment near a park, groceries that support cooking at home, one streaming service, gym plus good shoes, a $40/month local music space. He trims the low-RoE car lease into a used hatchback and bikes most errands. Savings rate jumps from 18% to 32% without austerity. In three months, he feels more "FI" even though the portfolio hasn't doubled. Why? His days already look like the life he's aiming at and the money is catching up to the design.

This is the quiet superpower of designing first: you stop letting averages tell you what happiness costs. You find out what *your* happiness costs and then you fund that, one cup at a time.

Reflection Pause

- ☐ Write your perfect Tuesday in five lines. What stays even in a busy week? What can disappear without grief?
- ☐ Circle one fixed monthly cost that doesn't earn its keep. If you trimmed it permanently, how much sooner would your FI number arrive (cost × 25)?
- ☐ Pick your ritual: what day and time will you sit for your Koffee Method? What's the first +1% nudge you'll make this week?

Make the Date Move

The above section gave you a blueprint: a perfect normal Tuesday, priced honestly, supported by a weekly Koffee ritual. Now we take that design into the engine room. We're going to turn your Tuesday into targets, levers and a simple cockpit you can fly without a spreadsheet hobby. Think of this section as the part where your plan starts pulling the FI date towards you; quietly, measurably and without drama.

Start by turning your story into a baseline. If your *perfect Tuesday* adds up to $60,000 a year (no number is too small or too big, it's just your number), your *first-draft FI* target is $60,000 × 25 = $1.5 million. Don't think of this as a prophecy but rather a stake in the ground. Then, take a snapshot: total net worth, amount already invested, your current savings rate (how much of after-tax income you keep) and your rough stock/bond mix. You'll refresh this snapshot quarterly, not daily. The goal isn't to be precise from get go, but rather have a direction to move.

Most people try to shave years off their FI date with clever (or sometimes YOLO) investments. The quieter truth is savings rate moves the calendar faster. When you permanently lower spending, you win twice - you save more now and you shrink the lifetime target your portfolio must support. As landmarks: saving ~20% often implies ~25-30 years to FI, ~40% can mean ~12-15 years, ~50% can be ~8-10 years. The market will do what it does; your monthly gap is the lever you actually control. Every permanent $1/month you trim knocks roughly $25 off your FI number and lifts your savings rate at the same time. That forgotten bundle, the second car you barely drive aren't really moral questions but rather timeline questions.

Tinker with the three levers in 90-day sprints so that improvement feels human and builds habits. You don't need a life overhaul. Just need 90-day experiments that stick. Rotate through the 3 levers; **Spend, Earn & Invest;** one lever per quarter.

- **Spend (anchor fixed costs):** Pick one recurring cost that doesn't earn its keep and replace, downshift or delete it. If you cut the cable $180/month bundle you barely notice, you save $2,160/year and drop your FI target by ~$54,000 (2,160 × 25). Your savings rate inches up, and your calendar moves forward without a whiff of austerity. In case there's no recurring cost to tweak, no worries; you will revisit next sprint.

- **Earn (widen the gap):** Choose one income move that's plausible in 90 days: a raise conversation, a cert that bumps your rate, a small retainer client you actually enjoy. If you add $50/month after tax and route it automatically to investments, that's $600/year of extra fuel. Your savings rate climbs and compounding works it's magic; your years-to-FI shrink materially.

- **Invest (remove friction, not joy):** Rearrange one thing where it lives. Move bond/REIT exposure into tax-advantaged accounts; keep broad, low-turnover equity ETFs in taxable. You won't "feel" this monthly but reducing tax drag by even 0.3-0.5%/yr compounds into months, sometimes years, off the journey. Boring is powerful.

Run one sprint at a time. Keep what works. The goal isn't a perfect quarter; it's a quarter that nudges the date.

Also, don't chase a single magic date. Rather, build a **cone of outcomes** instead. Set a conservative real (after-inflation) return for your base, say 4–5%. Then sketch a softer decade (3%) and a stronger one (6%). Re-estimate your years-to-FI under all three. The cone narrows as you (1) raise your savings rate, (2) lower fixed costs, and (3) add optional income capacity. You're trading fantasy precision for a more realistic confidence.

When you want acceleration without whiplash, test one speed-up:

- **Geo-experiment:** Try working remotely for 1–3 months in a cheaper, walkable area. If your run-rate drops $1,000/month and happiness rises, that's $12,000/year off spend and $300,000 off your FI target (×25). Keep it if love > friction.

- **House-hack:** Compress the biggest fixed cost creatively for a season (only if you can).

- **Windfalls routing:** Split RSUs/bonuses 50/50. Send half to meaningful life upgrades while the other half moves to fast-track FI. The split prevents feast-or-famine choices.

- **Mortgage fork:** If prepaying principal supercharges sleep, do it on purpose. If investing wins on paper but keeps you anxious, discount the paper win. Peace is part of the return.

Keep in mind that timelines fail not from math, but from shocks. Make the timeline durable with three quiet guardrails:

- **Cash buffer: 6–24 months** of spending, tuned to your comfort and job stability. Small buffers create brave choices.

- **Dynamic withdrawals (preview for later):** When you reach FI, use a spending band (e.g., 3.5–4.5%). In rough markets, lean low for a year; in great markets, let spending float up. Flex beats fear.

- **Barista plan:** Decide now what part-time role you'd happily take if markets wobble right at the finish. Optionality is a feature, not a failure.

A worked multi-sprint example to feel the math:

You priced your Tuesday at $60,000/year. Your FI target is ~$1.5M. You've invested $350,000, saving $2,000/month (~24% savings rate). Base-case cone: ~19–21 years to FI at 4–5% real.

Sprint 1 (90 days): tiny shifts on all three levers
- Spend: You retire one low-RoE subscription and switch a plan, trimming $50/month. That lowers annual spend by $600, which drops your FI target by ~$15,000 (600 × 25) to ~$1.485M. It also frees $50/month to invest.
- Earn: You add a small, enjoyable retainer worth $100/month after tax, auto-routing it to your brokerage.
- Invest: You move bonds/REITs into tax-advantaged accounts and keep broad, low-turnover equity ETFs in taxable. No new cash today, but you've shaved ongoing tax drag.

Net after Sprint 1: monthly investing rises to $2,150 (+$150), FI target ~$1.485M, cone nudges earlier by roughly ~0.5–1 year (partly the extra $150/mo, partly the lower target, with a little long-run help from reduced tax drag).

Sprint 2 (next 90 days): repeat the rhythm, add a notch
- Spend: Another $50/month comes off a fixed bill you don't value. Annual spend falls to $59,400; FI target to ~$1.485M → $1.485M – $15,000 = ~$1.47M. (Stacked total trimmed so far: $100/month, or $30,000 off the FI number.)
- Earn: A tidy upskill/negotiation lifts take-home by $150/month, again auto-invested.
- Invest: You swap one active fund for a broad, low-turnover ETF, dialing down surprise distributions. Still no cash change today, but a touch less tax friction going forward.

Net after Sprint 2: monthly investing climbs to $2,350 (+another $200; now +$350 vs. baseline), FI target ~$1.47M, and the cone shifts a further ~1–2 years earlier (compounding the extra cash flow and the smaller target, with incremental tax efficiency).

Sprint 3 (next 90 days): small, stacked, sustainable

- Spend: You right-size a recurring service, freeing $50/month. Annual spend drops to $58,800; FI target falls again to ~$1.455M. (Cumulative fixed-cost trim: $150/month → $1,800/year → ~$45,000 off the FI target.). Didn't find something to trim, no worries. You will revisit next sprint.
- Earn: A cleaner client package (or small price lift) adds $200/month after tax, auto-invested.
- Invest: You turn on 401(k) auto-escalation +1%, which, at your pay level, adds roughly $100/month to long-term, tax-advantaged saving.

Voice Check

Freedom doesn't arrive when a line on a graph hits a magic number; it arrives every quarter you move a lever on purpose. Trim one fixed cost that never loved you back and the date moves. Ask for a raise and split it with your future and the date moves. Stop donating basis points to taxes and the date moves again. You designed a Tuesday worth funding in the previous section; this section teaches that Tuesday to tug the future closer, one 90-day rhythm at a time.

<u>Net after Sprint 3</u>: monthly investing reaches ~$2,700 (+$700 vs. baseline), FI target ~$1.455M, and your cone pulls forward roughly ~2–3 more years (accumulating the extra $700/mo, the ~$45k lower target, and the quieter tax drag).

So, where do you land after 3 small sprints
- Monthly investing: $2,000 → ~$2,700 (+35% without lifestyle whiplash).
- Annual spend: $60,000 → $58,800 (you cut noise, not joy).
- FI target: $1.5M → ~$1.455M (about $45,000 lower).
- Timeline: Cone tightens and moves earlier by roughly ~4–6 years total (range, not a promise), with most of the shift coming from steady cash-flow additions, the smaller target and a quieter assist from tax-efficiency moves.

The point isn't perfection; it's stacking small, boring wins. Each quarter, you nudge *all three* levers be it a $50 off a fixed bill, a modest income lift you actually like and one friction-removing investing tweak. None of these moves alone is heroic. Together, they quietly rewire the calendar.

You don't need a wall of charts or complex reports. You need three touchpoints:

- Monthly (10 minutes): Savings rate (this month and YTD). Fixed-cost total. Did the automatic transfers hit?

- Quarterly (30–45 minutes): Re-estimate years-to-FI as a range. Rebalance with contributions (not sales). One Coffee Method win captured. One 90-day sprint chosen.

- Annually (60 minutes, November): Tax tune-ups (Roth vs. Traditional mix, HSA, FSA/ESPP), benefits check, charitable timing and a yes/no on any speed-up you've considered. Reset your cone and pick next year's three sprints.

If a dashboard item creates angst, simplify it or drop it. The best cockpit is the one you'll actually look at.

When you work in 90-day loops, FI stops being a someday word and becomes a quarterly habit. That's the whole play: steady sprints, tiny dashboards and a Tuesday you're already living into.

Reflection Pause
- ☐ Using your current numbers, which 90-day sprint (Spend, Earn, or Invest) would shift your cone the most with the least pain?
- ☐ What single fixed cost could you retire permanently this month and how many dollars does that remove from your FI?
- ☐ When will you do your first FI Dashboard check-in (date/time) and which metric will you track first: savings rate, fixed-cost total, or years-to-FI range?

Building the FI Engine

Design gives you direction. Sprints move the date. Now you need the engine that runs without your daily supervision. Think of this as the conveyor belt that moves money from paycheck to freedom with minimal touching. It's not fancy, just frictionless.

Start with one page you can sketch on a napkin. Across the top, write your flow:

Paycheck → (Taxes/Benefits) → Core Bills → FI Contributions → Near-Term Goals → Fun

That's the entire machine. You're going to automate each arrow so the default is *forward*.

Step 1: Route the paycheck (so right dollars never hit checking)

Anything you want to keep should leave *before* money feels like "spendable." That means:

- 401(k)/403(b) + HSA/IRA: Choose percentages on payroll, not promises in your head. If you're split between Roth and Traditional, set the ratio now (e.g., 60/40) and revisit in November.

- ESPP (if offered): Pick a calm percentage that you'll barely notice (3–10% for most) and create an auto-sell plan on the first eligible date. The discount becomes cash, folded back into the engine.

- Withholding tune-up: If you're running a side hustle, either bump W-4 withholding or schedule quarterly estimates. Pick one lane so April is a summary, not a surprise.

Your Koffee Method meeting doesn't decide whether you'll save this month; it decides by how much.

Step 2: Build buckets (so each dollar knows its job)

One checking account is a tornado of intentions. Buckets give every dollar a home and a purpose.

- Emergency Bucket: 3–6 months of expenses (more if that helps you sleep). This lives in high-yield savings and gets *left alone*. It turns crises into inconveniences.

- Near-Term Goals Bucket (2–5 years): Vacations, a car replacement, education certificates, a mini-sabbatical. This also lives in high-yield savings or short-term treasuries. Preferably, no market drama allowed.

- FI Bucket (Long-Term): Broad, low-cost stock/bond funds in tax-advantaged and taxable accounts. This is the engine.

- Curiosity/Alternatives Bucket (Small): Your shiny-things allowance (crypto, collectibles, angel bets) fenced by a hard cap. You get to play without risking the foundation.

- Giving Bucket: If generosity is part of your perfect Tuesday, automate it. The habit matters more than the amount.

Buckets remove the monthly debate and Dollars stop arguing with each other.

Step 3: Set the investment rails (glidepath you can live with)

Your FI bucket needs a rule you can explain on a walk. Try this template and adjust for comfort:

- Accumulation years: Equity-heavy (e.g., 80/20 or 70/30 stock/bond) across global, low-cost index funds.

- Transition years (5–10 years from FI): Glide toward 60/40 or 65/35 to reduce sequence-of-returns risk (bad markets right when you start withdrawals).

- At FI: Keep enough bonds/cash to cover *several years* of planned withdrawals (your comfort band), with the rest in equities to fight inflation.

You're not chasing perfect. You're picking a mix you can hold during both headlines and holidays.

Step 4: Automate the calendar (so progress shows up even in busy seasons)

Create three recurring dates; let them be gentle and consistent.

1. **Monthly (10 minutes):**
   o Are the automatic transfers landing?

o Savings rate this month and YTD (write the number, don't judge).

o Any fixed cost to retire permanently?

2. **Quarterly (30–45 minutes):**
   o Rebalance with contributions and sales.

   o Update your years-to-FI range (your cone).

   o Choose one 90-day sprint (Spend, Earn, or Invest) and write the tiniest first step.

3. **Annually (60 minutes, November):**
   o Benefits open enrollment: HDHP/HSA fit? FSA/DCFSA? Commuter?

   o Roth vs. Traditional mix for next year, based on current bracket.

   o ESPP percent and sell plan confirmed.

   o Charitable timing (DAF/appreciated shares) if you itemize.

   o Re-price your perfect Tuesday and refresh the FI number.

If a ritual starts to feel heavy, shrink it. Consistency wins.

Step 5: Raise-and-bonus rules (pre-decide the split)

Lifestyle creep is gravity; you need thrusters. Two simple rules:

- 50/50 Split: For any raise or bonus, send half to life upgrades you'll truly feel, half to FI. That preserves joy and accelerates the date.

- +1% Auto-escalation: Every January, increase retirement contributions by 1%. You'll adjust only if life demands it. Otherwise, it compounds without negotiation.

When money shows up unexpectedly, it should already know where to go.

Step 6: Friction for right things (and lube for good things)

Make good behaviors easier than bad ones.

- Lube: Automatic transfers the day after payday; cards on file for utilities; autopay on your smallest student loan or the mortgage principal add-on you chose on purpose.

- Friction: Remove saved cards from impulse-buy sites; 48-hour wait on purchases over \$___; freeze your credit by default; keep the Curiosity bucket in a separate brokerage so you don't "accidentally" rebalance into speculation.

Systems beat moods.

Step 7: A tiny playbook for rough markets

There will be quarters when screens are red and podcasts predict doom. Tape this to your desk:

- I rebalance with contributions.

- I do not sell what I bought for 10 years after 10 months.

- I raise cash from Near-Term bucket, never by dismantling the engine.

- If I feel itchy, I write instead of trade. (A one-pager on "why I own this" note calms better than a login page.)

- If a sabbatical will keep me from panic, I allow it. Barista FI is a feature, not failure.

Your plan is built for weather, not only for blue skies.

A quick "from messy to humming" ...Before: Checking account doing everything. Savings "leftovers" some months, nothing others. Investments in a random mix of funds, dividends turning into cash and drifting to lunch. ESPP un-enrolled because "I'll read that email later." Raises disappear into nicer everything. Anxiety spikes every April.

After: Paycheck routes 10% to a 401(k), 5% to Roth 401(k), 5% to HSA; ESPP at 5% with an auto-sell on the first day it's allowed. Checking only pays core bills. Two automatic transfers fire the day after payday: \$400 to FI brokerage (global stock ETF + bond fund), \$150 to Near-Term goals. Curiosity bucket capped at 5% in a separate account. Monthly: ten minutes, one number. Quarterly: pick one sprint. Annually: November hour. Same income; an entirely different level of calm.

__What about "one-time" decisions?__
Some levers you only pull occasionally, but they shape years:
- *Refi or re-amortize the mortgage if rates and costs make sense.*
- *Consolidate accounts to reduce mental clutter.*
- *Standardize fund choices (one global stock ETF, one bond fund).*
- *Document access (password manager + one-page "where everything lives" for your partner or executor).*

These are set-and-forget upgrades. You feel them every month without thinking about them.

The point of an engine isn't just to go faster; it's to go farther without stopping. When money moves through the same lanes, month after month, your savings rate rises quietly, your FI cone keeps inching left and your days start looking like the Tuesday you designed long before a spreadsheet declares you "done." You'll still have noisy weeks and messy months. But the machine keeps rolling.

Because in the end, financial independence isn't a heroic leap; it's a conveyor belt you assemble with a pen, a few percentages and three calendar reminders. Once it's humming, your main job is to enjoy the ride and choose the scenery.

Reflection Pause

☐ Which link in your current flow breaks most often? Routing from paycheck, bucket boundaries or calendar rituals?

☐ If you adopted only one rule this quarter (50/50 raise split, +1% auto-escalation or a 48-hour wait on big buys), which would change your year the most?

☐ When will your first "November hour" be and what's the one decision you'll pre-decide before you get there?

Risks, Myths & Guardrails

Financial independence is a freedom project, not a fragility project. Your goal isn't to build a glass sculpture that shatters with the first wobble but to build a canoe that flexes with the river. This section is your calm checklist of what can go wrong, what people often get wrong and the simple rails that keep you from drifting into the rocks.

The risk everyone whispers about: sequence of returns

Markets don't hand out returns in straight lines. If the first years of your withdrawal phase coincide with a bad market, you're selling shares at lower prices to fund life. That's <u>sequence risk</u>. It's not a reason to avoid FI but a reason to <u>buffer and flex</u>.

- Buffer: Hold 6–24 months of spending in cash or short-term treasuries as you enter FI. The exact number is personal: job optionality, stress tolerance, other income streams. That cushion means you can pause selling stocks during ugly quarters.

- Flex: Use a guardrail withdrawal instead of a rigid "inflation raise no matter what." Example: start around 4%. If your portfolio drops below a threshold, dial spending to ~3–3.5% for a year. If markets run hot, allow a raise up to ~4.5%. Tiny adjustments beat big worries.

Think of it as trail mix for the hike. You don't carry the whole pantry; you carry enough to keep moving through the lean patches.

Healthcare: the dragon that looks bigger than it is

The uncertainty of medical costs scares many people into postponing freedom forever. Swap fear for a plan.

- Bridging years: If you leave an employer plan, you'll weigh COBRA (costly but simple) versus ACA marketplace plans (subsidies may apply depending on taxable income). The surprising lever: controlling taxable income. A mix of Roth and taxable assets allows you to keep Modified Adjusted Gross Income in a band that can qualify for meaningful subsidies.

- **HSA as buffer:** If you've treated your HSA like a stealth IRA, you have a medical-only sidecar that grows tax-free and pays tax-free. Even a modest balance reduces the "unknowns."

- **Part-time with benefits:** This is why Barista FI is powerful. One enjoyable part-time role with health coverage can close 80% of the anxiety gap while you live 100% of the lifestyle gains.

You don't need certainty; you need options. Healthcare planning is mostly arranging which options you can turn on.

Kids & college: don't sacrifice future-you to future-them

Loving your children doesn't require demolishing your retirement. Loans exist for college; they don't exist for age 70.

- **529s on purpose:** If college is a goal, fund a 529 modestly and consistently. Keep the asset mix age-appropriate and avoid overfunding so you don't crowd out retirement.

- **Scholarship mindset at home:** Model cost/value conversations. Many teens will surprise you with mature tradeoffs when they understand how choices move timelines.

The unglamorous truth: stable parents with breathing room are a bigger gift to a child than a prestige loan payment that stresses the family for a decade.

Mortgage fork: pay down or invest?

There's no universal answer. There's <u>math</u> and there's <u>sleep</u>.

- Math lens: If your mortgage rate is low and long-term expected returns on a diversified portfolio are higher, investing wins on paper.

- Sleep lens: If prepaying principal reduces anxiety and anchors your monthly "need," that emotional yield is real. The hybrid answer: maintain target contributions, then route a portion of windfalls (bonuses, RSU sales) to principal prepayment. You stack both calm and compounding.

Pick a policy once, write it down, and stop renegotiating it every podcast episode.

Tax drags and hidden friction

The short version: <u>location</u> and <u>turnover</u> matter more than squeezing 0.1% out of a fund fee.

- Hold broad, low-turnover equity ETFs in taxable.

- Park bonds/REITs inside tax-advantaged accounts.

- Don't let active funds with big capital-gain distributions live in taxable unless there's a specific reason.

Fewer surprises, more compounding.

Myths worth retiring

- <u>"FI is only for tech millionaires."</u> No. Rather, it's for households that widen the gap and let time work. Coast and Barista routes exist for a reason.

- <u>"You must be frugal forever."</u> Intentional ≠ deprived. High RoE spending survives; low RoE melts away. Your perfect Tuesday includes joy.

- <u>"You'll be bored."</u> Boredom is a scheduling problem, not a money problem. When work is optional, you design work you actually like.

- <u>"4% is gospel / 4% is dead."</u> It's neither. It's a starting lane, made resilient by cash buffers and flexible withdrawals.

- <u>"One wrong year ruins the plan."</u> Plans with buffers bend, they don't break.

Myths thrive in all-or-nothing thinking. Your plan thrives in both/and: both growth and safety, both work and leisure, both spreadsheets and soul.

Guardrails that make everything calmer

Write these down somewhere you'll see them when emotions get loud:

1. Cash & credit:
  - Emergency fund target = ____ months.

  - Credit lines unused but available (for true short-term cash-flow gaps), paired with a written "no carry" rule.

2. **Spending guardrails:**
   - Fixed-cost ceiling = $\$\_\_\_\_$/month. If lifestyle creep pushes above, review within 30 days.
   - Big purchases: 48-hour rule + second opinion from your future self (literally write a two-line note: why now, what's the *tradeoff?*).

3. **Withdrawal guardrails (at FI):**
   - Spending band = –% with triggers (market down X% → shift to low end next year).
   - Refill rule: if equities rally, top up the cash bucket back to target.

4. **Work guardrails:**
   - Pre-drafted Barista Plan (two roles you'd take happily, hours/week, benefits).
   - Asking scripts for reduced schedule or sabbatical ("pilot for one quarter; same output, new cadence").

5. **Review cadence:**
   - Monthly 10-minute check.
   - Quarterly cone update + sprint choice.
   - Annual November Hour (benefits, taxes, allocation, Tuesday re-price).

Guardrails don't limit freedom; they protect it. You get to be bold because you set your nets ahead of time.

A quick reality vignette

Nate hits his FI target right as the market stumbles. Old Nate would have panicked and sold. New Nate follows the playbook. He turns off equity sales for two quarters, lives from the cash bucket, trims travel by 15% (low RoE for Nate) and picks up a two-morning-a-week consulting gig that he enjoys. The plan doesn't break; it bends. Twelve months later, markets stabilize, the cash bucket refills and he returns to his preferred cadence - unchanged goals, lower blood pressure.

That's the whole point. Independence is not the absence of uncertainty; it's the presence of capacity - money capacity, time capacity & emotional capacity. Risk never goes to zero. But your plan doesn't need zero risk. It needs rails.

Reflection Pause

- ☐ Which risk spikes your anxiety most right now - sequence, healthcare, or income gaps - and what's the smallest guardrail you can add this month to ease it?
- ☐ Write your mortgage policy in one sentence (pay down, invest, or hybrid). How will you avoid re-litigating it every time rates move?
- ☐ What's your Barista Plan? Name two real roles you'd take for benefits or meaning if markets wobble right as you reach FI.

Case Paths - Relatable Mini-Vignettes

By now, you understand that financial independence isn't a single lane; it's a network of quiet streets. Each path keeps the same principles: widen the gap, automate the engine, protect the downside, but the scenery changes with the season of life. These short stories show how different people translated "a perfect Tuesday" into timelines that actually fit.

1) Coast FI - Early Push, Gentle Glide

Asha & Will, both 29, leaned into their first five working years like a well-planned sprint. They lived in a walkable neighborhood near work, shared one used car, cooked on Sundays and automated 30–35% of their income straight into broad index funds across a 401(k), Roth IRA and a small taxable account. Their Koffee Method was simple: once a month they canceled one low-RoE cost and nudged contributions +1%.

At 34, their invested balance hit a number their spreadsheet labeled Coast Point. If they never contributed again, the existing pile would likely fund retirement at 60–65, assuming moderate returns. That flipped a switch. Asha shifted to a nonprofit job she loved that paid less but matched her energy; Will reduced to four days a week. They didn't stop saving entirely but the pressure vanished. The *feeling* of FI showed up a decade before any official milestone, because their days were already shaped like the life they wanted. The early push bought them a long glide.

Why it works: A front-loaded savings rate stacks compounding when it's most powerful. Coast FI trades "more money later" for "more life now," without abandoning future security.

2) Barista FI - Benefits and Breathing Room

Mateo, 41, was a product designer who hit a wall after a merger. His perfect Tuesday looked like deep work in the morning and a long bike ride after lunch, not back-to-back stand-ups. He'd saved consistently, but healthcare felt like a trapdoor. The phrase "Barista FI" gave him a lever: cover most expenses from investments and a small consulting roster and use a part-time role for structure and benefits.

He pitched his former manager on a two-days-a-week design systems contract and applied at a local university for a part-time staff role with health coverage. Two months later, his calendar had pillars: Tues/Thurs consulting, Wed at the university, Mon/Fri for long focus blocks and the bike. His savings rate dipped but so did his *stress rate*. The portfolio kept compounding. A year later, he realized something gentle: he wasn't chasing "never work again." He had already arrived at optional work now - the version of FI that made him smile on weekdays.

Why it works: Part-time benefits plus intentional income turn healthcare and identity into features, not bugs. Optionality beats all-or-nothing thinking.

3) Late Starter - Compressing the Timeline without Misery

Rina, 46, had done everything right for everyone else. Raised two kids, supported parents, moved for her partner's job while her own savings lagged. When the nest started to empty, she wrote her perfect Tuesday: Pilates, coffee with a friend, client calls in the afternoon for a small consulting practice, dinner at home. Pricing it landed near

$52,000/year; lower than she feared. That number made the math feel human.

She attacked fixed costs first: refinanced the mortgage, moved from two cars to one and replaced a $210 cable/phone bundle with a streaming + cell plan. Savings rate jumped from 12% to 28% without touching restaurants or travel. She took a course to refresh her credentials, picked up a 10-hour/week contract and routed every dollar of that income to a Roth IRA and taxable account. Within 24 months she was saving ~38% and felt momentum for the first time in years. Her FI cone shifted from "probably 67–70" to "comfortably 60–62" and her stress dropped faster than her age climbed.

Why it works: Late doesn't mean lost. Permanent fixed-cost trims + modest income lift can reclaim a decade with dignity.

"Social" validation?
None of these paths look like a viral headline. They look like notebooks, routines and tiny conversations with yourself. They look like the Koffee Method, a +1% nudge and a quiet refusal to let fixed costs dictate your future. The shape of FI is personal; the engine is universal.

---

4) High Earner, High Spender → Intentional Spender

Dev & Noor earned well into the six figures in Seattle. Raises had slipped into lifestyle by default with bigger apartment, nicer car, nicer wine, nicer everything. Their money never felt *bad*, just *busy*. When they finally priced a perfect Tuesday, they noticed luxury had crept into places that didn't raise their RoE. They didn't need six streaming services and two gym memberships they never used; they wanted long dinners with friends and two big trips a year.

They set a rule: 50/50 on every raise and bonus - half joy, half FI. They right-sized housing (same neighborhood, less space), switched to a one-car household with a car-share backup and redirected the savings to max 401(k)s, fund HSAs and automate a taxable contribution the day after payday. ESPP shares sold on schedule to cash and re-invest. Within a year their savings rate climbed from 18% to 36% without austerity. Their FI date jumped forward by seven years. The bigger surprise: they felt *richer* while spending less, because dollars were buying the days they actually valued.

Why it works: Intentional upgrades + capped fixed costs + raise rules convert high income into real freedom instead of busy furniture.

5) Sequence-Proofing at the Finish Line

Nate & Lila, early 50s, hit their FI target in a headline-scary year. Markets wobbled; friends said "wait it out another five." They opened their playbook instead. They kept 18 months of spending in cash, shifted their withdrawal from 4% to 3.4% for year one and picked up a small seasonal contract Lila enjoyed. They paused international travel (low RoE that year anyway) and wrote "Refill when markets rally" on a sticky note.

Ten months later, the market had recovered enough to top up the cash bucket back to target. They nudged withdrawals to 3.7% and booked a modest trip to visit family. Work stayed optional. The plan didn't crack because their rules were written for weather, not just sunshine.

Why it works: Cash buffers + dynamic withdrawals + pre-decided "bridge income" keeps sequence risk from stealing the dream.

6) A Quiet Split: Mortgage vs. Market

Harper, 38, could never shake the worry about debt. The math favored investing but the *sleep* favored prepaying her 3.75% mortgage. She wrote a simple policy: maintain target contributions (401(k), HSA, Roth IRA), then route one-third of all windfalls to principal prepayment. She would reevaluate only each November.

Over five years, nothing felt dramatic and everything felt calmer. The balance fell; her monthly "need" dropped; her FI cone moved left because the lifetime spending target shrank. Peace turned into performance because she stuck with the plan through dull months and busy quarters alike.

Why it works: When the policy respects both math and sleep, adherence becomes easy. And adherence beats optimization.

Reflection Pause

- ☐ Which story felt most like your next season? Coast, Barista, Late Starter, Intentional Spender, Sequence-Proofing or Mortgage / Market split?
- ☐ What's the smallest policy you can write this week (raise rule, windfall split, cash buffer target) that would keep you steady for a year?
- ☐ If you borrowed one habit from these vignettes for 90 days, which would move your FI date the most with the least pain?

Freedom Is a Practice

Financial independence isn't a finish line you collapse over; it's a rhythm you learn to keep. You designed a Tuesday worth funding. You turned it into numbers you can actually move. You built a small engine that runs whether you're inspired or distracted. And you added rails so a windy year bends the plan instead of breaking it. That's the whole arc:

$$\textbf{design} \rightarrow \textbf{numbers} \rightarrow \textbf{engine} \rightarrow \textbf{guardrails} \rightarrow \textbf{repeat.}$$

What makes FI accessible isn't a giant salary or a perfectly timed market. It's optionality built one cup of coffee at a time. Every permanent trim to a low-RoE expense pulls the date forward twice: today's savings rise and tomorrow's target shrinks. Every 90-day sprint widens the gap without asking you to white-knuckle a new personality. Every guardrail converts fear into capacity: cash for a rough patch, a Barista Plan for benefits and identity, a spending band that flexes when markets don't cooperate.

You don't need to do everything this quarter. You need something small and repeatable this quarter. FI grows from habits that are almost boring: +1% to contributions in January, one zombie bill canceled in March, an ESPP auto-sell you never think about again, a November hour where you re-price your Tuesday and reset your cone of outcomes. The magic is not in any one tactic. It's in the cadence that keeps the tactics alive.

If you're waiting to feel "ready," flip the question. Ask what would make you feel steadier: three more months of expenses in cash? A script to ask for a four-day pilot? An automatic transfer that removes your best intentions from the temptations of checking? Choose steadiness. Choose the system. Let the system choose the date.

Some seasons will ask for acceleration (a sprint year where you save 40–50% and jump the timeline). Some will ask for kindness (aging parents, small kids, burnout). Financial independence respects both. It's not a vow of scarcity; it's permission to align money with the days you actually want, long before a spreadsheet declares you "done."

So, here's the end of this chapter and the start of the rest: Keep your Tuesday close. Keep your levers small. Keep your engine humming. And keep your guardrails visible. Freedom will stop feeling like a cliff and start feeling like a practice you already live.

Worksheet - My FI Blueprint

Fill it in pencil. Revisit quarterly. It's not a contract; it's a conversation with future-you.

1) My "Perfect Tuesday" (five lines, priced)

- **Notes** (what I actually do on a great normal day):

  ____

- Annual spend to support it (housing, food, transport, health, joy, giving): $_____________

2) My FI Numbers

- **FI target (first draft)**: Annual spend × 25 = $_________
- Lean/Comfort guardrails: $________ (Lean) | $________ (Comfort)
- Today's snapshot: Net worth $_________, Invested $_________, Savings rate ____%

3) Cone of Outcomes (pick a base and a range)

- **Real return assumptions**: Base _____% | Soft decade _____% | Strong decade _____%
- **Years to FI (range)**: ______ - _____ years (Update this each quarter; celebrate direction, not precision.)

4) Buckets & Boundaries

- Emergency: target ____ months in HYSA
- Near-Term (2–5 yrs): goal(s) + monthly auto-save $_________
- FI (long-term): % to 401(k) ____ / IRA ____ / Roth ____ / taxable ____
- Alternatives cap: _____% of investable assets (hard ceiling)
- Giving: Auto-Contrib $_________ /mo (DAF or direct)

5) Investment Policy (plain words)

- Mix while accumulating: _______ % stocks / _______ % bonds (global, low-cost index funds)
- Glidepath (5–10 yrs from FI): target ________ % / ________ %
- Rebalance rule: with contributions; review quarterly

- Location rule: bonds/REITs in tax-advantaged; broad equity ETFs in taxable

6) Savings-Rate Levers (90-day sprints)

- Spend - fixed cost to retire permanently: ________________

  $____/mo → FI – $____ × 12 × 25

- Earn — one credible lift (raise/retainer/skill bump):

  ____________________ +$____/mo auto-invest

- Invest — friction to remove (location/fees/tax drag):

  ____

  Sprint dates: _/_/_ → _/_/_ (Q1) | _/_/_ → _/_/_ (Q2) | _/_/_ → _/_/_ (Q3) | _/_/_ → _/_/_ (Q4)

7) Automation Map (set and forget)

- **Payroll**: 401(k) ____% | Roth split ____% | HSA $____/mo | ESPP ____% (auto-sell)

- **Transfers** (day after payday): $____ → FI brokerage | $____ → Near-Term

- **Withholding**/estimates for side income: W-4 bump ☐ Quarterlies ☐ (reminders on: _/_, _/_, _/_, _/_)

8) Raise & Windfall Rules (pre-decide)

- 50/50 rule: half to life upgrade I'll feel, half to FI ☐

- Mortgage policy: pay down ☐ invest ☐ hybrid ☐
  (explain: ________________________________)

- ESPP: sell on schedule ☐ route to FI ☐

9) Healthcare Plan (so benefits don't stall momentum)

- **Bridge option**: COBRA ☐ | ACA marketplace ☐ | Part-time w/ benefits ☐

- **HSA balance** today $________ | invest ☐ or keep receipts file ☐

- MAGI target for subsidies (if using ACA): $__________

10) Guardrails (make the date durable)

- **Cash buffer**: ___ months (min) | refill rule: __________________

- **Withdrawal band** (at FI): ___-___%, "down-year" dial-back ☐

- **Barista Plan**: roles I'd take for benefits/joy:

  1) _______________ 2) _______________

- Big purchase rule: 48-hour wait + one-paragraph justification ☐

11) FI Dashboard Cadence

- **Monthly (10 min)**: savings rate YTD ____%, fixed-cost total $____, transfers landed ☐

- **Quarterly (30–45 min)**: update cone ☐; rebalance with contributions ☐; choose next sprint ☐

- **Annually (Nov, 60 min)**: benefits ☐, Roth/Traditional mix ☐, ESPP % ☐, charitable timing ☐, re-price Tuesday ☐

  Next Koffee Method date: ___/___/____

  Next Quarterly check: ___/___/____

12) One Small Action This Week

I will ____

____ by ___/___/____

(examples: cancel $X bundle; +1% 401(k); open HSA; set $200 auto-transfer; book raise conversation.)

X

The Sandbox Percent: How to Experiment Without Blowing Up Your Plan

When you see headlines about big companies making "bold bets," it can sound like they woke up one day, rolled the dice and magically landed on the next big thing. Nothing can be further from the truth and that is certainly not how it works.

Microsoft didn't just slam a giant "Buy" button on AI and hope for the best. They'd already been pouring money, people and time into artificial intelligence for years. Partnering with companies like OpenAI was part of a bigger pattern: take a small slice of a very large budget and say, "This part is for experiments. We expect some misses. We're here for the learning and the few big hits."

Nvidia did something similar. They started as a graphics chip company. Then they leaned into GPUs for games. Then for AI. Then for data centers. Now they're looking at what comes next like quantum and other frontier tech.

Not every project becomes a blockbuster. But year after year, they **fund the sandbox**: research labs, new chips, strange ideas that might be useless or might reshape an entire industry.

Pharma companies live in this world every day. They spend billions on drug trials knowing most of them will fail. That sounds insane until you remember that one successful drug can both change lives *and* pay for a decade of experiments. They're not being reckless. They're being systematic about risk:

- Don't bet the whole company.
- Set aside a slice for experiments.
- Learn fast. Double down on what works.

Big companies have a grown-up word for this: Research & Development. But underneath the jargon, the idea is simple:

> "We keep a small portion of our money for trying new things on purpose."

Now zoom out from Microsoft, Nvidia and pharma. And zoom into your kitchen table, where you're deciding what to do with this month's income. Most of us have only two modes:

1. **Be sensible.** Save, pay bills, invest in something "safe."
2. **Or go YOLO.** Throw money at the latest shiny thing and hope it moons.

What almost nobody talks about is a quiet third option: Having a tiny, intentional sandbox in your money life where experiments are not only allowed, they're *planned*. That's what this chapter is about.

I call it **The Sandbox Percent**:

> *A small slice of your disposable income, usually 1–2%, that you set aside on purpose for experiments and learning.*

Not for rent. Not for groceries. And Not for your long-term, boring, reliable index funds. This is your personal R&D budget. Want to try a new asset class? It lives here. Curious about a platform or a collectible or a strategy? It starts here. Know it might fail but feel like the learning is worth it anyway? Perfect. This is exactly the place.

In the rest of this chapter, I'll walk through my own 10-year "sandbox log", all the little experiments I ran with small amounts of money, how some worked, some flopped and what I learned along the way. But before we get into my story, hold onto this idea:

Big companies don't stay ahead by being perfectly safe or permanently lucky. They stay ahead because they **protect most of the plan** and then give a **small, well-fenced corner** of their money permission to explore.

Your money deserves the same. That corner is your Sandbox Percent because grown-up money still needs a sandbox

My Sandbox Story: 10 Years of Tiny Experiments

Before I ever called it the Sandbox Percent, I was already doing it. I didn't have a fancy name or a fixed 1-2% rule. I just had this quiet habit of taking small amounts of money and saying, "Okay, this part is for curiosity. If it all goes wrong, I'll be annoyed, but life will go on. If it works, I'll learn something (and maybe make some money)." Looking back, it almost reads like a 10-year experiment log.

2015 – Individual Stocks: "I Can Pick Them Myself"

In 2015, my sandbox was individual stocks. I read articles, watched charts, followed companies, and tried to spot the "winners." Some picks did nicely. Others, not so much. But this wasn't retirement money on the line; it was sandbox money.

What I really got wasn't a perfect portfolio. I got a feel for how earnings reports move prices, how hype builds and fades & more importantly, how it *feels* to watch your own money zigzag every day

Lesson: stock-picking is part numbers, part emotions. And the emotions are louder than you think.

2017 – Lending Platforms: $100 of Curiosity

In 2017, I tried something different: a lending platform (like LendingTree–style, peer-to-peer concepts) with roughly $100. The goal wasn't "get rich." The goal was: "What actually happens when I lend money to strangers through an app?"

I watched repayments, added more funds, small defaults, interest coming in slowly. On paper, the returns were okay. Emotionally, I realized it was a slow, steady grind, with real default risk built in. Not really me.

Lesson: high yield comes with a story and with strings attached.

2018 – Crypto & CDs: Roller Coaster Meets Park Bench

2018 was the year I put crypto on one side of my sandbox and CDs (Certificates of Deposit) on the other.

If crypto was a roller coaster, CDs were the park bench.

- Crypto: wild swings, big narratives, constant news.
- CDs: fixed interest, no drama, painfully calm.

On a spreadsheet, it was just two different return profiles. In real life, it was two very different emotional experiences.

Lesson: I started to see my own risk tolerance more clearly; not in theory, but in how I slept at night.

2019 – HSA Investing & Stock Trading: Building Systems

By 2019, my experiments shifted from "Which stock?" to "What system?" I played with HSA investing (using a health savings account more intentionally) along with different stock trading styles and rules. Instead of random moves, I tried having simple guidelines: when to enter, when to exit, how much to risk.

Lesson: I realized I enjoy frameworks more than frenetic trading. I like understanding *why* I'm doing something, not just chasing price moves.

2021 – Rally: Fractional Collectibles

In 2021, my sandbox wandered into the world of fractional collectibles with platforms like Rally. Suddenly I wasn't just buying stocks; I was buying shares of stories. Tiny slices of rare and unusual things. Think partial ownership of an inscribed first-edition copy of *The Time Machine* by H.G. Wells, a book over 125 years old and often credited with introducing the idea of time travel to the world.

This scratched a different itch:

- Part of me loves history, objects and narratives
- Part of me loves seeing how markets price those stories

Lesson: there *are* ways to combine passion and investing, as long as it lives inside a small, well-fenced sandbox.

2022 – Masterworks: Art as an Asset Class

In 2022, I tried fine art investing through Masterworks. I wasn't planning to become an art critic. I wanted to understand how does art behave in a portfolio? How long might money be tied up? And How would I feel if this took 5-10 years to play out?
This pushed me to think more long-term and more illiquid than a typical stock or ETF.

Lesson: some sandbox experiments are really slow-burn R&D. You enter knowing the payoff (and the lesson) might be years away.

2024 – Building My Own Collections

By 2024, my curiosity moved from platforms to physical collections of my own. Art, artifacts, collectibles I personally cared about.

This was a big shift. Now it wasn't just thinking: "Will this go up in value?". It was also:

- "Do I enjoy owning this?"
- "Would I still be happy with it even if it never 3x'd?"
- "Does this feel like a collection or just clutter?"

Lesson: the sandbox isn't only about financial return. It can also be about meaning, joy and identity, as long as the money part stays measured.

2025 – Options & Futures: High-Voltage Experiments

By 2025, my sandbox included options and futures, definitely the high-voltage section of the playground. I didn't start here; I arrived here after nearly a decade of smaller experiments. By then, I knew:

- How much volatility I could handle
- How disciplined I was (or wasn't) with rules
- How dangerous leverage can be if you get overconfident

So, I approached options and futures with extra-thick guardrails and even stricter limits.

Lesson: some tools are powerful enough that they *only* belong in a tiny, well-controlled sandbox, never anywhere near your core plan.

Looking back at 2015–2025, it might seem like a random collage of ideas: stocks, lending, crypto, CDs, trading, fractional collectibles, art, physical collections, options, futures. But underneath it all was one quiet pattern:

I kept most of my money on a solid path and used a small, intentional slice to learn, experiment and explore. Some of those experiments brought profit. Some brought losses. All of them brought data about me - how I think, what I enjoy and what I should probably avoid.

That is the heart of **The Sandbox Percent**.

In the next section, we'll zoom out from the timeline and talk about what these experiments actually taught me and how you can get those lessons without having to copy every step.

Reflection Pause
- ☐ When something new and shiny pops up (AI, crypto, NFTs, hot stocks, fractional investment platforms or whatever comes next), what's your usual reaction?
- ☐ What made you think, "I wish I had just tried a little bit, just to see"?

Some Bets Win, Some Just Teach
If you scroll back through that 10-year sandbox log, it can be tempting to circle the "winners" and cross out the "losers."
- "This one made money, good."
- "This one lost money, bad."

That's how we're trained to think. But what actually happens in real life is different. Some experiments *did* make money. Some quietly fizzled out. A few hurt enough to leave a mark. And yet, when I zoom out, I don't see a neat list of good and bad decisions. I see a decade of paid lessons. Some paid me in returns, some in wisdom. Both matter.

Think about the tuition you pay for education. We don't say, "That year of college was a failure because I didn't cash out for a profit right away." We understand that tuition is money we spend to learn how things work, discover what we like and don't like and build skills with confidence.

Your Sandbox Percent works the same way. When an experiment goes well, you earn some money *and* a lesson. When it doesn't, you still bought information and a deeper understanding of your investment style:

- "This style stresses me out."
- "This asset doesn't fit my personality."
- "This platform looks good in ads but not in practice."
- "I don't actually enjoy this game as much as I thought."

That doesn't make the experiment pointless. It makes it tuition. The key difference from regular tuition? You're keeping the cost small and contained, inside that 1–2% boundary.

Offsetting Bumps with Bigger Picture

*A shift that happens once you embrace The Sandbox Percent: You stop judging yourself trade-by-trade and start thinking in **portfolios**. Instead of: "This one play was down 40%, I'm terrible at this.", you start asking: "Across all my experiments this year, what actually happened?"*

Maybe Crypto went sideways, a small stock idea did well, a collectible held steady and an options experiment cost you some tuition. Individually, those results look noisy but together, they form a pattern:

- *You learned how different assets move.*
- *You discovered which ones match your temperament.*

- *You identified which ones are "never again" and which are "worth exploring more."*

And if your sandbox stayed at 1–2% of disposable income, those bumps didn't derail your financial independence journey. They were speed bumps in the sandbox, not craters in your main road.

One surprising lesson from a decade of sandboxing is identifying things you're *good* at but don't actually want more of. You might run an experiment that makes money, looks impressive on paper but leaves you exhausted, wired or constantly checking your phone. Technically, it "worked." Practically, it doesn't scale into a life you actually want.

The sandbox gives you the space to notice that. You get to say:
- "I can do this but I don't want my future self-chained to this screen."
- "Yes, the returns are nice, but the mental rent is too high."

Because your money plan isn't just about returns. It's about how you live while you earn them. That's just as valuable as discovering something you *do* want to scale.

On the flip side, some ideas you tried "just for fun" quietly earn a promotion. Maybe a small collectible category keeps doing well. A niche you understand (like your own industry) becomes a natural edge or a platform or strategy feels simple, sane and sustainable.

You notice patterns like :
- "This barely stresses me."
- "I enjoy reading and learning more about this."
- "I could see myself doing this 10 years from now, not just 10 weeks."

Those are signals where your sandbox is telling you: "Hey, there might be something here for your long-term playbook." You don't have to jump all-in. But you can give that area a bit more attention, a bit more allocation, a bit more thought.

This is how a **personal money style** is born. Not from copying someone's portfolio on the internet, but from years of tiny, lived experiments.

At the beginning, most of us approach experiments with "I hope this one works." After a while, if you use the sandbox percent wisely, that shifts to: "Whatever happens, I'm going to understand myself better." You stop trying to be the hero of a single trade and to author a long, coherent story. That doesn't mean you enjoy losing money. Nobody does. It just means:

- When something wins, you ask: *Why did this work for me?*
- When something loses, you ask: *What did this teach me? What guardrail was missing?*

Either way, you move forward a little sharper, a little calmer and a lot more intentional.

In the next section, we'll step back one more level and talk about why The Sandbox Percent deserves a real seat in your plan. Not as a guilty secret or a side hobby, but as a deliberate, powerful part of how you grow.

Reflection Pause
- ☐ Where does your "experimenting energy" go today? Random Amazon buys, new gadgets or nothing at all because money feels too serious to play with?
- ☐ What's one area of money you're genuinely curious about, but slightly afraid of?

Why The Sandbox Percent Belongs in Your Plan

By now, The Sandbox Percent might still sound like a "nice-to-have", a side hobby you squeeze in after all the serious stuff is done.

But I'd argue the opposite. If all you ever do is follow generic advice, buy whatever the internet says is safe and never test anything for yourself, something important goes missing. You might be doing the right things on paper but you never really learn how you react or what kind of money life actually fits you. That's where The Sandbox Percent quietly earns its place. It doesn't replace your core plan. It completes it. Let's break down why.

1. Learning by Doing (Not Just Reading)

You can read twenty articles about crypto volatility or watch ten videos about options or listen to five podcasts about real estate. They'll all teach you something.

But the day you put even a small amount of your own money into one of those ideas, the experience changes completely. You begin to own. You're not just reading about price swings, you're feeling them. You're not just nodding along at "long-term mindset," you're testing it on a red day. You discover your real reaction when a position is up 40% or down 30%.

The Sandbox Percent turns money from a theory into a conversation:
- between your brain and your emotions,
- between your plans and real-world outcomes,
- between "what should work" and "what actually happens for me."

That kind of learning sticks. And because it's capped at 1–2% of your disposable income, the tuition bill stays small.

2. Finding *Your* Money Style

There's no single correct way to manage money. Some people genuinely enjoy analyzing companies. Others would rather watch paint dry than read an earnings report. Some people thrive with a bit of risk and action. Others sleep best when everything is boring and automatic.

You don't discover your style by filling in a five-question risk quiz. You discover it by trying things in tiny, reversible ways. Maybe you find that you like having a small slice in something spicy, but not too much. Or collectibles and art make you feel connected and engaged, where trading futures makes you feel wired and stressed. Or you have an

Oracle instinct where you're great at spotting overhyped trends and prefer to bet against buzz, not ride it.

The Sandbox Percent gives you permission to explore all that without pretending to be someone you're not. Over the years, you end up with a money plan that feels less like a costume and more like a well-worn favorite outfit: it fits, it moves with you and you're not constantly tugging at it.

3. Asymmetric Upside Without Wrecking the Core

Big crazy wins don't usually come from the safest corners of your plan. Your emergency fund will never be 10×. Your broad index fund is not meant to be a lottery ticket. Your sandbox is where you keep the ideas that *might* have outsized upside:

- A small allocation to a new technology
- A niche you understand better than most
- An asset class that's still early or misunderstood
- A speculative experiment that could either fizzle or fly

If you put 50% of your money there, that's gambling. If you put 1–2% of your disposable income there, that's R&D.

The beauty of The Sandbox Percent is that if the experiment fails, your life doesn't. If it works, it can meaningfully boost your net worth and your confidence. And either way, the rest of your plan keeps quietly compounding in the background.

You are not betting your future on a single moonshot. You are giving yourself structured, repeatable chances to find things that work unusually well for you.

4. Slow, Gentle, Compounding Growth in Wisdom

Most money advice talks about compounding only in terms of dollars. But there's another kind of compounding going on if you use your sandbox wisely: **compounding of insight.**

Year 1, you might run one or two experiments and mostly learn what *not* to do. Year 3, you've already ruled out a few approaches that don't fit you. Year 5, you've found one or two strategies you actually like and understand. And by Year 10, you have a personal playbook that no blog post could have handed you.

Each small experiment adds to that. The losses teach you where your blind spots are. The wins teach you where your strengths are. Over a decade, even if the sandbox is always just 1–2% of your disposable income, the wisdom it generates can dramatically improve how you handle the other 98–99%.

You might avoid a huge mistake because a small early experiment taught you to spot red flags. You could double down, in a measured way, on something that suits you perfectly. You may let go of envy, because you know which games you've tried and chosen to walk away from. That's not just financial growth. That's emotional growth around money.

So, when you think about The Sandbox Percent, don't picture a side quest that sits outside your "real" plan. Think of it as the learning engine behind your plan, the place where your curiosity has a safe playground and the quiet lab where "what everyone says" is tested against "what actually works for me."

In the next section, we'll get more concrete and talk about **how to keep this sandbox safe**. The guardrails that let you experiment boldly *without* waking up one day realizing the sandbox somehow took over your whole beach.

Reflection Pause
- ☐ What is one R&D thing you've already tried with money (good or bad)? How did it work out for you?
- ☐ When it comes to money, where do you feel like you've mainly stayed in "theory mode" so far?

The Sandbox Safety Rules

By now, The Sandbox Percent might sound exciting. A little corner of your money where experiments are allowed? New ideas? New assets? New ways of learning? Beautiful. But we cannot skip the fences, right?

A sandbox without walls isn't a sandbox but just sand blowing all over your house. The whole point of The Sandbox Percent is that you get to play *without* wrecking the rest of your financial life. That only works if you put in a few simple, firm safety rules. Let's walk through them in plain language.

Rule 1: Never More Than You Can Afford to Lose

This is the golden rule, the one everything else sits on: **Your Sandbox Percent is small.** Usually 1–2% of your disposable income and no more. Disposable income here means what's left after paying off rent or mortgage, groceries and bills, debt payments, core savings and retirement contributions

Whatever remains is your flexible money. The sandbox gets just a tiny slice of *that.* If you're just starting out or feel nervous, you can start even smaller. Start with 0.5% of disposable income, or a fixed, low amount each month you'd be okay never seeing again. The test is simple: "If this entire sandbox went to zero, would my life still function? Would I still sleep at night?"

If the answer is no, the sandbox is too big. Shrink it until a total loss would sting, but not scar.

Rule 2: Go Slow on Purpose

Just because you *decided* your Sandbox Percent is, say, $1000 a month doesn't mean you need to throw all $1000 into something tomorrow. One of the most powerful moves you can make is: *slowing yourself down.*

You can let the sandbox balance build for a few months while you read and observe. You can start with one tiny position or one micro-experiment and add to it gradually as you understand more. Think of your sandbox like a TV series and not a viral clip. You don't have to cram all the drama into the pilot episode.

Going slow helps you notice your impulses ("I want in now!"), see patterns before you commit more and avoid chasing every shiny thing that pops up in your feed. You're not trying to be the fastest experimenter but aiming to be the longest-lasting.

Rule 3: Time-Box Each Experiment

Here's where most people get stuck: they start something "for a while" and then never really decide what happened. An easy fix is to make sure every sandbox experiment gets a time frame. You literally tell yourself: "For the next 3 months, my sandbox will focus on X." or "I'm giving this idea 12 months to play out and teach me something.". It could be 6 months trying a new platform, 9 months exploring a type of collectible or 12 months learning a trading style or options strategy. At the end of that window, you pause and ask:

- What actually happened?
- How did this feel day to day?
- Did it deserve more attention, or less, or none?

Time-boxing keeps you from drifting. It turns each experiment into a season, with a beginning, middle and end. And it gives you a built-in moment to choose between "This was good, I'll keep a small version of it," or "Thanks for the lesson, I'm done with this now."

Rule 4: Don't Be Afraid to Book Losses

One of the hardest skills in money (*and in life*) is knowing when to stop watering a dead plant. With sandbox experiments, this shows up as "It'll come back, right?" or "I've already put so much into this...". That is the **sunk cost trap** talking.

The whole point of The Sandbox Percent is that it's okay for some experiments to fail. That's built into the design. So, give yourself permission to close something that clearly isn't working for you or move on from ideas that cause more stress than they're worth. Say, "This was tuition. I've collected the lesson."

Booking a loss doesn't mean you're bad with money. It just means that you value your future decisions more than your past ego. You're freeing that money and your attention to fuel the next, smarter experiment.

Rule 5: Keep Your Core Off-Limits

This last rule is simple, but non-negotiable:

Your sandbox and your core plan do not mix.

That means you DON'T raid your emergency fund to "double down" on a sandbox idea, you DON'T stop retirement contributions to chase something speculative and you DON'T "borrow" from rent or groceries to chase one more play.

Your core is boring on purpose. Cash is for emergencies, regular retirement investing for your *Future You* and debt payments are to keep the roof over your head. That's the foundation that lets you even *have* a sandbox.

If you ever catch yourself thinking "Just this once, I'll pull from my core to add more to this sandbox idea...", that's your warning light. Sandbox experiments should **never** depend on money that keeps your life stable. If they do, it's not a sandbox anymore. It's gambling on your foundation.

Put together, these rules keep The Sandbox Percent what it's meant to be:

- **Small, on purpose**
- **Slow, thoughtful experiments**
- **Clear start and end points**
- **Freedom to walk away**
- **Zero impact on your essentials**

With these fences up, you can explore with curiosity instead of fear.

In the next section, we'll turn this from theory into a simple, practical setup: how to choose your Sandbox Percent, pick your first experiment and run your own mini "season" of learning.

Turning The Sandbox Percent into Something Real

At this point, The Sandbox Percent is a nice idea in your head. Let's turn it into something real in your money. You don't need a new app, a complex spreadsheet or a 20-step system. You just need a few simple decisions, written down somewhere you can see them. Think of this as creating your first Sandbox Season.

Step 1: Pick Your Percent (Start Small)

First question: *What's my Sandbox Percent?* You don't need to overthink it. If you're just starting: pick 1% of your disposable income. If you're more experienced and calmer about risk: you might go up to 2%. If you feel nervous, even 0.5% is okay. It's about the habit, not the size.

For example: after all your essentials, debt payments and core savings, let's say you have $5,000 of flexible money per month. 1% of that is $50, 2% is $100. That might sound tiny and that's actually perfect. The goal here is reps not bragging rights. Write it down: "My Sandbox Percent is *% of my disposable income, which is about $ per month.*" The numbers are for reference, if you are comfortable, feel free to increase the initial fund. However, remember Rule 1 (*Never More Than You Can Afford to Lose*) from the previous section?

Step 2: Choose One Experiment for This Season

Next, give this first season a theme. Resist the urge to try five things at once. You want to actually learn something and not create chaos. Some ideas could be

- "For this season, I'll dip my toes into crypto."
- "For this season, I'll try a very basic options strategy I've studied."
- "For this season, I'll explore one fractional investing platform."
- "For this season, I'll test a simple trading rule."

Pick the one that you're genuinely curious about, willing to study a bit and would like to understand better a year from now. Write it down in plain language: "For the next season, my sandbox experiment is: ______."

Step 3: Set a Time Frame

Now put a boundary around it in time. A good starter range is usually 6 months if you want something more active and 12 months if the thing you're testing moves slowly (like some collectibles or long-term plays). You're not promising to hold the same position for that entire period. You're just saying: "This is how long I'll give this *idea* space in my sandbox." Write it: "This Sandbox Season runs from __________ to __________."

This gives you a natural review point instead of drifting forever.

Step 4: Track the Story, Not Just the Numbers

You don't need to build a massive tracker. A simple page in a notebook, a notes app or a tiny spreadsheet is enough.

You want to capture two kinds of things: 1. The basics (What you put in, what you bought and rough current value); 2. The feelings and lessons (When did you feel excited, anxious or bored?; What surprised you?; Did you find yourself checking prices every hour or forgetting about them for weeks?)

Numbers tell you *what* happened. Your notes tell you *how you experienced it*. Every month (or every quarter, if that's easier), spend 5–10 minutes and jot down:
- "What changed?"
- "How did this make me feel?"
- "What did I notice about myself?"

That's where the real gold is. Don't rely on memory; human memory has a way of remembering the angst on the worst red days and forgetting the quiet, steady lessons and wins along the way.

Step 5: Close the Season and Decide What's Next

At the end of your 6 or 12 months, don't just roll on automatically. Close the season. Ask yourself a few simple questions:

1. Money-wise:

   o Did I make money, lose money, or roughly break even?

   o Was the amount at risk comfortable, too small to care, or too big for my nerves?

2. Emotion-wise:

   o Did this experiment add stress or energy to my life?

   o Was I obsessively checking things or did it blend in smoothly?

   o Would Future Me thank me for continuing this?

3. Learning-wise:

   o What did I learn about this asset or strategy?

   o What did I learn about myself?

   o What guardrails would I add if I repeated this?

Then make one of three decisions:

- **Promote it:** "This fits me. I'll keep a small version of this in my sandbox or even give it a slightly bigger, still safe space."

- **Park it:** "This was interesting, but I don't need more of it now. I'll keep the learning and maybe come back later."

- **Retire it:** "This is not for me. I'm closing this out and moving on. Lesson learned."

Write that decision down. That's the moment your experiment turns into wisdom.

You can run one Sandbox Season per year, or two per year if you like shorter cycles. Over time, these small, structured experiments stitch together into something powerful. They provide a clearer sense of what you enjoy, a sharper eye for fads and hype, a more honest understanding of your own reactions and a personal money style built from experience, not just advice

In the closing section, we'll zoom back out and place The Sandbox Percent inside the bigger picture of your life: not as a 30-second highlight reel, but as one more way to make your long, 60-year money movie worth watching.

Your 60-Year Movie

If you judged life only by your feed, you'd think money is one big highlight reel. Someone turned $500 into a fortune. Someone quit their job on a Tuesday and "never looked back." And someone bought the perfect thing at the perfect time and now lives on a beach. It all looks like a trailer: loud, fast and over in 30 seconds.

But your real life? That's not a reel. It's a long, 60-year movie. In a 60-year movie:

- Some years are quiet. Nothing dramatic happens and that's okay.
- Some years are confusing. You're in the middle of the plot twist, not the happy ending.
- A few moments turn out to be big turning points but you only notice them later.

You don't get to choose when the movie starts. You don't get to choose when it ends. But in between, you get more say than it feels like on a bad day. You get to choose to build a steady backbone for the story. An emergency fund so surprises don't knock everything over, regular savings and retirement contributions that keep the future moving forward and basic protections so one bad month doesn't become a bad decade That's the main storyline. It's not flashy, but it keeps the movie running.

And then, alongside that, you can choose to keep a small, playful side plot; your **Sandbox Percent**; that tiny 1–2% of your disposable income you set aside for experiments and learning. The part of your money life where you're allowed to be curious, try things, make mistakes and come back wiser. Some of those sandbox experiments will work. Some will not. What matters is that they stay small and contained, while your core plan stays steady and boring on purpose. Over time, you'll realize you understand yourself better around money, you're less spooked by headlines and hype and less tempted by "all-in" stories, because you know you can try "small and smart" instead.

We can't control every twist in the movie. We can't control when the credits roll, but we *can* decide not to live our whole money life chasing

30-second miracles. We can build a calm, sturdy core and give ourselves a fenced-off sandbox where learning, experimenting and small failures are not just allowed, they're part of the plan.

Remember:

Life is not a 30-second Insta reel. It's a long, usually enjoyable, sometimes messy, 80-year movie. We can't choose when we come in or when we leave but we *can* choose to make the best of the time, money and chances we do get. The Sandbox Percent is simply one way to do that on purpose.

Toolkits

Rituals, Checklists & One-Pagers

This section is your quick-reference companion to the book. The chapters teach the ideas; the Toolkit helps you run them. Come here when you want to reset your money in an hour, make a decision without overthinking, or build a small habit that sticks. You don't need to use everything. Pick one page that makes next month easier.

Toolkit A: The 12-Month Money Tune-Up (Make April Boring)

Money gets messy when it runs on memory. This tune-up is how you stop reacting and start steering. You'll do three small things on repeat: a 10-minute monthly dashboard, a light quarterly reset and one focused November Hour that sets your benefits and taxes before the year ends. The goal isn't perfection. It's predictability.

1) The 10-Minute Monthly Dashboard (the heartbeat)

Once a month, ideally the first weekday after payday, write three numbers and do one tiny action.

The three numbers

- **Savings rate (this month + YTD):** How much you kept vs. after-tax income. Round. Direction matters more than decimals.

- **Fixed costs (monthly):** Housing, insurance, utilities, phone, internet, subscriptions, car payments, anything that renews without asking.

- **FI cone (range):** A soft/base/strong estimate for how many years you are from "work optional," based on your current annual spend × 25 and your invested balance.

The one tiny action

Pick one "click":

- increase an auto-transfer by $25–$50, or

- cancel/replace one low-RoE recurring bill, or

- fix one automation pipe that didn't land.

Add one sentence

- **One win:** "Canceled $19 app." "ESPP auto-sell turned on."

- **One next click:** "Shop insurance next Tuesday." "Raise 401(k) 1% in January."

That's the entire dashboard. Ten quiet minutes prevents ten loud mistakes.

Dashboard template:

Month: _____________

Savings Rate: _______% (YTD ______%) Target __________%

Fixed Costs: $______________ | Goal ceiling $______________

FI Cone (yrs): soft _______ | base _______ | strong __________

Buckets: Emergency $_______ | Near-Term $_________ | FI $__________

Pipes: 401(k) ____% (Roth ____ / Trad _____) | HSA $______/mo | ESPP _______% (auto-sell □)

Transfers: $_________→ FI | $_______→ Near-Term | $_____→ Giving

One Win: ___________________

One Click (by __/_____): ____________________

---

2) Quarterly Maintenance (keep the gains, gently)

You don't need a new "sprint plan" here, that's in the FI chapter. This is lighter: one primary tune, plus two micro-tweaks so nothing drifts.

Each quarter:

- **Primary tune (30–60 min total):** one meaningful fix
- **Two micro-tweaks (15 min each):** one Spend, one Earn, one Invest touchpoint

Q1: Spend-Lock

- Primary: renegotiate/replace one fixed cost (insurance, phone, internet, subscriptions).
- Micro-tweaks:
  - Earn: send a 1-page impact note; book a career conversation.
  - Invest: redirect new contributions to fix asset location (no selling required).

Q2: Earn-Resilience

- Primary: one income move that won't colonize your calendar (raise talk, role scope, small retainer).
- Micro-tweaks:
  - Spend: retire one "zombie" subscription.
  - Invest: simplify one account setting (DRIP on/off, auto-rebalance, contribution split).

Q3: Invest-Housekeeping

- Primary: reduce drag (fees, complexity, poor asset location).
- Micro-tweaks:
  - Spend: confirm fixed-cost ceiling still holds.
  - Earn: refresh one signal (portfolio, cert, skill proof).

Q4: The November Hour + Rest

Run the annual tune-up (next section). Otherwise, coast and keep the dashboard heartbeat.

---

3) The November Hour (Open Enrollment + Tax Tune-Up in 60 minutes)

This is the hour that makes April boring.

Minutes 0–20: Health plan choices

Pick the plan that fits *your* year, not an average year. Compare:

- premiums
- deductible/out-of-pocket max
- employer contributions (especially HSA)

If HDHP + HSA fits, set your HSA contribution and turn on investing above the cash floor. If it doesn't, pick the richer plan with zero guilt. Calm beats clever.

Minutes 20–40: Payroll switches

Set next year's defaults:

- 401(k)/403(b) % (+1% if you can)

- Roth vs Traditional split (see rule below)
- HSA/FSA/DCFSA contributions
- ESPP % and auto-sell rule
- confirm beneficiaries

3-line Roth vs Traditional rule

- High current bracket, likely lower later → lean Traditional
- Modest bracket now or likely higher later → lean Roth
- Unsure → split (e.g., 60/40) and revisit next November

Minutes 40–60: Make April boring

- Tune withholding so refund/bill is small.
- If side income exists: pick one lane—W-4 bump or quarterly estimates.
- Spot-check asset location: bonds/REITs in tax-advantaged; broad equity ETFs in taxable.
- Set your charitable plan (monthly auto-give or bunching if you itemize).

Write one sentence at the end: **"My April goal is: small refund, no surprises. My plan is: _______________________________."**

---

4) The 20-Minute Automation Reset (once now, then each November)

- payroll contributions set (401k/HSA/ESPP)
- day-after-payday transfers set (FI + near-term + giving)
- alerts on (new payee, big transfers, failed logins)
- 48-hour rule note for big buys
- beneficiaries checked
- "where things live" note updated

Toolkit B: Money Psychology (Decision Hygiene That Sticks)

Your money plan fails for the same reason diets fail: not because the math is wrong, but because your brain is human. This toolkit isn't therapy. It's **decision hygiene**, small rules that keep you from making expensive choices in a tired moment.

1) The Big Four (the usual suspects)

Loss aversion: losses feel heavier than gains, so we cling or panic-sell. **Present bias:** "future me" is a stranger; "today me" is persuasive. **FOMO:** other people's highlight reels trick us into urgency. **Anchoring:** first numbers stick (home price, stock high, salary baseline), even when they shouldn't.

The goal isn't to eliminate these. It's to build guardrails so they don't drive.

---

2) The ICED method (a 2-minute decision filter)

Before any meaningful money decision, run ICED:

I - Intent: What job is this money doing? (Security, freedom, joy, learning?)

C - Constraints: What must remain protected? (Emergency fund, FI transfers, debt minimums)

E - Evidence: What facts matter? (fees, tax impact, true cost, alternatives)

D - Delay: Can it wait two sleeps? If yes, it should.

If a decision can't survive two sleeps, it's not a decision but a craving.

---

3) The 48-hour rule (the best anti-regret tool)

Pick a number: purchases over $______ wait 48 hours. During the wait, write two lines:

1. "This will improve my Tuesday by ______."

2. "The tradeoff is ______." (less investing, less travel, higher fixed costs, etc.)

If the answer still feels calm after two sleeps, it's probably aligned.

---

4) Three pre-commitments that beat willpower

These are tiny but powerful because they run automatically.

Auto-escalation: +1% to retirement contributions each January (unless life demands a pause).

Raise rule: 50/50 split, half to life upgrades you'll feel, half to FI (automated).

Subscription rule: new recurring expense must replace an old one (net zero).

You're not limiting yourself. You're preventing drift.

---

5) Scripts for real life (partners + social pressure)

Money arguments are often values arguments in disguise. Use simple scripts.

Partner check-in (10 minutes):

- "One win from this month?"
- "One stress point?"
- "One decision coming up?"
- "Do we need a 30-minute Coffee session this weekend?"

When friends influence spending:

- "That sounds fun, let me and get back to you."
- "We're doing a lighter season right now, but I'm in for coffee/walk."

When family asks for money:

- "I can do $________ one time." (bounded)
- "I can help you plan it." (support without open-ended funding)

---

6) The down-market playbook (what to do when headlines get loud)

Write this once, follow it when emotions spike:

- I don't sell long-term investments because of news.
- I rebalance with contributions.
- I stick to my spending band / guardrails (if in retirement).
- If I feel itchy, I write the reason I own this instead of trading.

Markets are noisy. Your rules should be quiet.

Worksheet — The Decision Hygiene Card (wallet-size)

My top bias: loss aversion □ present bias □ FOMO □ anchoring □

My 48-hour threshold: $__________

My non-negotiables (protect first):

emergency fund □   FI transfers □ debt mins □   insurance □

ICED quick check: Intent: __________ | Constraints: __________ |
Evidence: __________ | Delay: 2 sleeps □

My default rules: +1% Jan □ | 50/50 raises □ | ______________□ |
______________□| ______________□

Two easy trims in a "tight month": 1) __________ 2) __________

One sentence I'll use under pressure: "Let me sleep on it and decide tomorrow."

Toolkit C: One-Page Retirement Paycheck QuickStart

Retirement isn't a magic day where money becomes a fountain. It's a new job your money takes on of paying you, predictably, through good markets and bad. This page is a simple, non-scary starting plan, enough to begin, not enough to overwhelm.

1) Pick a spending band (guardrails, not a rule carved in stone)

Start with a range, not a single number:

- Low gear (bad market year): ~3.5%

- Cruise (normal years): ~4.0%

- High gear (great years): up to 4.5%

If markets are rough early in retirement, you spend in low gear for a year. If markets are strong, you allow yourself high gear. This flexibility is how you avoid panic-selling.

2) Build two buckets (so you don't sell stocks in a storm)

- **Cash bucket**: 12–24 months of planned spending (HYSA, money market, short-term treasuries).

- **Growth bucket**: everything else in a simple diversified mix (often 60–70% stocks / 30–40% bonds, adjusted for your comfort).

Refill rule: When markets have a strong year (or after a rebound), refill the cash bucket back to target by trimming gains from the growth bucket.

3) Withdrawal order (simple default)

A common starting order is:

1. **Taxable brokerage** (dividends, then sales as needed)

2. **Tax-deferred** (Traditional IRA/401(k))

3. **Roth** (last, as a tax-free "ace")

Why this often works: it lets taxable accounts keep compounding, gives room for tax planning and preserves Roth for later years or heirs. It's not the only order but it's a solid default.

4) Two tax levers that matter (keep it simple)

- **Roth conversions window:** In years when income is unusually low (early retirement before Social Security/required distributions), converting some Traditional → Roth can reduce lifetime tax.

- **Low-bracket gain years:** Some years allow you to realize capital gains at low rates, useful for "resetting" cost basis.

You don't need to execute these perfectly. You just need to know they exist and revisit them each year.

5) Your safety valves (so the plan doesn't feel brittle)

- **Barista/bridge plan:** one part-time option you'd enjoy if you wanted benefits or extra cushion.

- **Spending dial:** a short list of "easy trims" you can pull in a down year (travel scale-back, delayed big purchases).

- **Debt policy:** decide between pay down for sleep, invest for math, or hybrid; then stop renegotiating its monthly.

60-second checklist

- My planned annual spend: $__________

- My spending band: _____% – ______% (default 3.5–4.5%)

- Cash bucket target: ______ months

- Growth mix target: ____/_____ (stocks/bonds)

- Withdrawal order: Taxable → Traditional → Roth (or my variant)

- Refill rule written in one sentence: ________________________ ____

- Two easy trims for down years: 1) __________ 2) __________

- Annual review month (same as my "November Hour"): __________

Glossary

401(k) / 403(b)

Employer-sponsored retirement accounts in the U.S. You contribute from your paycheck (often before taxes) and many employers add a match. Think: "retirement bucket with payroll autopilot."

401(k) match

Free money your employer adds when you contribute. It's usually the highest-return move available because it's an instant gain.

ACH transfer

A standard U.S. bank-to-bank transfer. Useful and common but it can take a day or two to settle.

Active investing / active fund

Trying to beat the market by picking stocks or using a manager who trades frequently. It can work, but fees and taxes often eat the edge.

After-tax income (take-home pay)

What lands in your bank account after taxes and payroll deductions. This is the "real" number you live on.

Asset allocation

How you split investments across categories like stocks, bonds and cash. This matters more than picking the "perfect" stock.

Asset location

Which investments you place in which accounts. A simple goal: keep tax-inefficient assets (like many bonds) inside tax-advantaged accounts and broad stock index funds in taxable accounts.

Barista FI

A flavor of financial independence where your investments cover most expenses and you choose part-time work for benefits, structure, or enjoyment. It's less "never work again" and more "work is optional and lighter."

Bonds

Loans you make to governments or companies. Bonds usually swing less than stocks and are often used to stabilize a portfolio.

Brokerage account (taxable)

An investing account without special retirement tax rules. It offers flexibility but you may owe taxes on dividends and gains.

Capital gains

Profit from selling an investment for more than you paid. In the U.S., long-term gains (held >1 year) are often taxed at lower rates than short-term gains.

Cash bucket

Money kept in safe, liquid places (HYSA, money market, short-term treasuries) to cover near-term spending so you don't sell long-term investments in a market dip.

CD (Certificate of Deposit)

A bank product where you lock money for a set time in exchange for a fixed interest rate. It's usually safer, but less flexible.

Coast FI

A stage where you've already invested enough that, if you stop contributing, your portfolio can still grow (over time) to support retirement. You may keep working for current expenses but the pressure to save aggressively eases.

Compounding

When money earns returns and those returns earn returns too. It's slow at first, then powerful with time.

Credit score

A number lenders use to estimate risk. It affects loan approvals and interest rates. The basics: pay on time, keep utilization low and avoid unnecessary new debt.

Credit utilization

How much of your available credit you're using. Lower is generally better (often under ~30% and ideally lower).

Credits

Amounts that reduce the tax you owe directly. Think: "this lowers the bill, dollar for dollar."

Curiosity cap

The maximum amount you allow yourself to put into high-risk or speculative bets (crypto, collectibles, concentrated stock picks, etc.). It's your sandbox fence: you can play inside it but it protects the foundation from one bad season.

Deductions

Amounts that reduce taxable income. Think: "tax is calculated on a smaller number."

Dividend

A payment some companies or funds distribute to investors. In taxable accounts, dividends can create a tax bill even if you reinvest them.

Emergency fund

Cash set aside for life surprises (job loss, medical bills, urgent repairs). This is the buffer that keeps you from using debt or selling investments at a bad time.

ESPP (Employee Stock Purchase Plan)

A plan that lets employees buy company stock, often at a discount. Many people use an "auto-sell" rule to turn the discount into cash and diversify.

ETF (Exchange-Traded Fund)

A basket of investments that trades like a stock. Many ETFs track indexes and can be low-cost and tax-efficient.

Expense ratio

The annual fee a fund charges, expressed as a percentage. Small fee differences compound over time.

FI (Financial Independence)

When your investments and other income can cover your living costs, making work optional.

FI number

A rough target amount needed to fund your lifestyle. A common first draft is annual spending × 25 (based on a 4% rule starting point).

FI cone

A range of possible timelines to FI (soft/base/strong scenarios). It's a way to think in ranges instead of pretending you can predict markets.

Fixed costs

Bills that repeat regardless of mood: housing, insurance, utilities, phone/internet, subscriptions, car payments. These shape how "heavy" your monthly life feels.

FOMO (Fear of Missing Out)

The feeling that other people are getting richer faster, so you should jump in now. It's a common cause of expensive mistakes.

Guardrails

Pre-decided rules that protect you when emotions run hot—like a spending band, cash buffer, or a "no new fixed costs" rule.

HSA (Health Savings Account)

A U.S. account available with certain high-deductible health plans (HDHP). It has strong tax benefits and can be used for medical expenses; many people also invest the balance.

HDHP (High-Deductible Health Plan)

A health plan with lower premiums but higher out-of-pocket costs before insurance kicks in. Often paired with an HSA.

Inflation

Prices rising over time, which reduces what your money can buy. It's why cash alone usually can't be the long-term plan.

Index fund

A fund designed to track a market index (like the S&P 500). Often low-cost and diversified.

Insurance premium

The amount you pay to keep insurance active (monthly or yearly). You're paying for protection against rare but expensive events.

IRAs (Traditional IRA / Roth IRA)

U.S. retirement accounts you open yourself. Traditional often gives a tax break now; Roth often gives tax-free withdrawals later, if rules are followed.

Itemized deduction / Standard deduction

Two ways to reduce taxable income in the U.S. Most people take the standard deduction; itemizing makes sense if certain expenses exceed the standard deduction.

Koffee Method

Your short money ritual, usually 10 to 30 minutes, done monthly or quarterly. You update a few key numbers, note one win and choose one next click. The point is cadence: small check-ins that prevent big surprises.

Liquidity

How quickly you can turn something into cash without a big penalty or discount. Cash is highly liquid; real estate is less liquid.

Margin / leverage

Borrowing money to invest. It can amplify gains and losses. In simple terms: a power tool to be used only with extreme caution.

Net worth

What you own minus what you owe. It's a snapshot, not a report card.

Opportunity cost

What you give up when you choose one option over another. Buying something today may mean delaying freedom later.

Out-of-pocket maximum

The most you should pay in a year for covered healthcare services under an insurance plan (not counting premiums). It's your worst-case cap.

Peer-to-peer lending

Lending money through a platform to individuals or small borrowers. Returns can look attractive, but default risk and platform risk are real.

Perfect Tuesday

A picture of a great normal day, not vacation nor fantasy. It's the day you'd happily repeat most weeks. Pricing your Perfect Tuesday helps you estimate what your life actually costs and keeps "enough" from being a moving target.

Return on Enjoyment (RoE)

A simple way to judge spending: *How much joy, ease or meaning do I get per dollar?* High-RoE spending makes your normal days better. Low-RoE spending is the kind you forget a week later but still pay for.

Roth (Roth IRA / Roth 401(k))

A version of retirement contributions where you pay taxes now and (if rules are met) withdrawals later can be tax-free.

Sandbox Percent

A small, pre-decided slice of your disposable income reserved for experiments and joy such as courses, hobbies, small adventures or "shiny" investments, *without touching your core plan*. It's permission to explore, inside a fence.

Savings rate

The percentage of your after-tax income that you save and invest. It's one of the strongest predictors of how quickly you can reach FI.

Sequence of returns risk

The danger of bad market returns early in retirement while you're withdrawing. A cash bucket and flexible spending help reduce this risk.

Spending band

A flexible range for spending/withdrawals (especially in retirement), instead of a rigid number. It's how you stay calm in rough markets.

Tax-advantaged account

Accounts with special tax benefits (401(k), IRA, Roth IRA, HSA). Great for long-term compounding.

Tax bracket

A range of income taxed at a certain rate. Not all your income is taxed at one single rate.

Tax drag

How taxes reduce your investment returns over time (often from dividends, interest, or frequent trading). Good asset location and low turnover help.

Treasuries (T-bills / T-notes)

U.S. government debt. Often used as a "safe" place for cash or short-term reserves.

Traditional (Traditional IRA / Traditional 401(k))

Contributions often reduce taxable income now; withdrawals later are generally taxed as income.

Withholding (W-4)

How much tax is taken from your paycheck. Adjusting withholding helps you avoid a big refund or surprise bill at tax time.

Windfall rule

A pre-decided plan for bonuses, stock vesting, inheritances, or large one-time income. A common version is 50/50: half to life, half to FI.

About the Author

Hemant Goyal is a wealth coach and product leader who helps busy professionals turn money into something calmer and more useful: choices; the ability to say yes to what matters and no to what doesn't. With a background in computer engineering and an MBA from University of Massachusetts (Amherst), he's spent his career building data and platform products in the tech industry - work that trained him to simplify complex systems and make them practical. He is a Chartered Wealth Manager™ (CWM) and Chartered Financial Manager™ (ChFM) and through his coaching practice, Kappa Koffee, has guided U.S.-based clients from many backgrounds on saving, investing, taxes and building habits that stick. His approach is simple, but powerful: build a strong foundation, automate the boring parts and learn to look beyond the hype; so, you can build holistic wealth and grow your money without losing your peace. Hemant lives in Redmond, Washington with his wife and daughter.